G000079597

Selling
to Major
Accounts

Selling to Major Accounts

Tools, Techniques, and Practical Solutions for the Sales Manager

Terry R. Bacon

AMACOM
American Management Association
New York•Atlanta•Boston•Chicago•Kansas City•San Francisco•Washington, D.C.
Brussels•Mexico City•Tokyo•Toronto

Special discounts on bulk quantities of AMACOM books are available to corporations, professional associations, and other organizations. For details, contact Special Sales Department, AMACOM, an imprint of AMA Publications, a division of American Management Association,
1601 Broadway, New York, NY 10019
Tel.: 212-903-8316   Fax: 212-903-8083

This publication is designed to provide accurate and authoritative information in regard to the subject matter covered. It is sold with the understanding that the publisher is not engaged in rendering legal, accounting, or other professional service. If legal advice or other expert assistance is required, the services of a competent professional person should be sought.

Library of Congress Cataloging-in-Publication Data
Bacon, Terry R.
    Selling to major accounts: tools, techniques, and practical solutions for the sales manager / Terry R. Bacon, Ph.D.
        p. cm.
    Includes bibliographical references and index.
    ISBN 13: 978-0-8144-1011-0
    1. Selling—Key accounts.   2. Customer loyalty.   I. Title.
HF5438.8.K48B33   1999
658.85—dc21   99-24260
                                                CIP

© 1999 Terry R. Bacon, Ph.D.
All rights reserved.
Printed in the United States of America.

This publication may not be reproduced, stored in a retrieval system, or transmitted in whole or in part, in any form or by any means, electronic, mechanical, photocopying, recording, or otherwise, without the prior written permission of AMACOM, a division of American Management Association, 1601 Broadway, New York, NY 10019

Printing number

10 9 8 7 6 5 4 3 2 1

Contents

Dr. Terry R. Bacon is President and CEO of Lore International Institute® and an internationally acclaimed consultant in strategic account management, business and professional development, and leadership. He has authored more than 80 books and educational programs for business professionals, including Facilitative Selling®: Helping Customers Buy, Leadership Through Influence, and Effective People Skills.

Lore International Institute® provides business and professional development training, consulting services, and multi-rater assessments to some of the world's largest organizations. Core competencies include strategic planning, selling skills, account management, proposal writing and development, interpersonal skills, leadership, negotiation, influence, facilitation, and coaching. For more information on Lore International Institute® programs and services, call 800-866-5548 or visit the Lore web site at www.lorenet.com.

To learn more about account management, contact the Strategic Account Management Association (SAMA), a nonprofit professional organization for individuals charged with managing national, global, or strategic accounts. Call 312-251-3131 or visit SAMA on the Internet at www.nams.org.

Preface

Several years ago, I attended a customer panel sponsored by one of my clients, and I heard a representative of International Paper report that the goal of the company was to form better relationships with fewer suppliers. In recent years, he said, International Paper had reduced the average number of bidders on any contract from 5 to 1.7! So of every three contracts awarded, one is a sole-source contract and the other two contracts have, on average, only two bidders.

According to the *Wall Street Journal* this movement to reduce the number of suppliers a company works with is gaining momentum. Xerox reported a 90 percent reduction (from 5,000 suppliers to 500); Motorola, 70 percent; DEC, 67 percent; and General Motors and Ford, 45 percent and 44 percent, respectively. An A. T. Kearney study reports that three-quarters of the corporations it surveyed were reducing the number of regular suppliers. Two-thirds were developing strategic alliances with select suppliers, and more than half were forming more single-source relationships.[1]

This trend may be the best evidence that the world of commerce is changing and that we must build stronger relationships with our key customers. That's what this book is about. It's based on my years of experience as an account manager, sales manager, and consultant to numerous Fortune 500 companies. The goal of this book is to present the processes, tools, and techniques I have discovered in working with dozens of companies— the best practices they have discovered that help them manage their most important customer relationships.

This book has two premises: (1) that you should invest more of your sales resources in the relatively small number of customers that generate a disproportionately large amount of your revenue and (2) that strategic account management makes the selling process more efficient and adds value to your organization and to your strategically important customers. The ultimate goal is a *mutual* increase in value, and that goal is not attainable without substantial investment.

If your organization does not now manage key customer relationships, you may find the transition to strategic account management (SAM) both

---

1. *Wall Street Journal*, 16 August 1991.

difficult and time consuming. It requires more than giving salespeople key account responsibility, and it is more than a process or a set of tools. SAM is a mind-set—a way of doing business. It must be *lived* by senior executives, not merely endorsed by them. It must permeate your company and all its functions. When only the sales department is responsible for customer relationships, SAM is doomed; when it is part of everyone's responsibility, it can enhance your profits and your key customers' satisfaction.

In *The Marketing Imagination*, Harvard professor Ted Levitt notes that, "The natural tendency of relationships, whether in marriage or in business, is entropy—the erosion or deterioration of sensitivity and attentiveness."[2] It is precisely for this reason that key customer relationships must be managed—and this implies responsibility. Someone who is generally called an account manager must be charged with managing the account and must be given the authority, resources, tools, knowledge, and skills to do it. The authority and resources must come from your company. The knowledge, tools, and skills are provided in this book.

In *Selling to Major Accounts: Tools, Techniques, and Practical Solutions for the Sales Manager*, I use the terms *strategic account, major account,* and *key account* interchangeably, although some people prefer one or the other depending on the scope of the strategic accounts they manage. Some people also use the terms *national account* or *global account,* which implies that their major accounts are national or global in scope. By and large, I won't use those terms unless I am specifically referring to national or international customers. The U.S.-based association for account management is called the Strategic Account Management Association (SAMA), and as a member of that organization I prefer to use the term *strategic account management.* However, the tools, techniques, and perspective that I discuss here apply whether your accounts are regional, national, or global. As Shakespeare said, "A rose by any other name is still a rose."

When I cite examples in this book, I use actual corporation names if the information about those corporations is public knowledge. However, if the examples are from my own client work, I avoid using actual names to preserve my clients' confidentiality. I relate many of my experiences with strategic account management in mini cases throughout the book. The company, customer, and people names used here are fictional, but the situations are not. Though you may find some of these situations hard to believe, they are based on fact.

This book is intended to be a practical resource guide for executives, strategic account managers, and their sales managers, so it is filled with tools, examples, checklists, and guidelines. These are by no means the only approaches to strategic account management nor are they the only tools that help account managers do their jobs. I've selected the tools I think

---

2. Theodore Levitt, *The Marketing Imagination* (New York: The Free Press, 1986), pp. 118–119.

work best, but it behooves everyone practicing strategic account management to discover, adapt, or invent the tools that work best for them.

I would like to acknowledge those who have contributed in one way or another to this book. Among the people who offered insights on account management were Lynette Demarest, Frank Hart, Kathy Uroda, Linda Simmons, Sean Darnall, Ron Ferguson, Ken Brown, Allison Anderson, Marlene Gebhardt, Howard Armstrong, Lat Epps, Greg Elkins, Kim Hibler, Stephanie Glidden, and David Pugh. They've been invaluable in helping me think through my ideas. Megan Morrissey, Don Scott, Joanne Jankowski, and Alan Lloyd helped me explore the possibilities of software for account managers, and Tom Fuhrmark and Mike Ellis designed many of the visuals. Finally, I received excellent editorial advice and assistance from Marci Braddock and Christi Crumpecker.

Thanks, too, to the numerous authors whose works have helped build the foundation of knowledge upon which this book is based. They include Theodore Levitt, Regis McKenna, Mack Hanan, Ken Langdon, Michael E. Porter, Jordan Lewis, Robert B. Miller, and Stephen E. Heiman. In their books and teachings, they have offered many useful perspectives on strategic account management. I also want to thank the best teachers one can have—my clients. During the past 20 years, they have helped me better understand the issues and problems companies face when managing business development efforts and have helped me develop or refine many of the tools and concepts I discuss in this book. While it would be impossible to mention all of them, some in particular stand out: Bill Hardin, Jim Osborn, Gerald Glenn, Bo Smith, Randy Harl, Bob Draeger, Dean Sackett, Jerry Gibbins, Curt Weaver, Jack Browder, Gary Marine, Skip Richardson, Sandy MacArthur, David Jones, Steve Knott, and Wayne Hudson.

Finally, I want to thank my wife, Karen Spear, for all the support she's given me and for the lost weekends and evenings when she had to fend for herself while I was writing. She said she'd be happy when the book was finished. Hey, Karen. It's done.

— PART I —
Introduction

We've come a long way from the world of Willy Loman—Arthur Miller's tragic central character in *The Death of a Salesman*. Loman (whose name suggests "low man"), the lonely drummer on the road pitching his wares to one buyer after another, has given way to complex, cross-functional team sales to multinational customers with multiple product lines, buying units, and locations. The buying cycle is longer and less predictable; sales calls take more time and must be made to more people in more locations; buyers are becoming more sophisticated; and the procedures and policies for purchasing have become dense, often to the point of being impenetrable, even to purchasing agents.

Furthermore, as many authors have pointed out recently, the role of the salesperson is becoming more difficult. Competing for internal resources to serve customers often is harder than making the sale itself. An account manager today must be as good at developing an internal network as building a web of relationships in buying organizations. It's not uncommon for a salesperson to gain the customer's buying commitment only to be constrained in delivering the product or service because of a maze of conflicting internal priorities. One of my clients had seven levels of authority between field sales reps and the president of the operating unit (we reduced it to two levels). Another client found that its operations division was not cooperating with the sales group because the goals that had been set for operations were based entirely on reducing costs and increasing operating efficiency, which conflicted with the sales team's need for more product demonstrations, site trials, and visits between the operations people in both companies.

According to Benson P. Shapiro and John Wyman, "Strategic account management responds to the needs of the customer for a coordinated communications approach while giving the seller a method of coordinating the costs, activities, and objectives of the sales function for its most important accounts."[1] Indeed, effective coordination and focus are the keys to managing complex sales. However, coordination across business, product, and functional lines does not come easy. It requires a strong commitment from the top down to integrate the sales function with other functions and to facilitate the level and kind of communication necessary to manage information flow to and from the customer and to initiate concerted action when prime opportunities arise. This is what strategic account management is all about.

Chapter 1 defines the concept more thoroughly, gives examples of what strategic account management is and what it isn't, and explores the idea that strategic account management is a form of investment management. In chapter 2, I discuss the roles and responsibilities of strategic account managers and the key executives who support them. Finally, chapter 3 describes the four types of relationships you can have with your customers—from vendor to strategic ally. One of the principal aims of strategic account management is to establish stronger bonds with your key customers, and chapter 3 describes the progression from the weakest to the strongest type of relationship.

---

1. Benson P. Shapiro and John Wyman, "New Ways to Reach Your Customers," in *Seeking Customers*, ed. Benson P. Shapiro and John J. Sviokla (Cambridge: HBS Press, 1993), pp. 8–9.

— 1 —

What Is
Strategic Account Management?

Strategic account management is the systematic development and nurturing of cus-
tomers that are strategically important to an organization's survival and prosperity.

Strategic account management has gone by many names, including large
account management, key account selling, major account selling, national
account management, global account selling, and national account marketing. Whatever it's called, it represents how companies focus their selling efforts on the few customers who constitute the largest proportion of their
sales. The concept originated in the 1960s with Union Oil,[1] but it probably
had its antecedents during the post–World War II years as the rapid
growth of the economy stimulated large-volume purchases among industrial organizations such as IBM, Dow Chemical, General Motors, Ford, and
the aerospace and defense firms, all of which became giant buyers as well
as sellers.

   As this book is being written, strategic account management is growing steadily throughout the corporate world. In a survey of 152 companies
conducted in 1997 by the National Account Management Association
(NAMA), researchers discovered that 51 percent of companies had formal
strategic account management programs, with an average of 19 strategic
accounts per company. The industries that led this evolution were manufacturing, services, finance/insurance, wholesale trade, and transporta-
tion/utilities[2]—the industries that traditionally have sold large-ticket
items or had large-volume sales to key customers. GE Aircraft Engines, for
example, manufactures and sells turbine engines that only a handful of
customers in the world could purchase. Similarly, the petrochemical group

---

1. Dan C. Weilbaker and William A. Weeks,"The Evolution of National Account Management: A Literature Perspective," *Journal of Personal Selling & Sales Management* XVII (1997): 50.
2. *NAMA Journal* 13 (1997): 2–3.

in Fluor Daniel has a limited number of potential customers, each of which can make very large purchases. In these companies, it makes sense to organize business development efforts through strategic account management programs.

Strategic Account Management as an Approach to Selling

As an approach to selling your products and services, strategic account management differs substantially from other common approaches. To clarify what strategic account management is, let's first look at what strategic account management is not:

- Retail selling, in which products are sold to wholesalers or distributors and promoted through advertising and packaging
- Mass marketing, in which products are sold directly to customers through mail order, the Internet, or similar mass medium
- Sealed bidding, in which vendors' bids are opened publicly and the lowest bidder wins

These common forms of marketing and sales do not lend themselves to strategic account management. For strategic account management to be useful to companies, the following conditions should be true:

The seller sells products or services to governments or other companies, not to consumers (although consumers eventually may purchase the product or benefit from the service).

Although price is important, it is not the only factor buyers consider when making their buying decision. They also look for added value, and they are willing to pay for it. Added value may come in the form of additional services, customization of the service, modification of the product, higher quality or reliability, specialized attention, and so on.

There is a repeated or continuous need for the products or services. In other words, it is not a one-time sale. This would apply whether the repeated need is short term (as in fleet sales to auto rental companies) or long term (large capital projects for manufacturers, such as the building or modification of a plant or refinery).

The seller has (or can have) an ongoing business relationship with the buyer. Indeed, for strategic account management to be useful, the relationship between buyer and seller should be an important factor in the buyer's purchasing decisions. Most buyers are more willing to buy from people they know and trust for the simple reason that buying anything incurs some risk, and that risk is reduced when they buy from people who have proven to be reliable in the past.

However, even if these conditions were true for all your customers, you still could not afford to use strategic account management for each of

them. Strategic account management requires a substantial commitment and investment. As Benson P. Shapiro notes, "Account management is expensive and difficult. It can be used only for major customers. And, to be effective, it must be seen as a philosophy of customer commitment, not as a collection of advanced persuasion techniques. Its essence is superior customer responsiveness based on outstanding support systems. It goes beyond selling."[3] There are two common alternatives to strategic account management:

1. *Territory approach.* All salespeople are assigned to a particular geographic area or region and are responsible for all customers within their area. The territory approach generally is most useful when the territories are small enough to be manageable and when no customers represent a disproportionately high amount of your sales volume. For territories to be manageable, they should be small enough and contain a limited number of prospects so that salespeople can visit each customer or prospect within a reasonable period of time. As a rule of thumb, a territory is too large if salespeople can't contact each customer or prospect every month or two (depending on your business). The territory approach is preferable when you're selling a commodity product or a largely undifferentiated service and where relationships are less important than price.

2. *Product approach.* Each salesperson focuses on a particular product or service and assumes responsibility for all customers or prospects with clear needs for that product. The product approach is most useful when the product is complex and requires the seller to have considerable product knowledge, and when the customer base is small (but geographically dispersed) and well defined. The product approach is preferable when the sales effort demands a seller with considerable technical expertise, as with the few software companies that sell highly specialized scheduling programs to intermodal truck lines. Obviously, relationships are very important under this approach. Consequently, the tools and techniques described in this book also apply to the product sales management approach, although instead of creating an account plan for strategic customers, the salesperson might create a product plan.

Strategic account management is the right sales management approach whenever you have sustainable relationships with customers, those relationships are critically important to your business, and you can differentiate yourself enough from your competitors' products to reduce or eliminate price as the sole driver of buying decisions. Strategic account management offers numerous benefits:

It enhances the value that you provide your key customers through the extraordinary service and support they receive, which helps build their loyalty. Because they receive favored treatment, they become more willing to share privi-

---

3. Benson P. Shapiro,"Managing Customers in a Rapidly Changing Environment," in *Seeking Customers,* ed. Benson P. Shapiro and John J. Sviokla (Cambridge: HBS Press, 1993), p. 130.

leged information, give you greater access to key people, and devote more time to you when you call.

It improves your ability to win new business because it helps you identify opportunities earlier and better position yourself for the win. Numerous studies have shown that the earlier you respond to an opportunity and the more you position yourself ahead of the bid, the more likely you are to win the contract award. On average, companies report a 40 percent incremental increase in business from key customers *because* they are treated and managed as strategic accounts.

It improves customer focus and helps you systematically build your most critical asset—your relationships with your key customers.

It helps you build stronger entry and exit barriers, so it protects your investment in your customers and inhibits competitors. A strong entry barrier makes it harder for competitors to gain a foothold with your strategically important customers, and a stronger exit barrier makes it harder for your customers to select anyone but you.

It helps you be more selective in choosing which opportunities to pursue, so it helps reduce your cost of sales. When you know customers as well as you do in strategic relationships, you know which opportunities are stars and which ones are dogs.

It improves coordination in your organization by establishing and nurturing cross-functional, customer-oriented networks. Further, it helps you coordinate multiunit selling efforts when different parts of your organization serve the same customer.

It helps establish a bias toward you in the customer's mind and can lead to the holy grail of business development—a partnership or strategic alliance with the customer.

It promotes the "zippering" of relationships between your company and the customer's organization, which refers to peer-to-peer relationships at all levels of the two organizations. The primary benefit of a zippered relationship is that if you build bias toward your company at many levels in the customer's organization, you are less at risk if a key person in the customer organization leaves.

It improves the quantity and quality of communication with the customer, encourages feedback from customers, and helps you measure customer satisfaction and respond to problems more effectively.

It encourages greater participation in business development by members of your company who otherwise might not have significant customer interface, and it improves team selling effectiveness. In particular, it helps ensure that your senior executives are intimately involved with key customers, as indeed they should be.

The importance of customer relationships was made clear to me in a study conducted by one of the world's largest engineering and construction companies. This engineering and construction firm wanted to understand better what factors influenced winning and losing bids, so they studied forty previous bids—twenty winners and twenty losers. They identified nearly thirty different factors that might have contributed to these wins and losses, such as being an incumbent provider of services, knowing the customer's key people, writing an outstanding proposal, and so on. The not-surprising outcome of the study was that the only factor that correlated with wins and losses was the strength of their relationships with the customer's key people. It's not that other factors didn't contribute to their wins, but the only thing that *always* correlated with wins and losses was the presence (or absence) of a strong relationship.

Another company doing business worldwide documented the remarkable impact of strategic account management on their sales efforts. They studied nearly 200 wins and losses in five business units and learned that when customer relationships were managed using strategic account management principles and techniques, they realized a *100 percent increase in wins*. In other words, they are *twice* as likely to win contracts using strategic account management methods to position themselves long term with strategically important customers. We'll learn more about this study later, because it will help us to understand precisely what tools and techniques have the greatest impact on your win percentage.

In their book *Keeping Customers*, John Sviokla and Benson Shapiro note that building profitable, loyal customers is a complex process involving seven management principles:

1. Put the customer at the heart of your business.
2. Manage the business from the customer's point of view.
3. Execute with quality.
4. Keep the relationship vibrant.
5. Turn sows' ears into silk purses.
6. Convert customer satisfaction into profits.
7. Measure what matters.[4]

Strategic account management is the fundamental embodiment of those principles and the best way to turn them from concept to action.

Strategic Account Management as Investment Management

One of the purposes of strategic account management is to make the best use of scarce sales and sales support resources. Companies don't have an infinite amount of time, people, and money to invest in sales, so they must choose where and how to invest their resources. Likewise, salespeople don't have unlimited time to invest in each of their accounts, so they also must decide where and how to invest their time, energy, and effort. Here

---

4. John J. Sviokla and Benson P. Shapiro, *Keeping Customers* (Cambridge: HBS Press, 1993), p. xv.

are the kinds of questions salespeople should ask when evaluating the level of effort they should invest in an account:

- How much business are we currently doing with this customer?
- What is the revenue potential of the account?
- How important is the customer to our business?
- Does the customer represent a target industry, sector, or location?
- Does this customer buy based on value, rather than price, and does this customer represent significant revenue volume?
- How profitable is our business with this customer?
- Is the customer biased toward us? Do we have significant sole-source opportunities with this customer?
- What is our level of risk in serving this customer?
- What is our current level of investment in this account?
- Do the current or potential returns justify that level of investment?

Good account managers invest the right resources, at the right time, and in the right amount to build their key accounts most economically. If they invest too little, they may fail to realize the account's potential; if they invest too much, their sales may decline because they will ignore some potentially good accounts while focusing on others. The key is to invest the right amount of resources to achieve their goals, and it is important to measure the return on your investment in every account.

What Salespeople Invest in Accounts

- Their time and energy
- Sales call expenses
- Marketing and sales overhead
- Proposal time/cost
- Technical people's time spent on proposals, sales calls, negotiations, etc.
- Senior executive time
- Marketing and sales literature costs
- Samples or demonstration costs
- Time and resources that could be invested in other customers (which represent lost opportunities)

— 2 —

The Roles and Responsibilities of Strategic Account Managers

Account management is either a position or a role, depending on how your organization manages strategic customer development. In some companies, project or technical managers play the role of account manager by assuming responsibility for some key customer accounts; in others, account management is a position filled by professional salespeople with strategic account management responsibility. When multiple operating units or divisions serve the same customer or when the account is too large for one person to manage, there may be an account team led by an account team leader. In any case, there should be one person responsible for managing the account or coordinating the team's efforts. In most companies, account managers and teams report to a sales manager. Often, there is also an executive sponsor for each key account—a senior executive who can represent the company to senior officers in the buying organization, review the team's account plans, advise them, and monitor their efforts.

The three key positions in a strategic account management system are the account manager (or account team leader), the executive sponsor, and the sales manager. The responsibilities usually assigned to each position are listed as follows.

Account Manager or Account Team Leader

The account manager is primarily responsible for developing and implementing specific plans to fulfill the company's strategic visions with major customers. An account manager has two key roles: to act as a *consultant* to the customer and a *strategist* within his or her own company.

The account manager's responsibilities to the customer include:

- Being the customer's advocate inside the company; ensuring that the customer receives the appropriate amount of management attention and added value whenever possible

- Being a capabilities expert; assisting the customer in identifying needs and defining solutions; directing the customer toward the right products or services
- Being a resource provider and problem solver; negotiating internally for resources to meet the customer's needs
- Being a door opener and facilitator; ensuring that the right people in both organizations get together
- Being a business analyst and consultant; being an expert on the customer's business and industry; knowing how the customer differentiates itself in its markets and creates value for its customers; taking a broader view of the business picture and helping the customer maximize its business potential within the areas served by your products or services

The account manager's responsibilities to the company include:

- Formulating strategies for building the account and maximizing your company's potential to do business with the customer
- Developing, maintaining, and implementing account plans that contain the strategies and action plans for maximizing the value of the account
- Gathering, analyzing, maintaining, and disseminating information; developing exceptional knowledge of the customer and competitors; being well versed in the customer's problems, goals, needs, and issues—including the biases and concerns of individual decision makers and key influencers
- Systematically building relationships with members of the customer's power base and within the company
- Positioning the company for prime opportunities by preselling the company's capabilities and solutions and gathering information that will make the company's approach better than competitors' approaches
- Overseeing proposal development; helping create offers that represent maximum affordable value to the customer; ensuring that proposals address the customer's key issues, needs, and requirements
- Facilitating contract negotiations and achieving a win for both sides
- Monitoring customer satisfaction; communicating the customer's concerns to those who serve the customer; communicating the company's commitment to the customer
- Facilitating future business with the customer; seeking out and helping the customer define new opportunities
- Coordinating the efforts of the groups that serve the customer to ensure a synergistic, companywide approach to the account

Executive Sponsor

In addition to an account manager, strategic accounts also should have an executive sponsor, a senior executive in the selling organization who oversees the account, represents the company to the customer's very senior people, and develops strong relationships with his or her counterpart in the customer organization. Executive sponsorship should not be a short-term commitment or a revolving door. Your executive sponsor should make a career-long commitment to the strategic accounts he or she sponsors. The executive sponsor's responsibilities include:

- Representing the customer to your company's executives and being an advocate internally for meeting the customer's needs and requirements
- Developing relationships with counterparts in the customer organization and communicating their interests, perspectives, and concerns to members of the account team
- Establishing strategic alignment between the two organizations at the executive level, which means creating shared values, goals, and expectations with customer senior executives
- Opening closed doors for the account manager; making high-level contacts and ensuring that the account manager can connect at high levels
- Monitoring the account manager's or account team's activities and advising appropriately
- Reviewing account plans and overseeing implementation of action plans
- Monitoring delivery of your company's products or services to the customer and ensuring that the customer is satisfied and that your company is addressing the customer's needs, problems, and concerns
- Greasing the wheels inside your company; ensuring a rapid response to customer problems, complaints, and needs for quick service or delivery
- Participating in proposal reviews, presentations, and negotiations with the customer as needed
- Overseeing key proposal efforts and participating in or leading review teams
- Participating in key proposal presentations and negotiating sessions
- Hosting key meetings and events, as needed
- Accepting personal responsibility for the success of the customer relationship

Sales Manager

In most cases, the account manager's direct superior is a sales manager. If the account manager is a project manager or technical person with operational responsibilities, he or she should still report to a sales manager for the portion of his or her role that pertains to managing strategic accounts. The sales manager typically is responsible for the following:

- Providing direct management of account managers
- Ensuring that the right people are assigned to strategic accounts
- Balancing account management responsibilities with other sales team responsibilities to ensure that account managers have the time, resources, and latitude to do their jobs

- Reviewing and managing budgets and expenses
- Managing the human resource functions associated with account managers and other salespeople, including recruiting, hiring, appraising, compensating, and firing
- Ensuring that account managers are trained properly and are skilled in the performance of their tasks
- Establishing metrics for evaluating account and account manager performance, monitoring those metrics, and reviewing goals and outcomes with the sales team
- Ensuring that sales support functions (including estimating, proposal development, etc.) are effective

In addition to these key people, account teams may be formed that require the participation and support of other people in the company, including engineers, project managers, scientists, administrators, customer service reps, etc. If these types of people are assigned to account teams, then they should bear as much responsibility for the team's success as does the account manager.

It is best to view strategic account management as a unified endeavor among all your organizational functions, an orientation toward managing your sales effort that focuses everyone's attention on building and sustaining strong relationships with your key customers, those whose business provides the lion's share of your revenues and on whom you rely most heavily, not only for your prosperity but also for your survival as an enterprise.

Managing an account requires the dedication and resources of many people in the company. In companies where account managers must fend for themselves and struggle to gain support, strategic account management usually fails. In companies where strategic account management is supported and strongly encouraged—such as 3M, Motorola, Xerox, Hewlett-Packard, and IBM—the results can be extraordinary.

— 3 —

The Four Types of
Customer Relationships

When you first approach a potential customer, the customer is likely to perceive you as a common supplier or vendor—one of many similar companies offering a comparable product or service. You probably will have to compete with other vendors and fight for your share of the customer's business, especially if a competing supplier already is well entrenched. Like everyone else, you will have humble beginnings unless your brand has such cachet that it opens big doors and establishes you from the get go. But in most cases you'll be vying for position with other vendors, and your goal will be to build an increasingly preferential relationship with the customer, one that ideally could position you as the customer's predominant or exclusive supplier. The holy grail of business is creating strategic alliances with the most attractive customers, and it is the ultimate of the four possible positions you can establish with your customers.

As Figure 3-1 shows, the four possible relationships progress from vendor to strategic ally. From the vendor relationship we strive to become the preferred supplier, and from preferred supplier to seek a formal or informal partnership with the customer. If we can, we aspire to become strategic allies—the most vaunted and impregnable position your company can be in. It's not always possible to create a strategic alliance with a customer, however. A number of factors may prevent it:

- Laws or regulations that prohibit such alliances
- Customer prohibitions, including cultural biases against alliances
- Time or resource limitations that prevent you from establishing alliances, even if you wanted to
- Competitors who are better matched to the customer or better positioned
- The nature of your product or service, which may not be strategically important to the customer
- Incompatibilities between the customer's goals, values, people, or style and your goals, values, people, or style

Figure 3-1. The Four Types of Customer Relationships

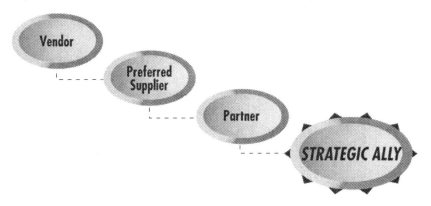

Where these factors do not create barriers, then strategic alliances usually are possible, and it's the goal of every business to move as far right on this relationship chain as possible. In his book, *The Connected Corporation*, Jordan Lewis defines a strategic alliance simply as "a relationship between firms in which they cooperate to produce more value (or a lower cost) than is possible in market transactions."[1] Lewis argues that alliances can result in 20 to 30 percent savings, but that many buyers are suspicious of close relationships with suppliers and fail to see or realize the many benefits of forming closer relationships with the companies who supply them. Indeed, until the Japanese popularized closer ties between companies, the tradition has been for companies to view their suppliers as a necessary evil and, conversely, for many suppliers to view their customers as a necessary evil. In this increasingly competitive world, however, those traditions are fading as more and more companies recognize the benefits of greater cooperation and trust.

The characteristics of the four types of relationships are described as follows.

Vendor

- You are one of many vendors or common suppliers and are treated the same as the others by the customer's key people.
- The sale is treated as an arms-length transaction.
- Many of your dealings are with the guardians or gatekeepers of the buying organization.
- You may have good relationships with some key people but not others.
- You have limited access to proprietary or confidential information. For the most part, you are limited to information that is in the public domain and thus accessible to all other vendors.

---

1. Jordan D. Lewis, *The Connected Corporation* (New York: The Free Press, 1995), p. 5.

- You must bid competitively on all contracts, and you must follow the rules. There are no exceptions made for you.
- If you aren't a specialty supplier, then you may have to price your products at a commodity level. In any case, price likely will be a strong consideration in the selection of a vendor.
- If your product is new to the customer, you will have to devote considerable time to service-related issues: installing the product, testing or debugging, establishing support, answering questions, training, and providing customer service.
- You have a low-to-moderate profile in the customer organization. Many key people either haven't heard of you or barely are aware of you and your products or services.
- You work under a series of discrete contracts or purchase orders. There is little continuity in the service you provide.

Preferred Supplier

- You have good relationships with a broad number of key people in the customer organization, and those relationships are influential in helping you get new business.
- You have many sole-source opportunities, do follow-on work to existing contracts, or supply some products and services on an ongoing basis.
- You are the supplier of choice. The customer is biased toward you, even on competitive bids, but may not be able to acknowledge it.
- You have an installed base, so much of your activity is devoted to problem solving, expanding, customizing, and responding to specific operator or user needs.
- Your price must be in the competitive range, but the customer will pay for added value or otherwise allow you a fair profit.
- You have a moderate-to-high profile in the customer's organization.
- You have access to a fair amount of proprietary or confidential information that other suppliers are not privy to. The information advantage enables you to get advanced warning of opportunities and changes that could affect your products or services.
- There is a continuity to the contracts you are executing with the customer, which establishes greater continuous presence at the customer's sites.
- There are good but not impenetrable entry and exit barriers so long as you continue to perform well.

Partner

- There are key contacts at multiple levels of both organizations.
- Relationships exist at the highest levels and are managed by key executives.
- You have a formal or informal agreement with the customer to provide products or services.

- You have many sole-source opportunities and continuous long-term contracts. In many cases, orders are placed without there being a formal purchasing process.
- There may be some co-location and/or sharing of people.
- You hold joint planning sessions and share ideas.
- Price is negotiated as part of your agreement.
- There are no competitors in key partnering areas—the customer views the relationship as a form of vertical integration.
- There are substantial entry and exit barriers.
- You have a high profile in the customer organization. Members of the customer organization acknowledge the special relationship between your two organizations.
- Your customer's customers are aware of your contributions to the products or services they purchase and come to rely on you and have brand name loyalty.

Strategic Ally

- You have a formal or informal alliance, which may be a joint venture.
- You have a very high profile—inside and outside the customer's organization.
- There are key contacts at all levels in both organizations, and executives of the joint venture come from both parents. The two chief executives co-lead the strategic alliance.
- There is absolute compatibility of goals and vision.
- Joint venture employees may be more loyal to the joint venture than to either parent organization.
- Both organizations strive for greater profitability through the mutual arrangement.
- Former competitors may become suppliers to the joint venture in areas neither parent serves.
- There are extraordinary entry and exit barriers, such as it might take a legal dissolution of the alliance to overcome them.
- The alliance seeks opportunities to maximize benefits to both organizations through integrated business activities.

It's worth noting again that achieving a strategic alliance may not be possible in your industry, with your products, or with your customers. Nonetheless, it is the rare circumstance in which it is not possible to achieve preferred supplier status, and that should be your minimal goal for each of the strategic accounts you manage. Indeed, if you aren't at least a preferred supplier for each of your strategic accounts, then those accounts (and the revenue and opportunities they represent) are at risk.

The movement from vendor to preferred supplier usually takes years, and if the customer is inclined to form a partnership or strategic alliance with you, that can take even more years. A senior account manager with one of my clients pursued Daimler-Benz for a decade before landing the account. Now, years later, he has a very close bond, built with a remarkable amount of time and patience on the relationship, and he won't stop investing effort into that relationship until he's retired. Such is the commitment you have to make to develop partner-like relationships with your key accounts.

Summary of Part I

Strategic account management is the systematic development and nurturing of customers who are strategically important to a company's survival and prosperity. The concept developed during the post-World War II years and is growing rapidly as more organizations recognize its potential. Strategic account management differs from the territory and product approaches to sales management, and it offers many advantages when you need to have sustainable relationships with customers that are critically important to your business. The key customers that provide most of your revenue and profitability should be viewed as critical assets, and strategic account management is a means of investing your scarce sales and sales support resources in this most important of assets.

In most companies, the strategic account manager acts as a consultant to the customer and as a strategist within his or her own company. Among an account manager's many roles are solving problems, building interorganizational relationships, gathering information, creating account plans, and positioning the company for prime opportunities. The other key roles in strategic account management are executive sponsors—the senior-level executives in your company who guide and support the account managers—and the sales manager, who is responsible for providing direction, monitoring progress, and offering support. Strategic account management should be a unified endeavor among all your organizational functions, and it requires the dedication and resources of many people in your company.

Finally, there are four types of relationships you can have with customers—from vendor to preferred supplier and from there to partner and strategic ally. The goal in managing a strategic account is to move as far up this chain as possible. It may not be possible to form a strategic alliance with a customer, but you should strive, at a minimum, to become your customer's preferred supplier.

— PART II —
The Foundations of Strategic Account Management

When strategic account management is well integrated into a company's selling systems and processes, it is more than an approach to selling, more than a set of tools or a way of regarding important customers. Indeed, it is part of the fabric of how the company does business. It's one of "the way things work around here." It grows out of the company's strategic vision of itself and is one of the programs articulated in the company's strategic plan—as important to the company as its plans for financing, marketing, research and technology development, manufacturing and quality assurance, customer service, and human resource management.

So one of the foundations of strategic account management is your strategic plan. Another is your determination of which accounts are strategic, as well as your selection of the people who manage your strategic accounts. Neither of these determinations is simple. Both require considerable thought, because they impact the way your sales force is structured and managed. And because strategic account management usually involves technical or operations people, it can impact how those areas are structured and managed as well. Finally, because strategic account management is best accomplished by teams of people focusing on key customers, one of the foundations of strategic account management is your concept for establishing and managing strategic account teams.

In this part of the book we explore the foundations of strategic account management—what must be in place before you can address the nuts and bolts of managing a strategic account. Chapter 4 discusses what it means to *manage* a strategic account. Chapter 5 explores the relationship between strategic planning and strategic account management. Chapters 6 and 7 describe how you identify which accounts to treat as strategic accounts and how you build an account team to manage them.

— 4 —

The *Management* in Strategic Account Management

What does it mean to *manage* a strategic account? During my years of consulting with organizations such as Siemens, Group Five (South Africa), Halliburton, Fluor Daniel, and Bechtel, I've discovered that the concept of *managing* a key customer relationship differs from organization to organization. That concept underlies everything else in this book, so it's important that we clarify what it means. To help us clarify the concept, it might be useful to imagine what *not* managing those accounts looks like. How familiar is this scenario?

> Although this customer's business constitutes a significant part of your revenue and profitability and you have a long-standing relationship with the customer, no single person in your company is assigned to look after the relationship or is responsible for its well being. A number of your people interact with the customer, at various levels, but they don't talk to one another, so information that might alert you to new opportunities is passed on only by happenstance. Occasionally, the same buyer in the customer's organization is visited by different people from your company, and your people aren't aware of it until the customer mentions it. More astonishing, on a few occasions, different groups in your company have bid on the same customer project—without knowing it— leading the customer to question which group actually represents your company. No one in the customer's organization knows the extent to which you are serving their various units, so no one knows your full capabilities. When key people in the customer's organization retire or otherwise move on, you are unprepared and have to start over with their replacements.
>
> You have no strategy for maximizing the value of this account and do not coordinate your selling and relationship-building efforts. Consequently, you are forced to react to change, which usually takes you by surprise, and you learn about many opportunities after they've been awarded to competitors. When you do learn about opportunities in time to bid on them, you don't undertake a coordinated effort to position yourself to win, and the people writing your proposals often don't know what the customer really needs, so your proposals usually focus on the features of your offer rather than how your offer meets the customer's needs and benefits them in unique ways. You have no plan for serving this customer and don't know enough to do accurate projec-

tions, so you can't anticipate the level of business you might receive from the customer. You are surprised when you lose some major bids—and eventually the account itself.

To me, the most incredible part of this nightmare scenario is that it describes the way many companies actually operate. At the most basic level, making an effort to manage your key customer relationships is common sense. Why would you do otherwise? The companies that don't manage their key accounts often have grown to maturity as market leaders in their industries and have commanded such a strong market position for so long that they have developed a culture of arrogance. "We are who we are" is their attitude, and they have a deep-seated belief in their ability to prevail in their markets *because they always have*. They generally don't realize until too late that things have changed. Other companies that fail to manage key accounts often have strong technical or operational cultures and correspondingly weak sales cultures. Many of them have the attitude portrayed in Kevin Costner's film *Field of Dreams*—"if we build it they will come." The power structure in these companies is based on technical managers at all levels who have demonstrated their ability to deliver the technical goods, and sales typically is viewed as a necessary evil. Such companies remain strong in their markets only until competitors can match them widget for widget—as inevitably will occur unless they can innovate faster than their competitors can match them, a tough game to play under any circumstances. By the time technical leveling has occurred, their cost structures are so high that they can't compete on price, which is often the only remaining discriminator.

The survivors in a tough marketplace are those companies that learn quickly enough to protect *all* their key assets, especially their key customers. In a very real sense, strategic account management is nothing more than good asset management. Unless you are careless or foolhardy, you always know where your wallet is. Likewise, you manage your strategic customer accounts. In business, they are one of your most precious assets.

In contrast to the nightmare picture I painted earlier, here is how it can look when you actively manage a strategic account:

> You have a long-standing relationship with a key customer, one whose business represents a significant part of your revenue and profitability. Consequently, several key people in your company are assigned to look after the relationship and are jointly responsible for its well being. One, a vice president of your company, is the executive sponsor of the account and maintains relationships at the most senior levels of the customer's organization. The other is the account manager, who coordinates all interactions between your company and the customer and ensures that information regarding new opportunities is passed on quickly to the people who need to know. This account manager also ensures that everyone of importance in the customer's organization knows how much and how well you are serving their various units, so they are aware of

and appreciate your full capabilities. You know well in advance when key people in the customer's organization retire or otherwise move on, so you are prepared for their replacements and are well positioned when such transitions occur.

Your account team, led by the account manager, has developed a strategy for maximizing the value of this account, so your selling and relationship-building efforts are coordinated effectively. You know of opportunities well before your competitors do, so you can be proactive in developing those opportunities, preselling your solution, and helping the customer's decision makers develop their decision criteria. Because of the depth of your knowledge about the customer's needs and wants, your proposals are very focused and specific, emphasizing the benefits of your approach and how you are differentiated from your competitors.

Your plan for serving this customer is sufficiently well developed to enable you to do accurate projections, so you can anticipate the level of business you will receive from the customer and can do sensible resource planning and allocation. Because you have sound action plans in place for capturing your greater share of the business, you are able to build a disproportionately high customer share. Over time, your relationship develops from being a preferred supplier to an informal partner, and, although nothing in life is guaranteed, your business with this customer is about as secure as it can be. You are maximizing the value of the account to your company—and maximizing the value of your products and services to the customer.

To reach these green pastures, you need to put the *management* into strategic account management, and that means performing many of the classic functions of management:

Understanding. Knowing the customer inside out; knowing your customer's markets and their customers; knowing how their industry works and how your products or services contribute to their business; knowing your competitors and understanding what they offer, how they differentiate themselves, and how they strive to gain competitive advantage; and knowing yourself, knowing your own strengths and weaknesses and how you are perceived by the customer.

Analyzing. Examining your performance in the account, drawing the right conclusions about your successes and failures, and learning from both; applying other analytical tools to develop a broader and deeper understanding of the customer's needs and how you can leverage your strengths and mitigate your weaknesses.

Prioritizing. Knowing where and how much time and resources to devote in the account given its size, potential, and relative importance to you and your company; managing your investment in the customer and allocating resources most efficiently.

Setting direction. Having a purpose; knowing where you want to take the account; having a vision that can be expressed in specific goals and objectives.

Taking initiative. Seeking and seeing opportunities that others don't see; creating energy around those initiatives and motivating others to join them; being proactive in looking ahead and establishing action toward shared goals.

Planning. Deciding how and when to approach the customer, where to focus your efforts, which of their needs to address, and what products and services to offer or develop; developing a strategy for realizing the account's potential; and identifying action steps necessary to implement your strategy.

Team building. Building a cooperative group of supporters and stakeholders in your company (and potentially in the customer's organization) that shares the vision, is committed to your aspirations for the account, and acts in a concerted manner to achieve them.

Coordinating. Synchronizing the activities of multiple people involved in the account; ensuring that people's actions are complementary and that actions are taken by the right people at the right time.

Communicating. Managing the flow of information to and from the customer's organization; ensuring that you have enough of the right information to assess the situation and act in a timely manner and that the customer has enough information about your company to make informed decisions.

Mobilizing. Managing momentum in the account; mobilizing more of your company's resources when necessary to respond to opportunities or problems; being efficient in your use of resources but always applying enough resources to meet the need.

Problem solving. Addressing delivery, installation, or performance problems with your products or services, on the one hand, and on the other being able to help customers solve problems on other issues within the scope of your expertise.

Attending. Being constantly aware of the state of your relationship with the customer and actively attending to customer satisfaction; knowing what the customer needs and is concerned about on an ongoing basis, understanding their key issues, and increasing the value they place on your interactions with them.

Measuring. Valuing your own company's return on its investment in this customer; satisfying your internal needs for a high return on that investment.

In summary, managing a strategic account means being systematic and proactive in developing and *working* the customer relationship so that you sustain the relationship at its peak value (to both you and the customer) for the longest period possible. It also means viewing the account as a business investment in which success is measured by your ability to minimize expenses (e.g., the "overhead" of time spent managing the account and performing non-revenue-generating activities) while maximizing your returns.

If this is such a great idea (and it is), why shouldn't you do it for all your customers? Very simply, it's too expensive. The investment in time and resources you would have to make for less important customers simply outweighs their potential benefit to you. You shouldn't discount those customers or prospects, but they do not warrant the degree of focus that strategic accounts do.

The sine qua non of strategic account management is your willingness to assume a leadership role in the account—to act rather than react, to create a vision and inspire others to adopt it as their own, to challenge the status quo, to innovate, and to motivate people in your own company and the customer's organization to support you. If you're not leading, you're following; and if you're following, you go where other people tell you to go, get what they choose to give you, and have potential only as great as the limits they set for you.

Unfortunately, many account managers lack the resources or authority to really manage their accounts. Mark Sebastiani is one. He's a strategic account manager for Pulp & Paper Products (3P), a large paper products supply firm. Mark manages two major accounts, the most important of which is Pacific Office Station, a national chain specializing in office supplies. Mark's company has developed an advanced point-of-sale system for managing inventory, and Mark knows that inventory management is a critical success factor in Pacific's industry. He thinks that his company has a lot to offer Pacific, but he is constrained by the sales budget and can't make the kinds of calls he needs to make in order to promote his system. At the National Office Supply Show in Los Angeles, he wanted to host a meeting between his company's senior people and key executives from Pacific, but management wouldn't approve his request because of other priorities. Some of the senior executives in 3P call on their friends at Pacific, but these executives never take Mark along and often don't bother to tell him about their calls.

Mark's counterpart in Pacific knows that he can't commit 3P to a contract. Mark doesn't even have the authority to negotiate a deal. When the negotiations begin, Mark is required to turn over the matter to his sales manager and 3P's Legal Affairs VP, who meet with the customer to seal the deal. No matter what Mark is called or how his job description reads, in reality he's a low-level functionary and matchmaker, and everyone knows it. When they want to get serious and talk business, they go over his head to where the real power resides.

Mark's case illustrates a fundamental fact about strategic account management: The companies that are serious about it ensure that their account managers have the authority and resources to really *manage* their accounts. This requires trust, and they develop that trust by assigning the right people to become account managers, giving them the right training, and then establishing management systems that give account managers the autonomy and authority to function as business leaders.

— 5 —

Strategic Account Management as an Instrument of Corporate Strategy

Strategic account management is one of the most important tools you have for implementing your company's strategic vision. Businesses exist to serve customers, and the group of customers that are your strategically important accounts usually provide a significant portion of your revenue; therefore, strategic account management constitutes the core of your raison d'être. Further, because strategic account management focuses primarily on your most successful customer relationships, it represents the fullest and most effective manifestation of your corporate strategy. A number of metaphors that describe the relationship of strategic account management to strategic planning come to mind, but I like the one represented by Figure 5-1.

It's easy to imagine strategic account management as the core of your customer relationships, the trunk out of which all major and minor customers branch. What gives strategic account management its foundation, what keeps it anchored in solid ground, are the various roots of strategic planning—your core competencies as an organization; your culture; your established markets and the installed base of your products in customer organizations; your brand image and consequent customer preferences and loyalties; your history of service to customers; and the product, service, distribution, or other differentiators that provide your competitive advantage. These roots provide sustenance to your strategic accounts in terms of focus, direction, style, and substance. In turn, your strategic accounts feed the roots—with profitability; information; new business; and, not least, encouragement. I don't want to carry this metaphor too far, but it does illustrate the foundational nature of strategic planning and how it is a crucial precursor to strategic account management.

Figure 5-1. Strategic Account Management as an Outgrowth of Strategic Planning

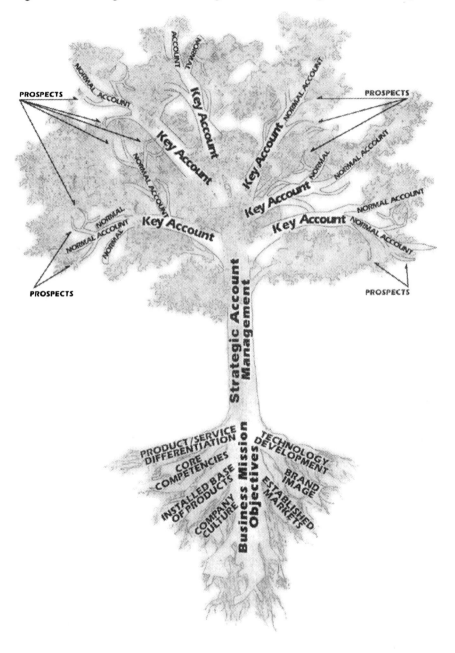

The Strategic Planning Process

Any company's business strategy seeks to answer these fundamental questions: *What business are we in now?* and *What should our business be in the future?* The answers to these questions indicate how the company views itself as a business entity and how its management anticipates changing in response to the dynamic social, economic, political, and competitive environment in which it exists. The strategic planning process—and its symbiotic relationship with strategic account management—is shown in Figure 5-2.

Figure 5-2. The Strategic Planning Process

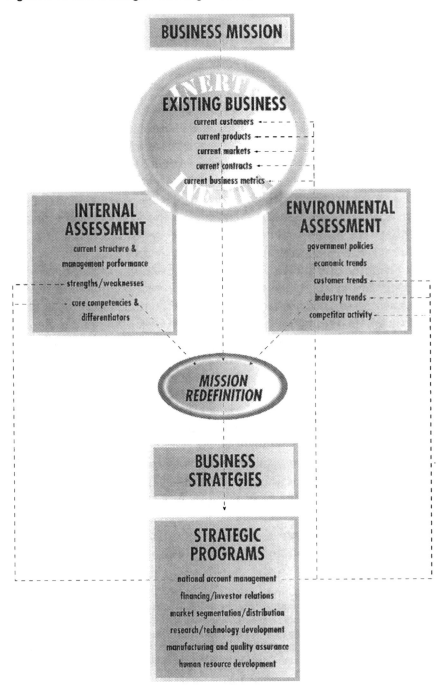

Redefining the Business Mission—The Forces of Inertia

The driving force in any business enterprise is its mission. Regardless of whether it is defined formally or informally, the mission or business purpose determines what business the enterprise is in, what core competencies it develops, what products or services it provides, what industries and customers it serves, which regions it serves, and how it seeks to sustain a competitive advantage. The mission represents how a company imagines itself and how it has grown, including which types of people it has attracted and retained. It also reflects what the company has excluded: the skills outsourced or considered irrelevant; the people not sought or hired; the products and services not offered; and the regions, markets, or customers avoided. In strategic planning, companies begin with their mission and are deeply rooted in what that represents. This is not to say that the mission cannot be changed, but companies develop considerable inertia in their development of products, services, markets, competencies, and identity as a business organization—and it takes powerful forces to overcome that inertia.[1] An IBM or Amoco can't decide overnight to become a different company, producing different products in different markets for different customers. This may happen over time, but radical shifts in identity and direction are virtually impossible except in small start-ups, where an infusion of new capital can fund radical shifts in direction in response to opportunities in the marketplace or technology breakthroughs. So the mission of the business is a strong inertial force, and it tends to keep companies moving in the same direction they've been moving. Collectively, the company's strategic accounts form a major part of this inertia, because they draw on the core competencies, demand a significant amount of management attention, and will, over time, cause the company not only to devote many of its resources to serving the strategic accounts but also to position its resources so that it can serve those customers most efficiently. In this regard, strategic accounts are a major force opposing change. Paradoxically, as we will see, they can also be a major force *driving* change.

Strategic planning has two purposes: to determine whether and how to redefine the company's mission, given changes in its operating environment, and to identify the business strategies and strategic programs necessary to accomplish its mission, which may or may not have been redefined. Much of the time, the company's mission doesn't change. But it's easy to imagine how the strategic planning session might have gone in a wagon

---

1. Inertia is defined as resistance to motion, change, or action. It is the tendency of a body at rest to remain at rest or a body in motion to remain in motion, moving in a straight line, unless acted on by an external force. I am using the concept to refer to a business entity's tendency to continue doing what it's been doing unless external forces compel it to change. All companies develop inertia, and the larger and more established they are, the stronger the inertial force and the more resistant they are to change.

wheel manufacturer at the beginning of the twentieth century. They might have anticipated a decline in the need for wooden wagon wheels and redefined their business as producers of automobile tires. Similarly, food manufacturers have had to anticipate or respond to rising demand for food products that can be prepared in the microwave (fast food for homes) and a corresponding decline in demand for food products requiring longer preparation time. In numerous industries, changes in customer needs or expectations, lifestyles, raw materials costs, and other factors force companies to either redefine themselves or die (as most wooden wagon wheel manufacturers actually did). But redefining the business is difficult. Companies have much invested in their existing business, and, as shown in Figure 5-2, their current customers, products, markets, and long-term contracts reinforce the current business mission and create powerful inertia, particularly if the company's current business metrics are favorable. When companies are performing at or near their expectations (which often are determined by industry performance benchmarks), there is little impetus for change. Indeed, it is easy to become complacent when the numbers look good. But even when the numbers sour, the organization's typical response is to look for problems to solve in their existing operating structure and systems: find more customers, develop more variations of the same products or services, explore previously untapped markets, and so on. In the flow of their existing business, there is little motivation for companies to redefine who they are and what they do. The need to generate cash to fund continuing operations is like a mighty river coursing through a valley that the river itself has created, and changing the direction of that mighty flow practically requires an act of God.

The company's strategic accounts contribute mightily to this inertia, because they represent the greatest share of current revenue and profitability. The proportions change from industry to industry and company to company, but it's not unusual for a company's strategic accounts to represent 80 percent of its business. Consequently, these key accounts are the largest drivers of current business metrics. When a company measures its performance, it is largely measuring the performance of those accounts. Likewise, the executives who decide whether and how to change the company's direction also are measured by key account performance. If those accounts appear solid, if the revenue stream is continuing and there are no warning signs, then there is little impetus for change.

Redefining the Business Mission—The Forces of Change

Three elements of the strategic planning process represent forces of change—forces that may compel companies to redefine their business, change their strategic direction, or abandon some strategic programs and initiate others.

In order of impact, these elements are an environmental assessment, internal assessment, and changes in the existing business, which are largely driven by changes in key account performance (see Fig. 5-2).

Environmental Assessment

The environmental assessment is the company's attempt to develop *out*sight (as opposed to *in*sight)—to understand the changes in the three domains, shown in Figure 5-3, that can affect their competitive posture. External changes generally are the most important, because companies have limited control over them. Overall economic trends and changes in government regulations or policies can have profound impacts on an industry. For example, deregulation of the airline industry resulted in massive restructuring of the industry, caused some carriers to fail, and stimulated the growth of numerous regional airlines serving smaller communities. Similarly, small business and minority set-asides in federal contracts have changed the way large government contractors bid on projects (in some cases causing them to no-bid opportunities they previously would have pursued or to partner with small businesses) and have stimulated the growth of many small contractors.

An environmental assessment also examines trends in the industries and markets the company it is serving. It uses market research to examine changes in customers' needs, buying practices, and consumer demographics. Of particular interest to the strategic planner are the industry trends that may signal changes in customers' demands. Will they need more or

Figure 5-3. The Domains of Environmental Assessment

less of my products or services in the future? Will they demand different features from the ones we offer today? How will their expectations change? For instance, the assessment may indicate that more manufacturers are outsourcing plant maintenance and that they prefer local providers. If you provide maintenance services, this may indicate the need to open local offices in targeted cities. Or the assessment may reveal that more retailers are relying on magnetic antitheft devices to curtail shoplifting, which may signal the need to change the way your products are packaged. Finally, the assessment should identify changes in competitor activity—strategic directions they are moving in and what these directions are likely to accomplish, new products or services competitors are introducing, contracts they have won or lost (and why), their evolving position in the marketplace (including customers' perceptions of them), changes in market share (and what those changes represent), and so forth. A thorough environmental assessment should provide a complete picture of the competitive environment in which your company operates. At its most extreme, an assessment can reveal such shrinking demand for a particular line of products or services that it compels the company to reduce or eliminate that line; more commonly, an environmental assessment reveals problems or opportunities that should be exploited through business strategies but that don't force the company to redefine its mission or undertake a more radical restructuring in order to accommodate changes in the marketplace. In any case, changes in the environment are a potent force for changes in strategy.

Internal Assessment

Internal developments, such as the development of new technologies, can prompt changes in a company's strategic direction. An internal assessment is a strategic planner's attempt to develop *in*sight by identifying problems and opportunities within the company's own systems and operations. The planner examines the company's strengths and weaknesses in every part of its value chain—the linkage of internal processes that constitute how the business builds value for its customers. The value chain normally includes engineering or product development, marketing, production or manufacturing, sales, distribution, and customer service, as well as various support activities such as procurement, human resource management, and finance. Form tends to follow function, so companies organize themselves in the manner that most efficiently enables the creation and delivery of value for their customers. At least, that's the theory. In practice, a company's structure is like an elephant chasing a gazelle, the latter representing the swift and often unpredictable changes in the marketplace. Although the elephant can keep sight of the gazelle and change direction accordingly, its movement is sluggish by comparison, and it never catches up. That's why companies rarely make subtle structural changes. When structure is changed—through reorganization or downsizing—to accommodate new marketplace realities, it tends to be noisy, abrupt, and disconcerting for everyone involved.

Strategic planning tries to anticipate these changes by noting how the company's current structure either facilitates or inhibits its ability to carry out its mission, and strategic programs, such as cross-functional teams, sometimes are initiated to make structure more responsive to a rapidly changing competitive environment. Similarly, part of internal assessment is an examination of the company's current leadership. Is it providing the vision and animation necessary to lead the company's workforce in the right direction? Is it sufficiently entrepreneurial where entrepreneurial action is necessary? Are there areas of the company where stronger leadership is required? Areas where the energies and visions of current managers have run their course, where a fresh spark of new leadership energy could move a function off center and create new excitement?

Finally, strategic planners examine the company's core competencies and differentiators. Does the company have the right set of core competencies to achieve its future aims? Should some competencies be outsourced? Should others be developed, perhaps through acquisitions? And is the company still well differentiated in its markets? Does it have clear advantage in areas critical to its competitive success? This latter question is an oft-neglected one during the strategic planning process, yet it is central to the fundamental questions being asked: *Where are we competitive now?* and *Where must we be competitive in the future?* (Note that these questions are similar to the two fundamental questions posed about the company's existence: *What business are we in now?* and *What should our business be in the future?*) These questions are similar because building a competitive advantage is the principal goal of a business enterprise. Any company's vitality depends on the competitive advantage it can develop and sustain. Nowhere is that advantage seen more clearly than in its strategic accounts, where its differentiation from competitors has enabled the company to secure a strong position.

Thus, the company's strategic account managers are primary sources of information on how its customers perceive the strengths and weaknesses of the company and its products or services. In the front lines of a major account, you quickly learn how important your core competencies are and how they help differentiate you from your competitors. You also clearly see when you are losing competitive advantage, when your products are falling behind the customer's evolving needs, when competitors begin making inroads to your customer through new products or services, or when some part of your value chain is failing to keep pace with the customer's expectations.

Changes in Existing Business

I said earlier that the existing business is a strong inertial force, but it is evident from this discussion that it also can be a force for change. When key account managers tell executives and strategic planners what they are hearing during their meetings with key customer executives, they become vital sources of information about how your industry is changing, how your customers are evolving, and what impacts these changes may have on the products and services you provide them. Ideally, the flow of information is like alternating current: the company's executives and strategic planners gain insight from industry and customer intelligence provided by account managers, whereas the account managers gain a broader perspective on the company's strategic directions, what impacts those changes will have on key customers, and what new products or services are forthcoming. The account managers then can use this information to position the company with its key accounts.

Are Your Channels Open?

During the strategic planning process in your company, do your strategic planners talk to the people who manage your strategic accounts? How do you ensure that the strategic planners are aware of your key customers' attitudes toward you and your products, of their perceptions of the value you provide, and of their evolving needs? Information from strategic account managers can influence your marketing direction, research focus, investment priorities, and other fundamental decisions made about the direction in which your company needs to go to retain and exploit its competitive advantages. One of my customers opened the channels by having its strategic planning staff interview all the account managers at the beginning of the strategic planning cycle. Another had its planning staff members accompany account managers into the field and interview key customers. If you don't have a planning staff, then the executives responsible for annual planning should be out in the field with your account managers. There is no better source of information on how your markets are evolving than the key customers who make the buying decisions that affect you. Within your own organization, the best sources are the account managers—not the engineers, the functional heads, or the CEO. Talking to the people who work with your customers continuously is the surest way to create strategic plans that reflect the realities of the marketplace.

Developing and Executing Business Strategy

Figure 5-2 shows the three forces of change converging on the next step in the strategic planning process: redefining the mission. In many cases, the mission will not need significant revision. If the company is performing well, no major changes have occurred in the competitive environment, and no signals from key accounts indicate the need for change, then the mission may continue as before, at least at the macro level—the broad definition of the nature of the company's business. At the micro level, there may be many changes, such as expansion into new markets, introduction of new products, different emphases in marketing and research, and so on. Microsoft made such a shift when they reacted to Netscape's introduction of an Internet navigator. Realizing that this represented a new form of software that could come to dominate personal computing, Microsoft swiftly created and introduced a competing product (Internet Explorer), which had not been part of its strategic direction. Although this new product did not redefine what Microsoft is, it did signal an important new direction for the software giant, a subtle revision to its mission. In other cases, where the company's performance is below par or other signals in the marketplace indicate the need for more radical change, then the mission may be redefined even at the broad level. IBM, which in the computer industry had been principally a mainframe manufacturer, did this when they introduced the personal computer (although they failed to recognize how radical a shift it represented and severely underestimated the important role that operating systems would play). Nonetheless, this is an example of a large corporation introducing a totally new product line related to, but still substantially different from, its core business.

Once the mission has been redefined, planners must determine how to accomplish it, and the result is a set of business strategies. In large corporations, business strategies at this level tend to have a broad scope and may be far-reaching, as these actual examples show:

- Expand into developing Eastern European markets by acquiring distributors and manufacturers in key market segments.
- Exploit our technology advantage in parallel-processed networks and use aggressive pricing to build rapid market share and establish a large installed product base with high exit barriers.
- Exploit the brand by diversifying into related products that convey an upbeat lifestyle to young adults.
- Develop a chain of food outlets offering fast and reasonably priced home-cooked, takeout meals to busy families.

Effective business strategies identify both your intent (*capitalize on the brand*) and the fundamental action needed to realize it (*by diversifying into related products*).

The examples I've given are not as extensive or detailed as many statements of business strategy; nonetheless, they express the two essential parts of strategy: intent and action. Business strategies are implemented through a series of strategic programs, which may include market research to explore consumer preferences, research projects to develop new prod-

---

Establishing Strategic Account Management

If your company is just now implementing strategic account management or is seeking to make strategic account management more integrated in the way you conduct your business, then it would be wise to establish strategic account management as a strategic program and to make managing strategic accounts one of your business strategies. The following strategy statement is generic but could serve as a blueprint for a business strategy that emphasizes the new direction you wish to take:

> Maximize the value potential in our existing business relationships by actively managing our most important accounts.

The strategic program you institute for strategic account management might have these elements:

- A cultural change program in which senior executives and line managers show a commitment to strategic accounts and communicate the importance of that commitment throughout the organization
- A reorganization of the sales force to assign strategic account managers and to build support structures around them
- A redistribution of authority that gives account managers primary responsibility for maintaining key customer relationships, and a realignment of communication channels so that all communications with key customers are focused through the appropriate strategic account manager
- Appropriate revisions to budgets, reporting mechanisms, performance metrics, and other systems
- Revisions to position descriptions and communication of expectations regarding the roles various people play in serving strategic account teams or (for executive sponsors) monitoring their progress and providing guidance and support

Strategic account management cannot be implemented effectively unless there is a commitment from the top and unless the company's structure and systems are modified in some fundamental ways. Strategic account management is not a quick fix, nor is it something you can overlay on top of existing systems. To manage your strategic accounts effectively, you need to commit to doing business differently.

ucts or technologies, marketing campaigns to promote new products or the brand itself, and manufacturing programs to streamline production and reduce costs. For our purposes, the most important strategic program is the company's initiative to manage its strategic customer relationships. In many companies, strategic account management is not explicitly identified as a strategic program, but it's treated as such anyway. In companies that are exceptional at managing strategic accounts, strategic account management is part of the fabric of how business is done, and its programmatic nature is reflected in the organization of the sales force, the compensation system, performance review systems, and position expectations at many levels—from the sales and operations people who manage key accounts or participate on account teams to the senior executives who are expected to make senior-level contacts with key customers and conduct periodic account reviews.

Strategic Account Management as a Competitive Strategy

Among the numerous benefits of strategic account management is its usefulness as an instrument of your strategy for building and sustaining competitive advantage. Once you have established your position with customers, your general aim will be to erect high entry barriers[2] against rivals who also are attempting to gain position with those customers and high exit barriers for customers who may seek to purchase competing products and services from your rivals. Strategic account management helps you sustain your competitive advantage in a number of ways:

1. The differentiation of your products or services from your competitors' products or services will create an entry barrier for rivals as long as your areas of differentiation match your customers' greatest needs and your rivals cannot show equivalent strengths in these areas. Conversely, if customers view your products or services as commodities, which any supplier can provide, then the switching costs for customers are low and any supplier can gain entry unless other entry barriers are in place.

One of the goals of strategic account management is to reinforce the differentiation of your products or services, if not in fact, then at least in perception. Of course, products can be differentiated in many ways, including such intangible differentiators as brand image, service or quality reputation, the impression of

---

2. Readers familiar with Michael Porter's *Competitive Strategy* will note that I am using these terms more tactically than he uses them. I use *entry barrier* to mean anything that hinders your competitors from displacing you in the account once you have established your position with the customer and *exit barrier* interchangeably with *switching costs* to mean anything that inhibits the customer from switching from you to a competitor.

convenience or ease in working with your company, and the strength of personal relationships. Account managers may not be able to create differentiation in technical areas of your products or services, but they can directly influence the customer's perceptions and can actively strengthen the quality of the relationships. In short, they can build intangible differentiation, which in itself can build customer loyalty and thus create an entry barrier.

2. By the time you have established a position with a customer, you will have climbed the learning curve with them and thus increased knowledge and trust on both sides. The opening stages of a business relationship are much like the opening stages of any relationship—people don't know one another well. Inevitably, there are fumblings, mistaken assumptions, and miscommunications. Theodore Levitt refers to this stage as a "courtship," and it is an appropriate metaphor. According to Levitt, "The sale merely consummates the courtship. Then the marriage begins. How good the marriage is depends on how well the relationship is managed by the seller. That determines whether there will be continued or expanded business or troubles and divorce, and whether costs or profits increase."[3]

Trust and comfort can grow as companies learn to work together, as they iron out the coordination issues, as they learn each other's operating styles, and as they discover and adapt to cultural differences. Beyond the relational aspects of bonding, there are technical factors as well: How must equipment be adapted? What configurations are preferred? What level of technical help is needed? Which details does the customer want to handle or outsource to other providers?

Once these relational and technical learnings have taken place, the level of comfort grows, and the trust that grows between buyer and supplier creates an emotional bond that also represents an entry barrier for rivals. Strategic account managers should manage this learning process, ensuring that the requisite levels of comfort are established. The company's technical managers and professionals clearly are involved in this process and are responsible for handling many of the issues that arise during the early stages of product or service delivery, installation, and operation. Nonetheless, there should be a single person (the account manager) who oversees and assumes responsibility for managing the learning curve. He or she should consciously attend to this process to ensure that the early relational and technical issues are resolved quickly and that trust grows stronger, thus erecting an entry barrier.

3. You may be able to develop a cost advantage through experience with the customer and through economies of scale. The cost of customizing solutions or products, for instance, and the various costs of learning should decline after the initial products or services are delivered or installed. You also may be able to realize efficiencies in production, inventory management, maintenance, and shipping. The account manager should be looking for these efficiencies and ensuring that the customer is aware of the cost savings accrued through continuing business with you. Rivals still would bear the costs of customization and learning and would not yet have realized efficiencies due to experience, so in theory their costs should be higher if they are offering comparable products or services. However, in present-

---

3. Theodore Levitt, *The Marketing Imagination* (New York: The Free Press, 1983), p. 111.

ing an aggressive offer to your key customers, they may strive to hide these costs. It's your account manager's responsibility to ensure that these hidden costs are exposed.

4. If you have an established position with key customers, you may have been able to create favorable locations or distribution channels, which can create an entry barrier to rivals who are not so well located. Companies in some industries, for example, will open a local office to serve a key customer. Once open, this site can provide a competitive advantage because of the proximity to the customer.

Similarly, you can gain advantage if your product forms an installed base that customers cannot abandon without unacceptable switching costs. The classic example is computer hardware. Once the hardware is installed, the software purchased and customized, the users trained, and the support and maintenance functions established, the cost of switching to a noncompatible system often is prohibitively high, and it forms a substantial entry barrier to rivals and exit barrier to customers.

You may also gain advantage if you and the customer share some functions or operations (for example, you have joint site inspection teams, quality assurance staffs, engineering or design groups, or similar joint functions). Depending on the nature of your business, such joint staffs can help ensure that your and the customer's needs for information and assurance are met more effectively than if you were conducting these functions separately. Joint staffs can create a barrier to entry for rivals.

It is important to realize that, in each of these instances, strategic account management reinforces your competitive advantage only to the extent that you communicate the advantages to your customers; highlight the added costs and difficulties of using competitors; and stress the benefits that accrue to the customer because of your favorable locations, installed base, or joint staff.

5. In each of the previous items, you also benefit from more and better information, including potentially "inside" information on the customer's problems, needs, and plans. Having more and better information enables you to anticipate changes and to position yourself to fulfill their emerging needs. Your account manager should provide superior knowledge of their organization—knowledge your competitors are less likely to have. Of particular interest are upcoming structural changes that may impact their needs, the decision-making processes they follow when they make buying decisions, and the biases and perspectives of the individuals involved in those decisions. Superior information also gives you insights into their systems, technologies, and administration of their business. An effective account manager ensures that you know the customer intimately and can use your knowledge to be there ahead of your competitors with greater insight into your customer's needs—which gives them more confidence in you—and offer a more focused, less risky solution.

6. The longer you work with a key customer, the greater your brand identification can become (if they view you favorably), and this can create strong customer loyalty. Clearly, if you are not performing, if your products have high failure rates, or if your services are not meeting their needs, then your brand can erode quickly. But if you are performing and they are satisfied with your products or services, then you are spoken about favorably. Their people don't think of this type of

product or service without thinking of you. The longer you serve them, the stronger this impression becomes.

At the extreme end of brand loyalty, customer representatives can't imagine not using you. The best account managers understand this and reinforce the brand whenever they can. They try to arrange joint presentations with key customers. They strive to put the name in front of key people as frequently as they can without overexposing the image. They ensure that key people remain aware of your history with them and the continuity of service that confers advantages they can't get elsewhere. With normal, smaller customers, the amount of access required to accomplish this may not be possible, but one advantage of strategic account management is the depth and breadth of access you typically have to the customer's key people.

7. No buyer–supplier relationship is without problems. Indeed, Theodore Levitt argues that "one of the surest signs of a bad or declining relationship is the absence of complaints from the customer. Nobody is ever *that* satisfied, especially not over an extended period of time. The customer is either not being candid or not being contacted. Probably both."[4] So the fact that the customer complains is not necessarily a bad sign. Paradoxically, it can convey advantage because in an established business relationship you should have well-defined problem resolution procedures and channels, which competitors attempting to penetrate the account will not have.

If you are addressing the problems and being proactive about learning from mistakes when they occur, you build more trust because of your candor and the initiative you are taking to improve your service. Now and then, some customer representatives may fall prey to the "grass is greener" syndrome as they listen to your competitors' promises, and it is your account manager's responsibility to ensure that the grass looks green on your side of the fence, too. Because of the importance of active problem resolution in maintaining customer relationships, some corporations, such as General Electric, have institutionalized procedures for joint problem solving with customers. GE's Work-Outs, which initially were intended only as internal team problem-solving efforts, were extended to include customers once their value became apparent.

8. Finally, a long-standing relationship with a key customer tends to create emotional barriers that inhibit customers from switching to your competitors. If you are serving your customers well, they come to depend on you. They rely on the quality and satisfaction you've been providing and will be reluctant to switch to another supplier because that level of satisfaction can't be guaranteed. In part, they fear the unknown, and in part they fear change. At a more personal level, they also may fear losing the relationships that have been established with your people. We all tend to feel more comfortable with people we know, and we are more inclined to be influenced by people with whom we have some affinity. Your long-standing relationships with key customers give you a sort of common history, which helps build an emotional bond.

---

4. Theodore Levitt, *The Marketing Imagination* (New York: The Free Press, 1983), p. 119.

That bond can be broken, of course. If there are compelling financial or technological reasons to switch to a competitor, then your relationships may not save the business, but if other factors are equal, relationships alone can make the entire difference, and often they can compel customers to give you the business even when your price is higher and your offer lacks some benefits your competitors can provide. Consequently, one of your principal roles is to manage the relationship with your key customers. If those relationships are strong, they can create a substantial barrier to your competitors.

One of the goals of strategic account management is to build your relationships to the point where the psychological switching costs are high (i.e., where the distress the customer would experience as a result of losing your relationship and starting over building new ones is so high they don't want to pay the price). Clearly, factors other than relationship quality must conspire if the switching costs are to be high. Your products or services must be important to the customer. The more vital they are to the customer's business and the more scarce the potential suppliers who can meet their needs, the more importance they will place on their relationship with you. In both the features of your offer and their benefits to the customer, customers also must receive the value they expect. Further, your price must be within the competitive range they consider reasonable for the value received. In most cases, your price need not be the lowest, but it must not be higher than the customer considers reasonable. If your price is the highest price, your customers must be able to justify it to the people they report to.

There are myriad ways in which strategic account management functions as an instrument of your company's competitive strategy. As one of your strategic programs, it helps you realize the vision articulated in your strategic plan. But more than that, it is a fundamental way in which you build and sustain a competitive advantage. It can create entry barriers that thwart your competitors' attempts to capture the business you have built with your key accounts, and it can create strong exit barriers that discourage your key customers from acceding to your competitors' promises. Done well, it not only can protect the revenue and profitability you realize from your key accounts but also ensure that your customers receive the maximum value from you. However, this cannot be done without a considerable investment of time and energy, and you cannot make that level of commitment to every one of your customers. So how do you decide which accounts are strategically important? That's the subject of the next chapter.

— 6 —

Identifying Strategic Accounts

Vilfredo Pareto, an Italian economist and sociologist born in 1848, contributed to a number of fields. His study of elite classes in societies was influential in the development of fascism (not his greatest achievement), and his work in statistics can still be seen in the use of Pareto diagrams, which are helpful in quality control analysis. But he probably is best known today for the Pareto principle (also known as the 80-20 rule), which suggests that, in many applications, 80 percent of the effects can be attributed to 20 percent of the causes. Applied to your management of customer accounts, the Pareto principle theorizes that 80 percent of your revenue can come from 20 percent of your customers. In practice, these numbers often are much more dramatic. One of my customers derives 74 percent of its revenue from just 4.8 percent of its customers.

Account Classifications

Whatever your actual percentages, it's helpful to divide your accounts into the three categories shown in Figure 6-1. In this hierarchy of accounts, perhaps 10 percent of the companies you sell to (or hope to sell to) would be considered strategic accounts. The next tier down, which consists of your normal customer accounts, might account for 30 percent of your total customer base, and the remaining 60 percent would consist of your prospects. Placing your customers in one of these three tiers helps you prioritize your efforts and pay the appropriate amount of attention to customers or potential customers at each level.

The three tiers of the pyramid shown in Figure 6-1 can be defined as follows:

Strategic Accounts

Strategic accounts are defined by the following characteristics:

- They are critically important to achieving your organizational goals.
- They provide a significant proportion of your current revenue.

Figure 6-1. The Account Pyramid

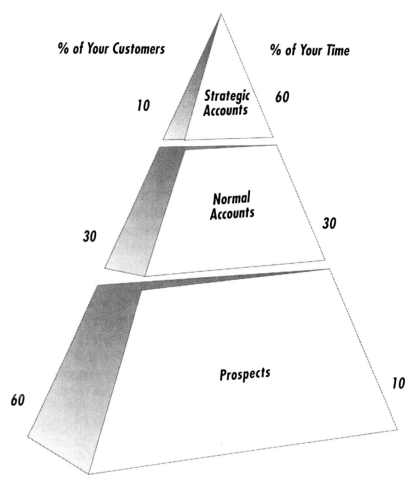

- Their loss would significantly impact your business and be difficult to re-cover from in the short term.
- Typically, you have an established, long-term relationship with them, and they have high potential for future business.
- Although they may represent only 10 percent of your customers and prospects, you should devote about 60 percent of your sales time to them.
- Because of their importance to your company, your most capable people should be responsible for managing their relationships.

Normal Accounts

Normal accounts are those that meet these criteria:

- They do not provide a significant proportion of your revenue, and their loss would not be damaging. (Losing *all* of them would obviously be damaging, but the loss of a single normal account typically is not critical.) Together, they represent about 30 percent of the customers and prospects you have, and you should devote about 30 percent of your time to them.

- For various reasons, they are not high-value, high-potential customers, at least in the short term.
- There may be moderate turnover among these customers, but they are replaceable through normal sales efforts that convert prospects into first-time customers.
- Sales to these customers are handled routinely by the sales force. However, when some normal customers develop more potential or generate an increasingly higher amount of revenue, they may become important enough to be reclassified as strategic accounts.

Prospects

Prospects are defined by the following parameters:

- They are not currently customers, but they need your types of products or services. You discover them through your normal prospecting efforts.
- You are talking to them, or they have shown interest in talking to you. In other words, they are more than *potential* prospects.

Gone Hunting

Salespeople sometimes are labeled as *hunters* or *farmers*. Hunters get their satisfaction from tracking and bagging the big bears. Nothing is more exciting for them than the hunt. Guns loaded, they head out into the field, searching for the next new big customer—the bigger deal than last time—and nothing thrills them more than when the customer says yes. "It was THIS big!" you can imagine them saying. Other salespeople are farmers. They like to work the soil, plant seeds, and see their hard work grow. They're happy when they can manage one good harvest after another, getting the maximum yield from the same forty acres.

Obviously, farmers make better account managers. The hunters are too focused on the next big kill. Farmers have the patience to work the territory, to make the repeated contacts over a long period, to hold the customer's hand when necessary, and to manage the details needed to maintain and build the account. Hunters typically lack patience and don't like to bother with the details. A sales force needs both, but a common mistake is to try to convert the hunters into farmers. Because the hunters are so flashy and often grab the limelight with spectacular wins, management assumes they should be handling the biggest accounts. But it's usually better to have the hunters hunting and the farmers farming.

- In most cases, they have unknown or uncertain potential. However, in some cases, their potential is known and is significant, but they currently are doing business with your competitors.
- Prospects are tracked by the sales force. If they are qualified and show potential, they receive more emphasis. Once a sale is made, they become normal customers. Although all salespeople may be responsible for tracking some prospects, in many sales organizations some people specialize in generating leads and qualifying prospects, turning them over to other salespeople once they reach a certain level of maturity.

As Figure 6-1 suggests, although your strategic accounts make up only 10 percent of your overall customer base, you should devote 60 percent of your time to them—and vice versa for your prospects. This makes good intuitive sense, but many sales forces don't do it. In trying to build their customer base, they often slight their key customers and spend far too much time chasing mirages, like the thrilling, big-ticket prospects that are always on the verge of closing but never actually do.

Classifying Customers

A more sophisticated tool for determining how to classify accounts is the customer classification system shown in Figure 6-2. I have seen a number of similar schemes for classifying customers, and they all work on essentially the same basis. They assume that customers and prospects can be characterized by their attractiveness, the business potential they represent, and their current or potential position with you. The virtue of this type of system is that it helps salespeople be more disciplined about prioritizing their time, and it helps the sales organization determine where best to allocate its resources. Before discussing which accounts are strategic, I will explain the evaluation categories.

Attractiveness

The first criterion is how attractive the customer is to you. Attractiveness, which is shown in the three rows in Figure 6-2, is a function of time and circumstance, so a customer who is not attractive now may be highly attractive in the future. Five factors affect the customer's attractiveness:

1. *Differentiation.* Relative to the customer needs, how well differentiated are you? Do your strengths match their needs? Are your weaknesses irrelevant or inconsequential? How well can you meet their requirements? How superior are your products or solutions to those of your competitors? Does the customer perceive that you are highly differentiated?

Figure 6-2. Customer Classification System

	High Potential		Medium Potential		Low Potential	
	Strong Position	Growth Position	Good Position	Entry Position	Limited Position	Exit Position
A – High Attraction	★★★★	★★★	★★	◆	◆	✗✗
	Well differed	Well differed	Well differed	Well differed	Well differed	Well differed
	Buy value	Buy value	Buy value	Buy value	Buy value	Buy value
	Biased to us	Biased to us	Biased to us	Biased to us	Biased to us	Biased to us
	Good access	Good access	Good access	Good access	Good access	Good access
	Few rules	Few rules	Few rules	Few rules	Few rules	Few rules
	High volume	High volume	Medium volume	Medium volume	Low volume	Low volume
	High profit	High profit	Medium profit	Medium profit	Low profit	Low profit
	Strong current relationship	High growth relationship	Good current relationship	High potential relationship	Limited current relationship	Declining relationship
	A1	A2	A3	A4	A5	A6
B – Medium Attraction	★★★	★★	◆	◆	✗✗	✗✗✗
	Okay differed	Okay differed	Okay differed	Okay differed	Okay differed	Okay differed
	Price & value	Price & value	Price & value	Price & value	Price & value	Price & value
	Neutral	Neutral	Neutral	Neutral	Neutral	Neutral
	Limited access	Limited access	Limited access	Limited access	Limited access	Limited access
	Flexible rules	Flexible rules	Flexible rules	Flexible rules	Flexible rules	Flexible rules
	High volume	High volume	Medium volume	Medium volume	Low volume	Low volume
	High profit	High profit	Medium profit	Medium profit	Low profit	Low profit
	Strong current relationship	Medium growth relationship	Good current relationship	Good potential relationship	Defensive relationship	Declining relationship
	B1	B2	B3	B4	B5	B6
C – Low Attraction	★★	◆	◆	✗✗	✗✗✗	✗✗✗✗
	Poorly differed	Poorly differed	Poorly differed	Poorly differed	Poorly differed	Poorly differed
	Price only	Price only	Price only	Price only	Price only	Price only
	Biased against	Biased against	Biased against	Biased against	Biased against	Biased against
	No access	No access	No access	No access	No access	No access
	Inflexible rules	Inflexible rules	Inflexible rules	Inflexible rules	Inflexible rules	Inflexible rules
	High volume	High volume	Medium volume	Medium volume	Low volume	Low volume
	High profit	High profit	Medium profit	Medium profit	Low profit	Low profit
	Defensive relationship	Low growth relationship	Defensive relationship	Low potential relationship	Defensive relationship	Declining relationship
	C1	C2	C3	C4	C5	C6

The A row in Figure 6-2 reflects situations in which you are highly differentiated, where the answers to all the above questions are positive. A customer is more attractive if your strengths match their needs. What makes them more attractive is that you can satisfy their needs more efficiently and effectively than your competitors can.

The B row reflects situations where you are somewhat differentiated but not completely, where your strengths do not match all the customer's needs, or where some competitors can offer similar features and benefits. Customers who might be more ambivalent about you are less attractive.

The C row represents situations where you are poorly differentiated. Here, you cannot match your strengths with the customer's needs. In fact, your weaknesses may match those needs, or you may not be able to meet the needs very well at all. Competitors may offer better solutions or have competitive advantages that make these customers less attractive.

2. *Value versus price.* Does the customer make buying decisions based primarily on value, price, or some combination of them? Value buyers are customers who will spend more money to get added value. All buyers consider price, of course, but value buyers are more willing to pay for added value than purely price buyers are.

In the B row, buyers will pay for value, but they must see it clearly demonstrated, and they tend to be very circumspect about what is value and what isn't. Typically, they will pay for some value items if the seller donates other value items. These customers are less attractive because they often negotiate hard on price, and they will shop around. Nonetheless, if you can offer convincing proof of the additional value, they will grudgingly pay for it.

The C row customers are principally low-price buyers, regardless of value. Their strategy typically is to specify a technical solution with certain requirements and standards, technically qualify the bidders, and then select the lowest-price offer. These are the least attractive customers because they treat suppliers as vendors and strive to eliminate value and relationship factors from the buying decision. If your products have built-in value enhancements, you may not be able to compete on price if a rival offers a stripped-down version of this product that nonetheless meets the customer's technical specifications. Typically, these customers are short-term thinkers, and the useful life of the products they buy typically is less than if they had spent more to buy a sturdier, more reliable, more versatile product. Consequently, their purchases often are more costly in the long term. However, these customers are being evaluated and rewarded for short-term results, so they make the kinds of decisions they're being rewarded to make. That may not help you, but that's how it is.

3. *Bias.* The third factor concerns how the customer views you—whether they are biased toward you, neutral toward you, or biased against you. This gets complicated because companies don't have biases, people do. So you have to consider the mix of people in the customer's organization who make or influence their buying decisions.

Obviously, the most attractive customers are those whose decision makers are biased toward you. They want to work with you, like your products or services, prefer your brand, or have personal biases because of their acquaintances or friendships with your account manager and others in your company.

A less attractive situation occurs when the customer's decision makers and influencers are essentially neutral. Perhaps they don't know you as well, or their experiences with you have not been uniformly positive, or they are striving to remain objective in their purchasing decisions.

The least attractive situation occurs when they are biased against you. Some of their key people may have had negative experiences with you or your products, or they may be biased toward your competitors.

4. *Access to key people.* How much access do you have to their key people, to their decision makers and influencers? Can you get to see them? Will they share their perspectives, hopes, and concerns? Can you learn enough about their needs and issues to create a highly focused solution?

In the A row, you have good access to key people, especially in the months and weeks before a purchasing decision. You can meet with them, learn their views, perhaps influence their selection criteria, and presell your solution. Clearly, this is a highly attractive situation.

The B row represents limited access. Perhaps you can meet with some of the key people but not all. Perhaps they place limits on your access or forbid you to discuss certain topics (such as their budget for this purchase).

Finally, in the C row you have essentially no access to key people. You may have limited or no access through your own incompetence if your account manager hasn't made the connections or hasn't gotten started on an opportunity early enough to learn who the key people are. But some customers deliberately limit suppliers' access to key people because they want to preserve the objectivity in the buying decision. It's a foolish prohibition because buyers *and* sellers gain from better information, but some customers don't see it that way, and they are not attractive prospects.

5. *Rules for buying.* The final factor concerns the customer's purchasing or procurement system. Is it flexible? Do they have few rules governing how buying decisions are made? Or are there inflexible rules that prohibit you from talking to key people at the right time?

Customers with inflexible rules (the C row) are difficult to deal with because they typically are very bureaucratic. Their stringent rules discourage creative solutions, and their insistence on following their procurement procedures can restrict the information flow between you and them. For instance, if they prohibit you from speaking to their end users or their technical evaluators, you may not be able to understand why they have specified certain requirements, whether variations or options are acceptable, or whether radically different solutions to the problem would be considered.

You have to use your judgment when deciding how attractive a customer is. Obviously, these five factors rarely are clustered as they are presented in Figure 6-2. You may have a situation in which you are well differentiated and the customer buys value, but they are neutral toward you, have restricted access to their key people, and have inflexible purchasing rules. Do your excellent differentiation and the customer's preference for buying value outweigh the other factors? You have to consider all these factors in aggregate and then decide which classification seems most warranted.

Potential

The second criterion concerns the customer's economic potential to you. In Figure 6-2, potential is shown in the three major columns across the top of the chart. The key is to ensure that you're looking forward, not backward. Customers who have provided significant revenue and profitability in the past are not necessarily high-potential customers, but they may appear to be. The tendency (and it's wishful thinking) is to assume that what's happened before will happen again. In any case, there are two primary factors that impact a customer's potential: volume and profitability.

1. *Volume.* How much future work does a customer represent? What is the potential volume of future sales? These seem simple questions, but the answer depends on how you measure potential volume, the time frame in which you measure it, and how certain you are about your estimates.

Volume typically is measured in sales dollars within a period of 1 to 2 years, depending on your business. However, in big-ticket items that recur less frequently, such as mainframe sales, global network implementations, or plant construction, it may make sense to focus on specific upcoming projects that occur once every 5 or more years. Conversely, with high-volume, low-cost items, such as cardboard containers, it may be more meaningful to measure the number of unit sales per month.

What Makes a Customer Attractive?

Besides differentiation, value versus price, and the other factors already cited, customer attractiveness also may depend on their financial condition, their position in their industry, and their future viability, which often depends on their sales trends; whether they are introducing new, innovative products; and the geographic distribution of their offices and markets. The customers who are acknowledged leaders in their fields are always more attractive because the prestige value of serving them can make you more attractive to other customers.

On a less tangible note, the compatibility of their values with yours also may factor into their attractiveness. Is this an organization you want to serve? Are they a showcase referral? The name you love to drop? Or, conversely, the name you hate to mention and wish had not been printed on your customer list? If it's true that you are known by the customers you keep, then you need to be selective about whom you serve. I've had customers who refused to serve potential customers in industries they felt were not compatible with their values, such as the arms or tobacco industries. If this matters to your company, then the customer's industry or products may determine which customers are attractive to you and which aren't.

However you measure volume, the difference between high, medium, and low volume will be apparent. The question is, how certain are you of your estimates? If sales history has been a good predictor of future volume, then you can achieve a fair degree of certainty if conditions have not changed. Look at the trends. Are they trending up or down? Or is volume predictably steady? You also can be reasonably accurate if the customer has budgeted for the purchases, they are critical to the customer's business, and no competitors are threatening your position. Otherwise, it is best to show your confidence level by indicating a range of potential volume (e.g., between $40,000 to $70,000).

Volume potential depends partly on the customer's size, but even more important on its unmet needs. A large customer with an installed base of your type of product has less potential than a similarly sized customer with no installed base and a growing need for the product. Furthermore, if your competitors are deeply entrenched in some business units, you may have little actual potential there, despite the overall extent of the customer's needs. So the question is always this: how much of the customer's potential volume could you capture if all conditions were *reasonably* favorable to you—assuming that your competitors get some of the business?

2. *Profitability*. How profitable are potential sales from this customer? What kind of margins have you historically achieved with this product or service and this customer? Profitability can usually be estimated more easily than volume because it tends to be less variable once you have delivered the product or service to the customer at a price you have agreed upon. Unless conditions have changed, your margins are likely to be predictable. If you have no historical data on margins with this customer, then you may need to rely on the standard margins in this industry for this type of product.

A customer's potential depends on the types of products or services you sell, the buying needs of your customers, and the conditions in your marketplace.[1] However you assess it, potential should reflect a combination of revenue volume and profitability. A high-potential customer offers both; a low-potential customer may be low in both areas, or it may offer low volume at high profitability or high volume at low profitability, neither of which represents strong potential if those conditions are static.

Position

The third criterion is the current position you have with the customer. Are you striving to build a relationship with them? Or are you already a strong, current supplier? Are you well entrenched and defending against competitors seeking to establish their position? Or are you in a declining rela-

---

1. Because volume sometimes is difficult to predict, some companies define potential according to other criteria, such as the number of locations the customer has, the number of services they are likely to need, the breadth of products they purchase, or the revenue potential from a minimum number of branch locations.

tionship, either because of reduced demand for your products and services or other problems that are leading the customer to buy from your rivals? The types of position are shown at the bottom of each box in Figure 6-2 and are described as follows:

1. *Potential relationship.* You currently are not serving the customer, but they have shown interest. Depending on the customer's size and the extent of their need, the potential may be low, medium, or high. [2]

2. *Growing relationship.* You have penetrated the account and established yourself as a supplier. You currently are growing the account and may have considerably more value to capture.

3. *Good current position.* You have a good relationship with the customer but more growth of the account is possible, perhaps by cross-selling products or services they need but aren't currently buying from you or by penetrating other divisions or buying units of their organization.

4. *Strong current position.* You are well entrenched with the customer and are maximizing the value you deliver to them as well as the value received from them. You have an excellent position and are harvesting the benefits of the strong relationship.

5. *Limited current relationship.* You have been selling to them for some time but have only limited penetration of the account and future growth is unlikely unless conditions change. Most often, this occurs because competitors are well entrenched in the other areas of the customer's organization that you could serve, so your position is steady but limited.

6. *Defensive relationship.* You have been selling to this customer, and your position may once have been good or strong, but it is now defensive. Poor performance or aggressive rivals are eroding the position you once had, and you may or may not be able to recapture it. In your defensive mode, you have been forced to lower price, so the account no longer has the potential it once did.

7. *Declining relationship.* You did serve the customer, but your position is declining, perhaps because they no longer need your services or because they have been cost cutting and it is no longer profitable for you to serve their needs. In the near future, you will likely exit from the account altogether.

According to Figure 6-2 there are eighteen classes of customers (labeled on the chart by a letter and number). Which of these customers would be considered strategic accounts? Certainly A1 (★★★★), A2 (★★★), and B1 (★★★), and probably B2 (★★). Without question, the three- and four-star customers are strategic, particularly because they represent high volume and profit. B2 customers will require more effort. You would

---

2. Later in this book I introduce a relationship life cycle model that explains these positions more thoroughly. I have not discussed the relationship life cycle here because it would add more complexity to an already complex discussion. However, position can be viewed in terms of one's position in the life cycle of a relationship with the customer. For more information, see chapter 12.

need to make them more attractive by improving your differentiation (if possible), convincing them to prefer added value in making purchasing decisions, and build your relationships so you have full access and can establish some bias in your favor. These are actionable steps that should be part of your account strategy.

A3 (★★) customers also may be strategic accounts. The only limiting factor is how much volume and profit they represent. If their potential remains moderate, they may not fall into the upper 10 percent of your customer base. C1 (★★) customers are more likely to be considered strategic accounts because of their high potential (volume/profit). However, their attractiveness is very low. It would take a Herculean effort, not only from your account manager but also your senior executives, to improve this situation, and that may not be possible because of the barriers the customer has erected (price buying, no access to key people, and inflexible rules). If you have better prospects, it may be wise to relegate C1 customers to normal account status and focus your strategic management efforts elsewhere.

On the other side of the chart, it is easy to dismiss the customers from hell—C6 (××××), C5 (×××), B6 (×××), and B5 (××). Their low potential and medium-to-low attractiveness don't leave much to recommend them. Yet it's not unusual to find salespeople chasing these night crawlers in the hope that they may metamorphose into butterflies. Unless you have a high tolerance for pain, it's best to avoid them. C4 (××) customers would not be good prospects except that they have shown interest in you (potential relationship) and they represent a moderate amount of revenue potential. They might be acceptable prospects if your sales team includes people designated to develop leads, but you would not devote significant time to them. Nor would you to A6 (××) customers, although—because they are so attractive—you would regret not being able to serve them more. These are probably companies that were good customers when they had greater need for your products. They are biased toward you, so the relationship probably is declining because they no longer need what you provide or they are in fiscal decline and no longer can afford your products at the rates you must charge.

The customers labeled with a diamond symbol (A4, A5, B3, B4, C2, C3) are neutral, neither strongly positive nor negative. Types A4, B3, and B4 are normal accounts. They aren't large enough to be strategic, but they do or can generate a moderate amount of revenue and may have growth potential. A5 is probably a low-level cash cow; it provides steady revenue but is not strategic because of its limited potential. C2 represents an exciting prospect because of its high potential, but the factors that make it unattractive suggest caution; it may not be possible to turn this one into a star. Nonetheless, this type of customer deserves attention and should be managed as a normal account until it shows signs of life, then it could become strategic. C3 customers don't have high potential, and you're in a defensive relationship with them. This is the type of customer that can sap a lot of your energy and never provide a decent return on your investment. However, if it's a signature account, it may be worth the fight.[3]

Obviously, it's possible for customers to be reclassified as circumstances change, and account managers can precipitate some of that change. It's generally not possible for you to impact the customer's potential because what they spend on your products and how much they're willing to pay for them are factors they have more control over than you do. But you can have some influence on a customer's attractiveness. You can try to increase your differentiation by customizing your products or services to their needs and requirements, or you can joint venture with other suppliers who sharpen your competitive edge, or you can introduce new products or services that offer benefits your competitors can't offer. You also can try to persuade them to buy value-added features and benefits. You can build the relationship and strive to create bias toward you and you can, through persistent efforts, improve your access to key people.

You also can affect your position with the customer to some degree. If you have a strong current relationship, you can work hard to keep it there; if you have only a potential relationship with the customer, you can strive to close that first sale and then deliver with excellence. So movement around this chart depends partly on the customer and partly on you. Table 6-1 summarizes the likely account status of each type of customer and the general strategy you might adopt with each one.

A customer classification system such as the one shown in Table 6-1 is a superb tool for sales managers. One of my customers uses something similar to ensure that salespeople are devoting the right amount of time and attention to each class of customer. The lessons learned from this kind of system may seem self-evident, but salespeople do chase dogs, and they have been known to cling to forlorn prospects far too long. This can occur because they have a friend in the customer's organization who keeps telling them that prosperity is just around the corner, or, more cynically, they've met a customer representative who wants to string them along for the free lunches. It happens. A system such as this helps you identify the criteria that make customers more or less important to your business so you can prioritize them and make the most intelligent use of your resources.

---

3. A signature account is a customer that would be highly prestigious to serve or a highly desirable account to have for any of these reasons: (1) they are best in class in their industry, the flagship corporation of their kind; in the software industry, Microsoft is an obvious example; (2) they are growing rapidly and are the darlings of Wall Street; the supplier that builds share with them early could be along for a great ride; (3) they dictate the standards in their industry; serving them would validate you with every similar company in their industry; (4) they have branches in all the areas you wish to serve or they have broad international presence that would enable you to expand internationally by riding on their coattails.

Table 6-1. Customer Account Status and General Strategy

Type of Account	Class	General Account Strategy
Strategic Account	A1	These are your signature accounts. Execute flawlessly and nurture the relationships throughout their organization but especially at the top. Seek a partnering relationship or strategic alliance if possible
	A2	These are high-growth accounts in a favorable environment. Try to convert them to A1 accounts by aggressively cross selling and building relationships throughout their organization
	B1	Work tirelessly to increase differentiation, gain access to more key people, and build bias toward you. Strong effort on your part can help make this customer more attractive. Try to make them A1s
	B2	Execute well in the areas you've penetrated, and try to convert them to A2s by promoting your differentiation, improving access to key people, and building bias. Also promote the added value you can provide
Normal Account	A3	Provide appropriate attention to these customers. Realize that it may not be possible to convert them to strategic accounts unless their needs change and their potential increases
	B3	Try to convert them into A3s by building differentiation, access to key people, and bias toward you. Sell your value-added enhancements but be competitive on price to grow your share of this customer's business
	C1	Try to convert them into B2s or B1s by aggressively building relationships wherever you have access. Success will likely require top-to-top connections, so involve your senior executives. Work hardest on access and overcoming the bias against you
	C2	Try to convert them into B2s using the strategies outlined for C1 customers. Exceed their expectations on the products you're delivering and try to accelerate growth in the account
	A5	Don't neglect your relationships with key people. These customers may be in decline, and their key people may go elsewhere, taking you with them. Otherwise, maintain the volume possible and seek other creative ways to serve them if possible
	A6	Try to convert them to A5s, but if the relationship continues to decline, find the least-cost exit strategy. Preserve the best relationships with key people
	C3	Many factors indicate that this is a dying relationship. To save it, you will have to be proactive in differentiating yourself from competitors and building relationships with key people. Is the account potential worth it? If so, try to convert them to B3s
Prospect	A4	These are excellent prospects. Strive to convert them to A3s by moving aggressively to close the first sale. Then execute well and consolidate your position
	B4	Try to convert them into B3s. Doing so will require better differentiation and steady work to gain access to key people and build bias in your favor
	C4	These are poor prospects, but with their potential they may be worth it if you can differentiate yourself well enough to remove the negative bias against you. Pursue only if your price enables you to generate reasonable return or if they would be signature customers and are worth the investment. Try to convert them into B4s
Dog	B5	If this customer's potential were higher, it would be worth the effort, but chasing this dog is probably fruitless unless their needs change, then try to convert them to B4s
	B6	With potential this low, the customer is probably not worth saving. Let the prospect die. Use your resources elsewhere
	C5	Hang on to this only if you're into pain and suffering
	C6	Get away as fast as possible, and don't let the door hit you in the back on the way out

When John Raymond joined Apex as Vice President of Sales, he inherited a sales force of 47 people dispersed in three regional offices and eleven district offices. As he toured the offices and got to know the people, he was impressed with their knowledge of the product and their work ethic, yet the group was only at 73 percent of goal, and sales had declined the past 3 years. The regional sales managers attributed Apex's problems to a decline in the market, but John knew that three of their major competitors had been increasing market share during Apex's decline, and Apex's products were not inferior. Something else was happening.

John found a clue when he began reviewing the business development tracking reports—a weekly listing of leads; prospects at various stages of development; and sales for each region, district, and salesperson. John noted that some high-ticket prospects had been on the books for 12 months or more. They made the pipeline look large, but there appeared to be no movement toward closure. When he called the salespeople involved, John heard a familiar story—that these were solid prospects but the projects kept getting delayed because of internal politics, disagreements over priorities, funding problems, and so on. The salespeople felt confident that these opportunities eventually would materialize but, when pressed, admitted that they didn't know when. To get the complete picture, John compared the business development tracking reports for each salesperson with their weekly call summaries, and he discovered that the salespeople were devoting an average of about 70 percent of their time to prospecting (some as much as 90 percent), no matter how viable those prospects were. When he inquired about the more questionable prospects, he learned that they wouldn't even qualify as wishful thinking—more like the shadows of wishful thinking! "Then why are we chasing these dogs?" he asked. It turned out that the salespeople received twice the incentive for bringing in new customers than they received for getting repeat business from existing customers. Now it made sense. You get what you pay for.

To turn this situation around, John overhauled the incentive plan, set up a customer classification system, required each salesperson to classify his or her accounts and justify their classifications, and then assigned account managers to each of Apex's newly designated strategic accounts. Salespeople were required to submit activity plans for upcoming months based on the priorities established by their account classifications, and long-range prospecting was assigned to a small group of hunters in each regional office whose personalities and talents were best suited to finding and developing leads. Within 3 months, overall sales had improved by more than 40 percent and repeat business from Apex's strategic accounts had jumped even higher. Knowing where to focus your time and resources is one of the secrets to effective management of business development.

Can prospects ever be considered strategic accounts? Frankly, there is no simple answer to this question. Some sales managers argue that accounts are strategic only when they provide a significant portion of your ongoing revenue and profitability. Others argue that the most important factor is potential, and if a prospect has the potential to generate high volume and profits, then it ought to be considered strategic. It may depend more on the viability of the prospect, which is a function of the certainty of their need and how well your competitors are positioned with them. If the need is strong and your rivals are not well positioned, then there is a greater probability that you can realize the account's potential. In this case, you should manage the prospect as though it were a strategic account, using all the tools and concepts discussed in this book. However, if competitors are well entrenched and have long-term contracts with the prospect, then managing the account strategically may be wasting your resources, at least for now. In either case, it's a judgment call.

The sales manager typically determines which accounts are strategic and which are normal, although this determination may be influenced by operational or technical managers, the strategic planning group, and the senior executives. Customers can be reclassified at any time, but sales managers generally conduct a formal review of customer classifications during the annual planning cycle. Using a tool such as the customer classification system can help, but difficulties may still arise if the customer's organization is so large or complex that it's not clear which entity constitutes the account.

Handling Complex Accounts

CH2M Hill, Jacobs Engineering Group, and ICF Kaiser International are among the firms that may offer environmental consulting or construction services to the U.S. Department of Energy (DOE). If your company provided such services, would you consider DOE a strategic account? Or would it make more sense to consider DOE-Albuquerque (one of the agency's field offices) a strategic account, along with all the other DOE field offices you serve? Is DOE one account or seventeen accounts? Every company that sells products or services to large government agencies or large, multinational corporations faces this question. Is the customer one entity or many? Favoring the single-entity approach are these factors:

- The account team can develop tremendous expertise on the customer and can know how policy changes or funding decisions in one office are likely to affect others.
- The account team can better track key people as they are promoted, change assignments, or transfer from one office to another and so can better maintain relationships with those key people.
- The account team provides a single point of contact for all the customer's representatives; the customer always knows whom to call and will always get the same answer or solution.
- Account information will be consistent and is shared easily with the right people because it is maintained in one place. This should minimize communication and coordination problems.

- There is a single strategy for the account that is implemented and managed by a single group of people, the account team.
- A single account team leader (probably a senior person) is responsible for managing the account. The leader is supported by others, but the company vests account responsibility and authority in one place.

Given these advantages, it may be difficult to imagine why anyone would favor the multiple-entity approach, but it too is beneficial in many ways:

- The account managers can be located very near the customer's offices and thus establish strong local presence, which influences many buyers.
- The account manager responsible for a single customer site or office can give enough attention to the customer to develop relationships in breadth and depth. In short, when you are on site constantly, you develop much better relationships and have deeper, more specific knowledge of the customer's needs.
- You can develop account strategies that are much more targeted and specific than strategies created for a single, much larger entity whose individual offices may have differing priorities, needs, and decision-making styles.
- If the buying decisions are made at the field office level, then managing the account as a single entity may not be fruitful or necessary. For example, DOE-Albuquerque may not know or care what DOE-Oak Ridge is doing, and vice versa, so there may be no synergies to be gained by managing the account as a single entity.
- It simply may be beyond your capability to manage a single, nationwide entity with multiple offices and thousands of employees. If you lack the staff and resources to cover the whole, then common sense would suggest targeting the field offices you are most interested in serving and covering them exceptionally well.

As there are compelling reasons for both approaches, most companies handle complex customers by following these principles:

1. If any buying unit of a large organization by itself provides enough business to fall into the top 10 percent of all your customers, it should be managed as a strategic account.

2. If you serve multiple buying units of a large organization and the collective revenue from them falls into your top echelon of customers, then the organization itself should be managed as a strategic account.

3. If multiple buying units of a large organization provide a significant amount of business or are dispersed widely and must have strong local presence on your part in order to maintain them, then they should be managed as subaccounts, with a single person responsible for the overall account team.

4. If you are an emerging business or in an emerging market and have few or no strategic customers, then you should manage prime prospects as strategic accounts.

In any case, there should be a single point of responsibility in the company for managing the account and coordinating all the people and groups who interface with the customer. The more critical the customer, the more senior the account manager or team leader should be. In Fluor Daniel, for instance, corporate vice presidents often are charged with the responsibility for managing key customer relationships. Senior people don't manage accounts by themselves, of course. They are supported by a host of people who are members of, or work with, the account team.

When Joan Henderson was promoted to sales manager of Delta Engineering Corporation's Oil Field Services division, she faced an internal problem she hadn't anticipated. Delta's sales had been climbing about 7 percent annually, but they had lost a major customer last year and suffered the first decline in sales since 1990. A postmortem of the loss revealed that they were guilty of benign neglect with their major customers, assuming that the business would go on and not managing the accounts as they should. Meanwhile, an aggressive competitor had built strong relationships with the customer, who abruptly cancelled all orders with Delta and stopped returning phone calls. This loss led Delta to institute more formal strategic account management procedures, which Joan Henderson supported wholeheartedly.

After she assigned strategic account managers to the key accounts in her division, however, she realized that some of Delta's other divisions also served those customers. A case in point was Bedrock Oil, one of her key customers. Bedrock also was served by three of Delta's other divisions—Offshore Exploration, Refinery and Plant Maintenance, and Environmental Services. The problem was that none of the people from the four divisions serving Bedrock spoke to one another. Although there were many opportunities for synergy and cross selling, these individuals never met, did not consider themselves a team, did not share information, and weren't generally aware of each other's activities except when informed by the customer. As she investigated the problem, it became clear to Joan that coordinating their activities would benefit not only Delta but the customer as well.

It wasn't clear who should be responsible for the overall account. Should Joan's person be designated the account manager? The other sales managers objected to that idea because they didn't want to lose their autonomy in the account or compromise the key relationships they had established. They all felt that their people had to be responsible for developing the business in their divisions, yet everyone agreed in principle that Delta needed to manage the account in a more focused way and that better coordination was essential.

Their solution was to create an overall account team that comprised each of the salespeople in the four divisions who were responsible for their division's relationship with Bedrock. Jim Scoggins, a senior operations manager in the Oil Field Services division, was named as the account team leader. Because of his work with Bedrock, Jim had the highest-level relationships with key Bedrock

continued

executives, and his job became overseeing the activities of all four divisions and ensuring that they were coordinating their plans, strategies, and activities. Jim initiated monthly account team meetings with the four subaccount managers, and as a team they mapped out a coordinated approach to the customer.

During their first year as a team, they were able to grow the account by 17 percent and they unseated one competitor who had been providing maintenance services to two of Bedrock's refineries. Although it might seem unusual to name an operations manager as the account team leader, in fact Jim was the most logical choice. He knew the customer well, had a comprehensive understanding of their business and their technical needs, and was able to offer expert guidance to the subaccount managers from the four divisions.

— 7 —

Building Account Teams

Except in small companies with limited resources, account managers typically are supported by various people in the company, including managers or executives, other salespeople or sales support staffers, technical designers or engineers, installation or maintenance people, and customer service representatives. Functional managers sometimes resist assigning specific people to support key accounts, but having an account "team" that consists of a loose confederation of supporters is far less effective than having a team composed of members with specific account support responsibilities. In forming an effective account team, a sales manager must answer three questions: Who should be the account manager? Who else should be assigned to support the account manager? What must happen to ensure that the team works well together?

Identifying the Account Manager

Identifying account managers can be one of the most difficult decisions a sales manager has to make. In a large company, many people may have a vested interest in the customer, and a number of people may have developed personal relationships with customer representatives. Operations or project managers, because of their day-to-day interactions with customers, may know the customer better than anyone in sales. They may resist what they perceive as a salesperson coming between them and the customer. So this decision often is complicated by conflicting agendas, misperceptions, and legitimate functional concerns. It's not surprising that it's a difficult decision. You are entrusting the care of one of the company's most valuable assets—its key customers—to a select group of people. You want to be sure they are the right ones. In making this decision, there should be one overriding factor: *The account manager should be the person who is responsible and accountable for managing the revenue this account generates and developing the overall customer relationship.*

Because of this factor, operations managers should not be assigned as account managers unless their position description is modified to include revenue generation responsibilities (and you may need to change their compensation plan, too). Because salespeople are responsible for generating revenue, they typically are assigned as account managers, but people from management or other functional areas could be. However—and I can't stress this enough—they *must* be given the authority and then held accountable for growing or maintaining the revenue the account represents and achieving the other strategic objectives for the account.

Another factor in assigning the account manager should be *the customer's comfort level* with the person chosen. It should be someone with industry experience—someone who can speak credibly about your products and services, your competitors' offerings, approaches or products your customer's competitors are using, and trends in the industry that could impact how the customer operates or uses your types of products and services. It's possible but difficult to make up for a lack of industry knowledge, so most companies hire salespeople with specific industry experience. Equally important with experience is *personality and style*—the fit between the customer and the person you want to manage the account. Factors such as age and gender are never as important as intangibles such as operating style, demeanor, compatibility, and similarity in outlook and interests. The bottom line is that the key people in the customer's organization must genuinely like working with your account manager; must be comfortable with him or her; and must feel that he or she speaks the language, walks the talk, understands the issues, respects the customer's business and people, and is on their side. In short, they must come across as insiders, not outsiders, as helpers rather than sellers, as friends and associates rather than vendors.

The credibility and personality factors probably are the most important, but here are some additional criteria to consider when selecting account managers:

1. *Relationship development.* Account managers must be people oriented enough to be facile at building and maintaining a broad array of relationships throughout the customer's organization. Further, they must be capable of building relationships at the top. Most people can build relationships at what they perceive to be their level—engineer to engineer, first-line manager to first-line manager, and so on. But it takes boldness and the right perspective to build peer-like relationships with senior executives if you aren't one yourself. The person selected as a strategic account manager should feel comfortable moving throughout the customer's organization, having lunch with the engineers, conducting focus sessions with floor supervisors, having lunch with vice presidents, and meeting with the CEO. They must be able to converse on a range of topics, remember the small details of people's lives and business needs and perspectives, and bring people together where greater communication would be helpful. In short, account managers must be natural networkers.

2. *Strategic thinking.* Account managers must, simultaneously, see both the forest and the trees. They must be capable of attending to the tactical issues while

never losing sight of the broader, strategic vision. Even while managing the details of a half dozen ongoing initiatives, they must be thinking about how the strategic picture is changing and what they must do, in the short term and the long term, to manage the dynamic environment of the account. This is easier said than done. Many people are good tactical thinkers, excellent at strategizing how to pursue a particular opportunity; others are better strategists. It's rare to have both skills in one person—but essential in a good account manager.

3. *Resourcefulness.* Account managers must be adept at coordinating a company's internal resources and ensuring that the right things are in place at the right time. Do they have to be technically proficient themselves? This question is part of an ongoing debate about whether account managers should be professional sellers who have learned the company's products and how they are installed and used or former technical specialists who have been trained in selling skills. In many industries, it doesn't matter so long as the account manager can bring together the right resources at the right time. Account managers must know what they are talking about, but they need not be brain surgeons. However, if the relationship requires a brain surgeon, then the account manager should be able to get one. The fact is, the criteria listed here are much more important than technical skills. Customers will come to trust and rely on the account manager who listens to them, is responsive to their needs, and is resourceful—meaning that he or she can get the resources required in a timely manner. Many a technical guru doesn't listen, isn't responsive, and isn't resourceful except in his or her narrow field. What's most important is resourcefulness.

4. *Organization.* Given the magnitude of people, resources, information, and activities that must be coordinated, account managers must be masters of organization. They must be flexible and responsive to changes as they occur, so rigid adherence to plans is not desirable. But they nonetheless must be superb at prioritizing tasks, organizing people, and coordinating the flow of information to and from the customer's organization. They must be capable of setting and meeting schedules and driving to closure the things that can come to closure. Some salespeople are excellent in every other respect but aren't well organized enough to manage strategic accounts, where attention to detail and mastery of the ongoing flow of people, events, and information is an essential skill.

5. *Team leadership.* Finally, account managers must be capable of leading teams, particularly internal, cross-functional teams where they have no actual authority over team members and must use their influencing and collaborative skills to foster cooperation and build enthusiasm for the team's mission. Although it might be frustrating at times, they must be able to work with functional managers to get the resources they need, convince others to set aside their priorities in order to meet the customer's needs more expeditiously than they would otherwise, and entice senior executives to devote some of their scarce time to relationship-building activities with the customer's key people. As unbelievable as this may sound, building internal support and cooperation for your account activities often is much harder than persuading the customer to buy your products and services. Account managers must be internal leaders.

The competencies discussed here are the essentials. Among the other skills that sometimes are cited for account managers are persistence; interpersonal skills (assertiveness, listening, being sensitive to others, and managing conflict); creativity; writing and speaking skills; and organizational savvy. It should be clear that it doesn't matter if the account manager is a salesperson, an operations person, a manager, or some combination of these functions. What's important is the assigned account manager's industry experience, personality fit, networking and relationship skills, strategic thinking, resourcefulness, organizational skills, and ability to lead teams.

Supporting the Account Manager

In an interview regarding his role at Fluor Daniel, one of the world's largest engineering and construction firms, former CEO Les McCraw claimed that he spent the majority of his time on the road visiting customers. He represented the type of chief executive who understands the importance of top-to-top contacts between suppliers and customers, and the investment of his time with key customers is one reason why Fluor Daniel maintained its leading role in the engineering and construction industry. In world-class business development organizations such as Fluor Daniel, General Electric, and Hewlett-Packard, account managers are supported by representatives of every area who interface with key customers, beginning with the senior executives themselves. In many cases, corporate vice presidents act as account team leaders. But even when they don't have direct responsibility for managing key customer relationships, senior executives support the account managers by placing high priority on meeting with and serving key customers, providing strategic direction, and ensuring that key customers receive immediate attention from the functional areas that serve them.

Dan Springer felt like the proverbial fish out of water. As the newly appointed Vice President for Sales in Hammerhead Corporation, he quickly realized what it meant to work in an operations-oriented culture. Hammerhead manufactured a variety of molded plastic and metal products for the automotive, aircraft, and construction industries, and Hammerhead's management consisted almost exclusively of former operations managers. None of the corporation's senior management had a sales background. Nor had sales been considered essential. Until the early 1990s, Hammerhead had enjoyed a seller's market. Now, years later, times were tougher, and Hammerhead was losing market share to aggressive competitors whose products and services were not superior to Hammerhead's but were sold more effectively because the competitors had professional sales forces and executives who were more focused on selling. Hammerhead's management didn't seem worried, however. They felt that their superior reputation for quality would prevail, so although they paid lip service to sales by hiring Dan Springer and promising to support him, it was pretty much business as usual.

continued

Dan recognized that the only way to get ahead at Hammerhead was to be in operations, but he hoped that Hammerhead's management would come to grasp the importance of sales in today's marketplace. He knew that they would continue to lose orders to their competitors as long as they rested on their technical laurels and failed to match the aggressive sales and marketing campaigns of their competitors. So Dan launched a series of initiatives to invigorate their sales program. He identified their strategic accounts and assigned account managers (many of whom were operations managers because Dan had very few actual salespeople). Because of its size and importance to Hammerhead, Dan assigned himself as account manager for General Automotive, an account that represented nearly 15 percent of their annual income. Then his nightmares began.

Dan found it impossible to manage the account. The various operations managers who worked with General Automotive resisted Dan's efforts to become involved in the account. They protected their relationships with key customers, in some cases refusing to introduce Dan, and would not give him information they learned from customers unless he specifically asked for it. He was never sure who was meeting with the customer, what the meetings were about, or what opportunities were upcoming. His effort to establish a centralized database of information on the customer failed as soon as it was set up because only a handful of people contributed to it. Dan's frustration peaked when he tried to arrange a series of meetings between Hammerhead's CEO and a number of General Automotive's senior executives. Although the CEO was willing to meet with the customer's chief executive, he was not willing to spend an extended length of time on the road meeting with other, lower-level executives in General Automotive or anywhere else. "My job is to run this company," the CEO told Dan. "Yours is to go out and get the business."

Dan lasted less than 18 months at Hammerhead. Two years after he left, the company was reorganized by new corporate owners, who fired 90 percent of the senior executives, including the CEO. Today, Hammerhead still struggles as an operations-oriented company waiting for "the market to turn around," but a new group of young executives is seeking to balance its operational excellence with strong focus and capability in sales and account management. Unless support for account management comes from the top, it is nearly impossible to institute strategic account management methods and concepts, particularly in well-entrenched technical or operational cultures.

Beyond senior support, account managers should be supported by the people in the organization who have the greatest interface with the key customer and who have a vested interest in the success of the account. As Figure 7-1 shows, this can include representatives from marketing, manufacturing, research and development, shipping, accounting, and customer service. Ideally, the senior person in each of these functional areas who is responsible for the customer should be a member of the account team. The operating principle here is that account managers should have direct links to the functional people who are responsible for serving the account, the

Figure 7-1. Representative Account Team Structure

ones who can ensure that what needs to happen does happen and that the appropriate corners are cut, if necessary.

It's often helpful to differentiate between core and auxiliary team members. In Figure 7-1, for instance, the account managers assigned to Amoco's business units, such as the Rocky Mountain unit, would be core team members. However, the functional representatives (e.g., shipping, manufacturing) would play an auxiliary role. Managing the account typically is a full-time responsibility for core team members, and they would meet frequently to manage their day-to-day tasks and priorities. Auxiliary team members would be involved as needed but also would participate in annual planning sessions and monthly or quarterly account reviews.

In addition to support from other functional areas, account managers are often supported by other people in the sales group. Junior salespeople might be assigned to them, and they might receive dedicated sales support. The purpose is to leverage the account managers' time so they can focus on the highest-value activities. More junior people should coordinate the letter campaigns, update the intelligence files, coordinate internal processes, and do the other grunt work required. In some of the companies I've worked with, junior people act as apprentices on account teams, learning how to build and manage key relationships, account strategies, and action plans by working with and observing experienced account managers, who often are acting as formal mentors. In General Electric, this process is part of the ongoing education of new salespeople.

At Dell Computer, which has emerged as a strong player in the personal computer hardware market and is arguably best in class at serving its market segment, account executives are held in high esteem and are well compensated. Being the account executive for a top-ten account is a prestigious position. They receive considerable top-down support, so they get what they need to serve their accounts. And those accounts keep growing, year after year, because their key customers love the level of attention and service they receive. When problems occur, these customers know that they won't have to wait in line for Dell's normal customer service support. Would they receive the same treatment from other providers? Perhaps, but the fear that they won't is a powerful incentive for doing all their business with the provider they've come to depend on. What makes this work is Dell's commitment to managing strategic accounts and its executives' resolve to give favored treatment to their most important customers.

Preferential treatment for key customers is not necessarily spontaneous. Senior executives need to show their own commitment to these accounts by taking a special interest in them, going out of their way to meet with their counterparts in the customers' organizations, devoting time to discuss strategy with the account teams, and insisting that the functional areas treat key customers with special deference. Further, everyone in the company should know who the key customers are. From the shipping clerk to the receptionist, people should be aware when they are dealing with a key account. You wouldn't want any customer treated poorly, but there is a difference between good service and exceptional service, and your key customers expect and deserve the latter. That's why they remain key customers year after year.

Summary of Part II

Strategic account management is more than an approach to selling and a set of tools for building customer relationships; it is a part of a company's strategic vision and must be integral to the way the company conducts its business. Managing key accounts means viewing these important customers as investments and nurturing the relationships so that you sustain them at their peak value to you and your key customers for the longest period possible.

One of the foundations of strategic account management is your strategic plan, which defines your business mission and the strategic objectives and programs required to achieve it. Strategic account management is one of those strategic programs. It receives guidance and focus from your strategic plan while providing information to the planners that helps them understand your key customers' needs and changing directions. Because your strategic customers provide the majority of your revenue, serving their interests is crucial to your success, so strategic account management is one of the primary instruments of your competitive strategy.

Another foundation of strategic account management is determining which accounts are strategic. Strategic account management requires a significant investment of time, energy, and resources, so you must be selective in determining which accounts to manage strategically. An effective way to classify all customers is to assess them by their attractiveness to you, their revenue and profit potential, and your current position with them. Strategic accounts should be very attractive, have high potential, and give you a strong current or potential position. Prospects that are highly attractive and represent strong potential may not be considered strategic accounts, but they can be managed strategically using all the tools of strategic account management. Every strategic account should have a single point of responsibility in your company—an account manager who is responsible for managing the account and leading the account team. If the customer has multiple buying units, each of which has independent purchasing authority, then each buying unit might be considered a subaccount and have a subaccount manager. Collectively, this customer still should be considered a single strategic account; however, if any single buying unit represents a significant portion of your revenue, then it should be managed strategically by itself.

Account managers should be responsible and accountable for managing the revenue a strategic account generates and developing the overall customer relationship. The people who assume these roles must be credible in the customer's eyes and have an operating style that is compatible with the customer's culture. In addition, they must be competent at developing relationships, thinking strategically, coordinating resources, organizing activities, and leading teams. To be effective, they must be supported by others in your company who interface with the customer or provide functional support to the delivery, operation, and maintenance of your products or services. Principally, however, account managers must be supported from the top. From the CEO on down, executive awareness of, and support for, account management activities is fundamental to the success of strategic account management. Providing extraordinary support to key customers creates a special bond, because these customers cannot be certain of receiving such service elsewhere, and this keeps them coming back to you year after year.

— PART III —
Account Planning

Roman philosopher Lucius Seneca said, "Unless a man knows what harbor he is making for, no wind is the right wind." Likewise in key account management, sailing aimlessly through an account and heading where the next wind happens to blow you is seldom productive. Account management demands discipline, direction, and purpose. You have to know what's possible with the customer, where you want to take the relationship, and how you are going to get there. In short, you have to know what harbor you are making for. So, at the strategic level, account management is methodical, deliberate, analytical, and aspirational.

Day-to-day account management is more like rafting down an unruly river. It demands flexibility and responsiveness. From the calm of moving water you suddenly are plunged into the roar and tumult of rapids. Just as suddenly, the white foam disappears, and you can collect yourself through a long stretch of smooth water. But you sense a dull roar ahead, and it grows louder as you approach the next stretch of white water. Although you know the general course of your journey, what happens moment by moment can be unpredictable, and this is what it feels like in the day-to-day management of strategic accounts. Consequently, the discipline required at the strategic level can be at odds with the flexibility and speed necessary in the daily response to events, opportunities, and threats as they arise. But if you can't do both at once; you'll soon either be lost or hopelessly frustrated at your inability to work the plan. In this part of the book I'm going to talk about the discipline of planning. In part IV, we'll plunge into white water as I talk about implementing the plan.

Chapter 8 describes the account planning process and the logic of a strategic account plan, and chapter 9 discusses how you gather information from a variety of public and private sources. Chapters 10, 11, and 12 address the heart of the analytical effort in account planning: analyzing the customer, analyzing competitors, and analyzing your own position. Part III concludes with chapter 13, which discusses how you use the results of your analyses to develop a strategic account strategy.

— 8 —

The Account Planning Process

Reduced to its essentials, account planning has only two purposes: to analyze your competitive position with your key customer and to develop an account strategy that will maximize your business potential. The account plan you create during this process is important because it captures critical information, documents the problems you've solved and the decisions you've made, and enables you to communicate your plan to other people in your company. However, the plan is less important than the process itself, and you risk doing a stupid paper exercise if you think of the plan as the end in itself. The real purpose is to force your thinking along disciplined lines so you arrive at the right answers about managing the account.

As you develop an account plan, you look deeply into the customer's business and needs. You examine your own competitive position with the customer, as well as your primary competitors' positions. You try to determine the account's potential, forecast your business volume in the coming years, and identify trends in the customer's organization or industry that could impact their need for your products and services. Finally, you identify the actions necessary to enhance both the actual value you bring to the customer and their perceptions of your value. These activities are so important *in and of themselves* that you should do them whether or not you create an account plan. The plan is merely a vehicle for analyzing the account and documenting and communicating your intentions to others who need to know them.

Once an account plan is in place, consider it a guide, not a straitjacket. This was an early lesson for me. When I wrote my first account plan, I spent weeks on it, gathering and sorting intelligence, analyzing the data in depth, and producing a carefully crafted, fifty-page plan—which was out of date almost before the ink dried. As I began managing the account and walking the customer's hallways searching for people to meet, I became so caught up in the daily business of working my contacts and responding to requests that I lost sight of the plan. Three months later I realized I hadn't looked at it for a long time. When I had a moment, I sat down to reread it and realized that it was hopelessly out of date.

71

An account plan is like a snapshot. It's one picture, frozen in time, showing what you thought and intended when you wrote it. But things change. As you work the account, you learn more. Your assumptions are proven right or wrong. New opportunities arise. The customer's key people retire or are promoted, transferred, or replaced. Their business grows, their priorities change, and their needs evolve. Like white water, the picture is in constant flux, so you need to treat the plan like a living, evolving organism.

I learned from my first account plan to carry the action plans with me, to put them on my laptop, and to make them part of my time management software. When I began treating the plan like part of my "to do" list, it came alive, and I was able to work the plan as capably as I was working the hallways.

Annual Account Plan Revision

Notwithstanding its dynamic nature, an account plan should receive a major overhaul periodically. In most companies, account plans are rewritten annually as part of the organization's strategic or business planning processes. There are a number of sound reasons for doing this:

- Within a year of writing your plan, the information and assumptions you based your plan on will no longer be valid. You'll have a different product portfolio and a new strategic direction.
- The customer will no longer be the same. Their markets will have evolved and their needs and priorities will be different, which will impact how and where they spend their money (e.g., internationally, the price of paper runs in boom-to-bust cycles, which whipsaws not only the paper producers but the suppliers serving them).
- Your competitors will have changed. Although you may have the same rivals, their positions and strategies will have evolved as they responded to their opportunities or threats with this customer.

Perhaps the best reason for an annual rewriting of the plan is that it gives you an opportunity to step back and reflect on the account as a whole, to think about what has been working for you and what hasn't, and to reevaluate your account strategies in light of your successes and failures in achieving your objectives. When I step back to rewrite my account plans, I'm always amazed at how different the picture looks now.

As Figure 8-1 shows, the process for writing an account plan is not complicated. The first step is to gather information from a variety of internal and external sources. When you are well established with a customer, the two primary sources of information are the customer and your own people who have been serving the account. However, numerous other

Figure 8-1. The Account Planning Process

sources can enlighten you on customer issues, market and industry trends, and your competitors' activities with the customer, and these sources become more important when you are trying to develop new key account relationships. The information you gather is instrumental in your analysis of the customer and their industry and markets, your competitors and their positions with the customer, and your own position with the customer. The accuracy of your analysis depends mostly on the quality of your relationships with customers and the richness of the information you can get from them, as well as the depth and breadth of knowledge you glean from other sources. Clearly, if you have a partnering relationship with your key accounts, even informally, you can leverage the relationship to obtain better, more private information that your competitors may not have.

If you are well informed and do the analysis properly, you should be able to identify areas where you have the competitive advantage, as well as areas where you don't. You should be able to highlight the opportunities and threats you face. You should know where you stand with the customer's key people and which relationships you need to build further. Finally, the implications of your analysis should suggest how to prioritize your activities in the account, what you must do to build your relationships, and how to communicate the differentiated value you can provide.

Figure 8-2. The Logic of an Account Plan

EXECUTIVE SUMMARY

Highlights overall purpose and direction, including account objectives, and provides an overview of the customer. Can be presented separately from the rest of the plan.

Customer Profile

Describes the customer--key people, products, locations, markets, strategies, financials, and trends, as well as strengths, weaknesses, opportunities, and threats. Describes past, current, and projected needs.

Competitor Profile

Describes key competitors' strengths, weaknesses, current position, and strategies in this account.

Position Assessment

Analyzes your position in the account - history, current business, product life cycle, relationship life cycle, strengths, weaknesses, opportunities, and threats. Also profiles your relationships with key customer representatives.

ACCOUNT STRATEGY

Establishes your account objectives, based on the foregoing analysis, and details your action plans for achieving your objectives. This is the most dynamic part of the plan.

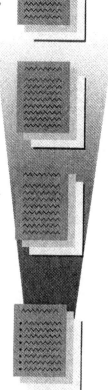

During the strategy phase of the process, you use your analysis to establish account objectives and to determine the actions required to reach each objective. Together, the objectives and action plans constitute your account strategy.

The Logic of the Account Plan

The account plan mirrors this process and is correspondingly simple in structure. As Figure 8-2 shows, most account plans open with an executive summary that provides an overview of the account and highlights the primary conclusions, namely, the account's potential, the account manager's goals, and the strategies for achieving those goals or objectives. Next is the analysis of the situation, which is presented in three parts: the customer profile, competitor profiles, and an assessment of your own competitive position. Because this part of the plan can be extensive, some account managers leave it out of the plan but make it available for whomever needs to see it. The analysis shows how you arrived at your account strategies, so it is important, but in the interest of keeping the plan simple, you may want to summarize the analysis in your plan and leave the detail in your files.

The heart of the account plan is the section showing your account strategy. This section should list your account objectives followed by the high-level actions required to achieve them. These actions constitute your account strategy. As we will see in chapter 13, there are several types of account objectives and several kinds of action plans that may be appropriate in any account plan. In essence, this section of your account plan states *what* you intend to accomplish in the account and *how* you are going to accomplish it. Your strategies should be based on your analysis of the customer, competitors, and your own position, so they are a logical outcome of what you learned as you analyzed the information you gathered at the beginning of the process.

— 9 —

Gathering Information

Information is the fuel that powers the account planning engine, and the defining characteristic of an effective account plan is that it displays insightful detail about the customer and your competitive posture vis-à-vis your rivals. The worst plans show no insight and reveal very little beyond what is already publicly known about the customer. Being skilled at information gathering is not simply a matter of knowing how to produce a lot of information. Today, it is relatively easy to become overwhelmed with data once you start looking for it. The volume of information available on the Internet alone is staggering. So anyone with the time and the inclination can generate information on customers that goes well beyond the point of diminishing returns. Rather, skill at information gathering is a matter of having access to the *right* information at the *right* time, particularly if your competitors do not have comparable access. Thus, one of the first and most important competitive advantages an account manager can build is access to *privileged* information, where I am defining *privileged* as information that is ARTful: *advantageous* (it helps you build competitive advantage), *restricted* (your rivals do not have it), and *timely* (you learn of it in time to take action that builds your advantage).

Levels of Information

Information gathering is a discovery process, and invariably you begin with public information that is not ARTful because it doesn't help you build advantage, it's accessible to everyone, and you typically learn about it too late to act. Nonetheless, when you're researching a new customer, it makes sense to visit their web site and send for their annual report and 10K. It's easy, too, to search for articles on them in back issues of *Fortune*, *Forbes*, *Business Week*, *Harvard Business Review*, and other such publications.

As you move beyond the obvious, public sources of information, you begin to discover some less accessible but still public sources, such as industry trade journals, analyst reports, and company or industry surveys such as *Hoover's, ValueLine,* and *Standard & Poor's.* These sources often provide a richer and more robust understanding of the customer's organization and industry. However, the best sources of information are inside the customer's organization. As you work with different customer representatives, they provide invaluable information on their directions, goals, problems, culture, processes, products, and needs. Indeed, if you aren't privy to these private sources of information, you will not progress beyond a superficial understanding of the customer. Most valuable to you, however, are the confidential customer sources—the people who give you privileged information that your competitors don't have. These deep private sources give you the most ARTful information available.

As this discussion illustrates, there are four different levels of information available on customers (see Figure 9-1). To truly understand the cus-

Figure 9-1. The Four Levels of Information

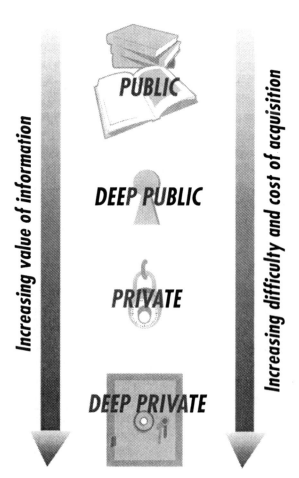

tomer, you must have access to information at all four levels, and you can't develop a strong, mutually beneficial relationship with a strategic account unless you have significant private and deep private sources. So one way to gauge how well positioned you are in an account is to identify your information sources at all four levels.

Level 1 (Public) Information

Level 1 (public) information is the easiest to gather and includes the customer's annual reports, 10Ks, advertisements, brochures, product descriptions, technical bulletins, catalogs, press releases, and web site. The customer generates these sources to reveal and manage the image they project to the public and, if they are publicly traded, to the investment world. Although this may help you understand how your customer wishes to be viewed, it offers little insight and has relatively little value because it is so widely known. Secondary sources in the level 1 (public) arena would include books about the customer; third-party comparisons of the customer's products and their competitors' products; and articles about the customer in the general press and in the business press (e.g, *Forbes, Fortune, Wall Street Journal, Business Week*). Among the most useful secondary public sources are Companies Online (www.companiesonline.com), Corporate Financials Online (www.cfonews.com), Forbes (www.forbes.com), News-Page (www.newspage.com), Wall Street Journal Interactive Edition (www.wsj.com), Barron's Online (www.barrons.com), Moody's Investors Service (www.moodys.com), Dun & Bradstreet (www.dnbcorp.com), the Motley Fool (www.motleyfool.com), Fortune (www.pathfinder.com/fortune/), Business Week Online (www.businessweek.com), Standard & Poor's (www.standardandpoors.com), Hoover's Online (www.hoovers.com), Kompass (www.kompass.com), and ValueLine (www.valueline.com). For an exhaustive list of other public sources, see Leonard M. Fuld's *The New Competitor Intelligence* (New York: John Wiley & Sons, 1995).

These secondary sources offer more revealing information about the customer because they aren't trying to put the customer's best foot forward, but they rarely provide the kind of insight or in-depth information necessary to truly understand the account. Nonetheless, it's imperative to master level 1 information. The annual report is typically a public relations effort, so it's intended to put a high gloss on the company. But information in the notes and explanations section at the end of the report often can be revealing. Here is where they will try to bury the bad news, so many account managers read annual reports from the back forward, ending with the CEO's message, which rarely is written by the CEO but can reflect key elements of the company's strategy. The 10K usually is much more revealing, and you can get it easily by calling their investor relations office and asking for a copy. It must contain any information that could affect the company's stock price, so the 10K must describe the nature of the business, key holdings, outstanding legal actions against the company, key people, assets held and for sale, acquisition strategies, and so on. I've found the 10K to be a much richer source of information than any of my customer's brochures and annual reports.

Level 2 (Deep Public) Information

Level 1 (public) information generally is free or available for a nominal fee; however, level 2 (deep public) information is more costly and less readily available. Most newsstands carry *Fortune* or *Forbes*, but keep in mind that your competitors stop at these newsstands or have the same magazines delivered to their offices. Deep public information is less visible. It includes subscription reports by industry analysts, industry journals (such as *Engineering News Record* for the engineering and construction industry), market research published by specialty firms such as Standard & Poor's (S&P) that analyze industries in depth, industry conference proceedings, federal government reports (such as Department of Commerce industry analyses), and various state and local government reports and public records. A number of subscription services provide Internet or press guides to companies and industries, including *ValueLine* and *Hoover's*. The on-line versions of these services offer some information, but deeper and more extensive coverage of companies and industries is available by subscription only. The S&P Industry Surveys, for example, profile fifty-two industries in depth, and there are numerous sources for company profiles on the Internet. What makes this information deep public is that, although anyone can access it, it is less well known; less evident to the casual observer; and more costly to acquire, both in terms of research time and actual expense. So you can gain a competitive advantage with deep public information because it requires effort and investments your competitors often don't bother to make.

If your customer is a public corporation or government agency, the amount of public and deep public information available is vast, and it would be inexcusable not to have it. It won't constitute privileged ARTful (advantageous, restricted, timely) information, but failing to have it could prove detrimental because this information provides a baseline of intelligence that every competitor needs. To compete, you have to play on a level playing field, as they say, and knowing the public information about your customer puts you on the level playing field. You won't be in the game unless you have this information, and it can signal trends or provide early warning of events you need to probe further. The two primary problems with public information are that it never reveals the whole truth and, by the time it's public, the insiders have already acted on it.[1] That's why you'll find the best information on levels 3 and 4.

Level 3 (Private) Information

Level 3 (private) information is not available to the public. It comes to you through various contacts in the customer's organization or from other sources who work closely with the customer, including:

- The customer's executives and managers (also retired executives)
- The customer's project managers, engineers, scientists, technicians, and others who provide information on the record to partners, suppliers, vendors, and others who serve the customer
- Your own technical, project, or service people who have been serving the customer (or your own employees who previously had been employed by the customer)
- Third-party suppliers, such as equipment or service providers
- Industry specialists or consultants who know the customer
- Government officials who interact with the customer

Private information begins to give you insight at the project, need, and budget level that is not available publicly. Consequently, it's here that you learn enough about the specific needs, desires, strategies, and plans of individual customer contacts to be able to formulate your own actions in response. Private information enables you to anticipate their needs, know how they intend to use your products, understand the differences in priorities and perspectives among their decision makers and the people who can influence them, and comprehend the potential alignment or misalignment between their needs and your possible solutions. When on site with customers—walking the hallways and talking to their people—you gain invaluable information that is fundamental to developing effective approaches and strategies to winning the business. The account manager doesn't do this alone, of course. There should be numerous people in your company who are talking to their counterparts. In the best of circumstances, the flow of information to and from the customer is continuous

---

1. I learned this lesson many years ago as an officer for the Defense Intelligence Agency in the Pentagon. For nearly a year, I worked the night watch, reading dispatches from overseas and learning of events as they were unfolding in other parts of the world through State and Defense Department classified messages. When I was off duty, reading newspapers or watching television news, I noticed that the public news agencies rarely learned of those events until days or weeks later, and they never reported the events as accurately as I learned of them through top secret sources. Similarly, and for obvious reasons, the sensitive information that is most useful to know about your customers rarely reaches the public, at least in all its objective detail, and by the time it has, the people who had the privileged information earlier have already acted on it.

and rich at all levels. This is the domain that most account managers work in. But it's not the *best* one.

Level 4 (Deep Private) Information

Information from level 3 (private) sources can be advantageous and timely, but it may not be restricted. If your competitors are doing their jobs (and you should always assume that they are unless you have evidence to the contrary), they will be working the hallways, too. They will have their own private sources and will be gathering much the same information. To develop competitive advantage through information gathering, you must also be operating at level 4 (deep private). At this level, all your sources are within the customer organization because no one else can know what they know—not the industry analysts, the consultants, or even former employees of the customer. These deep sources are your sponsors or champions— the people in the customer organization who trust you the most; who have built relationships with you; and who want you to win, not just because of your personal relationship (which can take you only so far) but because they are convinced that your products are right for their company and will yield the highest value and greatest return on investment.

Customers share deep private information only when they have substantial trust. It's usually confidential because it provides insight into the customer's strategies and changes in direction. Knowledge of it could give the customer's competitors an edge, so it can't be shared widely. It typically is given only to very trusted allies, partners, or key suppliers, and it's shared because customers believe that if you know it you will understand better their most private decisions and needs so you can serve them better. But your sources must trust that you respect the sensitivity and confidentiality of the information, that you will use it only to their advantage, and that it (and the fact that they gave it to you) will remain deeply buried.

Deep private information is controversial because it gives its holder considerable competitive advantage. Such information can include precise project requirements, insights on the evaluation criteria or the people who will make the buying decision, budgets, advance drafts of RFPs (requests for proposal), details of future plans, warning of changes in direction or priority, details of bid evaluations, or notice of contract changes. Clearly, having such information helps you, but in certain circumstances it can be improper or even illegal to possess it—precisely because it confers such advantage. If your customer is a federal agency, for example, the Procurement Integrity Act forbids possession of much of this information (in fact, it's illegal even to ask for some information). When working with publicly traded corporations, having the information might not be illegal, but if you buy or sell securities based on it, you might be guilty of insider trading. For all these reasons, deep private information is alluring but dangerous. Like the fruit of the forbidden tree, the knowledge you gain from it is tantalizing, but the penalty you might pay is harsh. The best advice is to remain on solid legal and ethical ground—but cultivate deep sources and get the information if you can. So long as you don't compromise your integrity or that of your sources or violate any laws or customer protocols, what you learn from deep private information can be extraordinary. Information at this level is highly privileged. It is ART in the fullest sense of the term—advantageous, restricted, and timely.

Remembering that there are four types of customer relationships (vendor, preferred supplier, partner, and strategic ally), it is obvious that the most privileged information is available only beyond vendor status. Preferred suppliers usually have access to a lot of level 3 (private) information and may have some level 4 (deep private) information, but vendors almost always are restricted to the public levels (1 and 2), although they may have some limited private information about the specific customer need they are responding to. Level 4 information is mostly accessible to partners and strategic allies, so one gauge of your relationship with a key customer is the depth of the information you have access to.

Turning Information Into Intelligence

Information does not become knowledge or intelligence until you verify and analyze it to determine its meaning and significance. As Leonard Fuld notes in *The New Competitor Intelligence*, information is not intelligence, but in the popular press, *data*, *information*, and *intelligence* often are used interchangeably. For information to become intelligence, it must be analyzed and you must derive the implications that will allow you to make decisions.[2] No matter what the source, it's best to evaluate the information, find confirmation from other sources as good journalists do, and then consider each piece of information in the context of everything you know about the customer. Properly analyzed and within context, intelligence helps paint the broader picture of what's happening and enables you to give the proper weight to everything you learn. Taken by itself, information can be false, misleading, or given too much weight. When you analyze it and discern its meaning in light of everything else you know, it can be invaluable as an aid to intelligent decision making. Finally, for intelligence to become useful, you must disseminate it in a timely manner to the people who need to act on it. As Fuld notes, "Much like a container of fresh ice cream, intelligence

---

2. Leonard M. Fuld, *The New Competitor Intelligence* (New York: John Wiley & Sons, 1995), pp. 23–24.

has a short shelf life. Use it and apply it, but don't ignore it. Once intelligence is allowed to sit around and not be used, its value declines rapidly."[3]

I'll talk more about the account manager's responsibilities for information management and intelligence gathering and dissemination in part IV of the book. Suffice it to say here that the person principally responsible for managing information flow to and from the customer is the account manager, and it's not an easy task, particularly in large accounts with many levels of interface between the buying and selling organizations.

---

3. Ibid.

— 10 —

Analyzing Your Customer

The primary difficulty many account managers have when they begin the analysis part of planning is distilling the wealth of information they've gathered about the customer into a coherent picture that yields insights about the account's potential and the right strategies for developing the relationship and the business. Although there no doubt are hundreds of ways you can organize and analyze customer information, at a minimum you should focus on your customer's industry and markets, direction, structure and management, performance, and need for your products (see Fig. 10-1).[1] The purpose of this analysis is to understand better the customer's business and needs, which in turn enables you to differentiate your products and solutions from those your rivals can provide.

The more you know, the better you can identify and meet their needs, offer the right products and solutions at the right time, and communicate your value in compelling ways. In this chapter, I'm going to describe how to analyze the customer and create a customer profile. As a starting point, we'll look at each of the areas shown in Figure 10-1.

Your Customer's Industry and Markets

Obviously, your customers don't operate in a vacuum. They compete within definable industries and have opponents who provide the same types of products and services. Understanding the competitive landscape in which your customer operates is fundamental to understanding the de-

---

1. Another useful way to analyze customers is to use the 7-S framework, which was developed by McKinsey & Company and is described by Tom Peters and Robert Waterman, Jr., in their book, *In Search of Excellence* (New York: Warner Books, 1982), pp. 9–10. According to this framework, managers have seven variables in building and operating an organization: structure, strategy, skills, staff, style, systems, and—underpinning the whole—shared values. Although this framework was intended as a diagnostic tool in management problem solving, it's a useful way to disaggregate the factors in a business that contribute to its strengths or weaknesses and to understand how the institution generates value and sustains itself.

Figure 10-1. The Domains of Customer Analysis

cisions they make as an organization, what needs they have, and how they strive to create value for their customers. Every business exists to serve its customers, and each of the rivals in an industry aims to compete in ways that differentiate its products from alternative products. As Michael Porter notes in *Competitive Strategy*, there are only three generic strategies: cost leadership, differentiation, and focus.[2] All three strategies may help to segment the market if there are buyers with different priorities and needs. In the retail clothing business, for instance, buyers whose priority is low cost will shop at particular outlets (Wal-Mart or J.C. Penney) and buyers whose priority is differentiation shop at the high-end niche stores (Ann Taylor, Talbots, Neiman Marcus). It's not possible for a seller to appeal to both segments simultaneously, so sellers must choose one strategy or the other.

---

2. Michael E. Porter, *Competitive Strategy: Techniques for Analyzing Industries and Competitors* (New York: The Free Press, 1980), p. 35.

The strategic possibilities may differ from one industry to the next, but cost, differentiation, and focus strategies operate to some degree in every industry. The strategy your customers select depends on the nature of their products, the nature and number of their rivals, and the economics of competition in their industry.

In his article, "How Competitive Forces Shape Strategy," Porter notes that "the nature and degree of competition in an industry hinge on five forces: the threat of new entrants, the bargaining power of customers, the bargaining power of suppliers, the threat of substitute products or services [where applicable], and the jockeying among current contestants."[3] Elaborating on these concepts is beyond the scope of this book, and Porter has already done so in his work. Suffice it to say that the five-forces model he describes has become a standard for analyzing the competitive forces in an industry, and it is a useful tool for analyzing your customer's industry. As you examine their industry, ask the following types of questions:

- *Is your customer's business in sync with developing changes in their marketplace?* Take it for granted that their industry is changing. Among the many forces that promote continuous change are advances in their own products, new and emerging technologies, distribution channel changes, government policy changes, changing demographics of the consumers, changes in raw materials pricing or availability, and their competitors' growth and development. If you assume that your customer's markets are dynamic, then the questions become (1) How will their markets evolve? and (2) How well positioned are they for the probable changes in their marketplace? Are their market and product strategies aligned with the direction their markets are heading? Dell Computer's decision to focus on mail-order customized computer purchasing was wise at the time because it reflected changes in how buyers were purchasing personal computers. They were in sync with market direction. In the early 1970s, however, Sears was not. It overlooked the changes in buyer preference signaled by the rise of K-Mart and Wal-Mart and began a long decline that only recently has been reversed through a painful period of self-analysis and realignment of their business strategy with the marketplace they're operating in.
- *Entry barriers.* Are entry barriers a powerful force in your customer's industry? How strong are those entry barriers? Do your products help build stronger entry barriers? For example, does your product help differentiate your customer's products? Does it increase the capital requirements for potential entrants into your customer's industry? Does your product help your customers achieve greater economies of scale? Or increase their access to distribution channels (while limiting their rivals')?
- *Threat of substitutes.* Are your customer's products threatened by substitutes? Can you help diminish that threat?

---

3. Michael E. Porter, "How Competitive Forces Shape Strategy," *Harvard Business Review* March–April (1979): 137.

- *Power of buyers.* Are the buyers a powerful force in your customer's industry? Can your products help diminish that power? Can you increase the buyers' reliance on your customer's products? Can you increase the significance and extent of their product differentiation?
- *Power of suppliers.* Are the suppliers in your customer's industry powerful? Can your products help increase your customer's dominance, increase switching costs, or reduce the threat of vertical integration from your customer's suppliers?
- *Rivalry among competitors.* Is there intense rivalry among competitors in your customer's industry? Can your products give your customers a stronger competitive position? What advantages do your products convey to your customers in ways that are meaningful to their customers?

The bottom line of this analysis is to understand how the changes in their industry and marketplace will impact them and how your products can help them achieve greater advantage. As their industry changes, they are likely to face new opportunities and threats. The increasing pace of technology change may impact their products in significant ways. So it's important to understand the landscape in which they compete and how that landscape is evolving. In turn, those changes could profoundly impact their need for your products and how much they value what you offer.

Maggie Hamilton is a strategic account manager for Universal Routing Services (URS), a Cincinnati-based firm offering services to the motor transport industry. URS provides global positioning system, real-time routing information, and analysis systems for motor carriers. For the past 3 years, Maggie has handled three major accounts, including Watkins Motor Lines, a 65-year-old trucking firm that reported revenues of $535 million in 1996. Watkins is a less-than-truckload (LTL) carrier, one of hundreds of trucking firms competing in the $18 billion LTL market. Although ninth in market share in its industry, Watkins is considerably smaller than the "big three": Roadway Express, Yellow Corp., and Consolidated Freightways, each of which grosses more than $2 billion annually.

In writing her annual account plan, Maggie began by updating herself on the motor transport industry. Her principal level 2 (deep public) sources were *Traffic World* (a logistics news weekly that analyzes the trucking industry), *Overdrive Online* (a weekly update on trucking), *Commercial Carrier Journal* (a monthly), and *Transport Topics* (a weekly publication of the American Trucking Association). In addition, she obtained the Standard & Poor's industry survey on "Commercial Transportation," as well as the Department of Commerce analysis of the industry. Her level 3 (private) sources included nearly a dozen Watkins executives at various levels and locations in the company and two consultants who frequently serve the trucking industry. She may have some level 4 (deep private) sources but won't discuss them.

Her research confirmed much of what she already knew, but she also learned some things that shed new light on her customer and its industry. The

continued

LTL motor carriers have had a tough decade. Although volume grew faster than the growth of industrial output, the carriers have suffered from excess capacity and competition from other modes of transportation, which has constrained profits. Also, the guaranteed overnight delivery of packages by Federal Express, United Parcel Service, and other such carriers is forcing motor carriers to offer similar guarantees and faster delivery. Coast-to-coast LTL shipments used to take 5 days, for example, and some carriers are now guaranteeing 2-day shipments. This is accomplished using sleeper teams (while one driver's at the wheel, the other sleeps). Maggie also learned most carriers are discarding the high-cost hub-and-spoke system in favor of "directional loading," in which loads are shipped directly from one location to another instead of to a hub. Intermodal shipping, which uses a combination of modes (truck, rail, ship, or airplane), also is on the rise. By maximizing intermodal traffic, some carriers have lowered their operating costs by 3 percent.

Two of the key drivers, so to speak, in this industry are fuel costs and labor. Truckers spend 12 to 17 percent of their gross on diesel fuel, so changes in fuel cost can dramatically impact profitability. Also, the industry averages a 150 percent turnover rate, so recruitment and training costs are high and experienced drivers are hard to find. Hiring inexperienced drivers means a higher accident frequency, which increases insurance costs and claims for damaged or lost cargo.

Maggie knows from her private sources that Watkins is launching a new premium service called Watkins Ultimate Service Advantage, which guarantees deliveries in 2 business days between Miami or Atlanta and southern California. This is all but impossible on the highways, so they are forming an alliance with an air freight service. Watkins' strategy is to use intermodal shipping to meet customers' demands for guaranteed, rapid, coast-to-coast shipments, and to accomplish that goal, she surmises, they will need two things she can offer. First, they must have a very complex and efficient scheduling system that routes a variety of LTL shipments from point of origin to the most expeditious air freight terminal. Second, they must have instantaneous tracking of shipments and know where every shipment is on a moment-to-moment basis. If they don't meet delivery guarantees, they don't get paid for the load. Consequently, their profits are tied directly to meeting their schedule guarantees. Because other carriers are looking at the same intermodal solutions, Maggie knows that time is of the essence. Her industry analysis confirms that she has a short window of opportunity in which to propose a software system that will give Watkins a rapid, fail-safe solution to scheduling and tracking their loads. This insight becomes a key feature of her account strategy.

Your Customer's Strategies and Synergies

The next critical area to analyze is your customer's direction—their vision; mission; strategies; plans; and intended synergies with partners, allies, and segments of their market. As they formulate their direction, they are responding to their view of their industry and marketplace and articulating the role they see themselves playing in their industry. Consequently, any time they change direction (by revising their corporate mission, strategies, or themes) they are signaling their response to the changing competitive environment they face. In 1997, for example, Texaco adopted a new tag line for its advertising: "Texaco—A World of Energy." This new theme reflected a new emphasis on themselves as a worldwide energy company as opposed to an American oil and gas company. Such themes reflect the way your customers view themselves and how they are positioning themselves in their markets. Here are the kinds of questions that can illuminate not only their vision and direction but also their strategies for getting there:

- What is their corporate mission or purpose statement? Has that changed recently? What does it imply about their strategic intent?
- What business are they in? How has that changed? What marketplace assumptions are implicit in their business definition?
- What are their CEO and other chief executives saying about the company, about their place in their markets, their growth strategies, or their vision of themselves in the future?
- What are their short-term plans and initiatives? What tactical decisions are they making in the short term to further their interests? What do those decisions imply about their need for your products?
- What opportunities are they pursuing in the short term? Which ones are they not pursuing and why? This last question usually is very insightful in that it reveals the selection criteria they are using and, hence, how they are defining their business interests.
- What is likely to threaten them in the short term? How are they responding to those threats?
- What are their long-term strategies? How will they seek to build their competitive advantages in the next decade? What products, technologies, and competencies are they building? As they realize their future vision, what are the implications for your products and services?
- How are they seeking to build synergy with partners and allies? Or with segments of their market? How are they going outside themselves to improve their competitive position? In early 1998, for example, Shell Oil Company and Texaco announced the formation and operational start-up of a new joint venture called Equilon Enterprises. Their intent was to merge their downstream interests in the western and midwestern United States by combining major parts of their refining, marketing, transportation, trading, and lubrication businesses. The downstream market had been tight for years, so an alliance between rivals in the business reduced competitive pressures for them and allowed both partners to find synergy. To deeply understand your customer, you have to know where marketplace pressures are forcing them to reach out.

This analysis of your customer's strategic direction is all at a fairly high level, of course, and it's only meaningful if they use your products strategically or if your products have broad impact on their business. If yours is a local business selling cafeteria services to one of their regional offices, then knowing how strategic forces are impacting their global business obviously is not germane to managing the account. Part of the art of account planning is knowing what level of strategic thinking is appropriate to managing your relationships with your key customers. It's common, however, for account managers to think too narrowly of their products and to fail to see what business purpose those products serve. Ian McMillan and Rita Gunther McGrath argue that most companies focus their energies only on their own products and services, while in fact "a company has the opportunity to differentiate itself at every point where it comes in contact with its customers."[4] Knowing your customer's strategic direction and taking a strategic view of your products can open up possibilities for differentiation you hadn't imagined. In her book *Visionary Selling*, Barbara Geraghty argues that when you sell at the C level (CEO, CFO, COO, etc.) of your customer organization, you must thoroughly understand their vision, purpose, and operating principles and show how your solutions further their interests along those strategic dimensions.[5]

Your Customer's Structure and Management

Next, it's important to understand the impact of the customer's organizational structure and management systems on how they operate, particularly in how they use what you sell and how they make buying decisions for your types of products. The types of questions you might ask are

- How are they organized? What does their organization reveal about how they manage their business and create value for their customers?
- Where do your products fit in? Where are they used? Who manages their use? How does their use impact other parts of their organization? How does it impact what they deliver to their customers?
- What systems do they have in place for installing, using, testing, monitoring, shipping, or decommissioning your products? How and when do they acquire the product? What is the life cycle of its use within their organization? Who interfaces with it?
- Where are their locations and facilities? Which of these locations and facilities use your product? Which don't, and why not?
- Who are their key people? Who can decide to buy the product from you? Who influences those decision makers?
- How well positioned are you with those key people?

---

4. Ian C. MacMillan and Rita Gunther McGrath, "Discovering New Points of Differentiation," *Harvard Business Review* July–August (1997): 133.
5. Barbara Geraghty, *Visionary Selling* (New York: Simon & Schuster, 1998).

- How do they buy your product or service? What is the buying process? What protocols or requirements are in place for purchasing your products?
- How complex or simple is the buying decision? How many people are involved? What steps have to be taken? What gates do you have to pass through to be selected?
- What criteria typically are most important to them in selecting a supplier? What are their recurring key issues, such as lowest installed or operating cost, ease of maintenance, greatest functionality, longest life, and customization or flexibility?

A customer profile should describe how they are managed; how the buying decisions are made; and who makes them, particularly in complex buying situations where there are multiple buying units and many levels of influence and decision making. In recent years, decision-making authority has been pushed lower and lower in many organizations. Today, plant managers can make buying decisions that 10 years ago were made by vice presidents of manufacturing. More people are involved in these decisions, so it complicates the selling process, especially when there now are multiple, independent buying units where previously there was one centralized purchasing group. Today, understanding how the buying decision will be made and who will make it is increasingly challenging. So one of the best practices in account planning is to profile the customer's key people.

Your Customer's Key People

There are a number of distinct roles in the buying process.[6] The first and most obvious is the *decision maker*. This is the person (or group of people) who makes or approves the buying decision. Decision makers are concerned primarily about organizational results and bottom-line business impacts. They also may care that the process looks fair and open, especially if the decision is subject to public scrutiny and oversight, but their primary concern is making the right technical and financial decisions. Clearly, it's essential to know who is the decision maker and to try to build an effective relationship with that person. However, decision makers today often have less latitude in their choices than you might think. In large or public organizations, their decisions must reflect the supporting view of others in their

---

6. In their book, *Strategic Selling* (New York: William Morrow & Company, 1985), Robert B. Miller and Stephen E. Heiman propose a similar scheme for identifying the types of people involved in a buying decision. However, their scheme is focused more on the tactical level of selling and does not classify all of the people who can influence complex sales in large organizations. In this book, I am elaborating on a framework devised by Dr. David Pugh, an expert on business development in large organizations. His scheme includes the broader range of people who impact buying decisions in large accounts, particularly the informal network of advisors within an organization and the external people or groups who often impact the buying decision in profound ways.

organization who have reviewed the offers and done the due diligence on the offerers. So perhaps it's equally essential to know who will influence the decision.

There are four common types of influencers: operators, advisors, gatekeepers, and externals. *Operators* are the people who will use or manage the product once it has been purchased. They typically set the specifications and evaluate the impact on operations or performance. Although it is common to involve them in buying decisions, occasionally they are excluded from such decisions. *Advisors* are the people who support and assist the decision maker. They often are senior managers, but they also may be nonmanaging professionals whom the decision maker trusts. It's easy to be blind sided by advisors because it's difficult to know who they are or how much influence they will exert. Another important group is the *gatekeepers*—contract managers, procurement officers, administrators, and other protectors of protocol and procedure. Their roles are to screen out unacceptable suppliers before the buying decision has been made and to enforce the provisions of the contract afterwards. They are concerned primarily that you and your offer meet the specified requirements and follow the rules. Typically, they can't say yes to a purchase but they can say no. The final category of influencers is the *externals*—people outside the customer organization who advise the decision maker or otherwise impact the decision. They include partners or allies of the customer, other suppliers, equipment manufacturers, attorneys, accountants, consumers, consultants, union officials, politicians or government officials, special interest groups, bankers, and the media. Depending on the type of product and the nature of the purchase, any of these types of external people may exert influence on the buying decision. If so, you need to know who they are, what their issues or perspectives will be, and what impact they are likely to have. If the externals have high visibility and their issues are politically sensitive, then their influence may be disproportionately high.

In addition to their functional roles, any of your customers, including decision maker, also can act as your sponsors. *Sponsors* are people in the customer organization who know you well and want you to succeed. Because they are biased toward you, they are willing to provide or interpret information, facilitate your access to key people, alert you to factors that may influence the decision, and warn you of obstacles and pitfalls. Clearly, it is critical to have sponsors within your key account. They are the people most likely to give you access to level 4 (deep private) information. The opposite role is *blocker*, a kind of antisponsor. Blockers either want you to lose or want no one to win. They may be biased toward another supplier, or they may think the purchase is unnecessary. Blockers often think the buying organization should try to solve the problem internally rather than seeking outside assistance. Or they think the solution is too expensive (no matter whom they buy it from) or they have other priorities for spending the money. In any event, you have to know who the potential blockers are and what their attitudes and perspectives might be.

Table 10-1. Rules of Key People in Buying Decision

Role	Involvement	Issues and Concerns
Decision Maker	Makes, or approves the buying decision; controls funding, often relies on others for information on the application, potential solutions, and tradeoffs; can sign or approve the contract or veto decisions of a selection team	■ Fits the budget; is affordable to own and maintain ■ Provides good return on investment ■ Increases productivity ■ Increases profitability ■ Improves performance ■ Improves cash flow ■ Achieves strategic goals ■ Builds competitive advantage ■ Heightens visibility or improves organizational image
Advisor	Assists or supports the decision maker; provides information and insight; highlights other organizational concerns or needs; assists in evaluating options and may recommend a solution or supplier	■ Satisfies the decision maker ■ Meets the needs of user ■ Impacts other operations minimally or favorable ■ Is the best buy for the organization ■ Provides the best solution across the board
Operator	will use, operate, manage, and depend on your product; consults with the decision maker; evaluates ease of implementation and use, impact on operations or performance; provides firsthand knowledge and experience; recommends potential and preferred solutions	■ Increases production or efficiency ■ Is easy to install and operate ■ Is compatible with existing systems and know-how or is easily adaptable ■ Expands capabilities or skills ■ Performs to standards ■ Makes the job easier, faster, or more cost effective ■ Eliminates or simplifies tasks ■ Flexible; has growth potential ■ Is state of the art ■ Reliable and quickly, dependably serviced ■ Is easy to learn
Gatekeeper	Screens out unacceptable products and suppliers; judges the parts of the offer; relies on standards, requirements, and rules; reviews for technical, contractual, or administrative compliance; helps to negotiate deals; usually can't say yes but can say *no*	■ Meets the specifications ■ Fits the budget and schedule ■ Meets legal, contractual, and regulatory requirements ■ Is easy to evaluate and administer ■ Has the best warranty or guarantees ■ Has no hidden costs ■ Places more performance responsibility on the seller ■ Minimizes or mitigates risk
Sponsor	Guides you to success; helps map out the power base and provides insights into individuals' issues and concerns; provides or interprets information; facilitates access to key people; alerts you to externals who may influence the decision; wants you to be aware of potential problems or obstacles	■ Satisfies organizational needs and solves the problem ■ Presents you and your solution in the best light ■ Capitalizes on the existing relationship with you or the installed base of your products in the organization
External	Serves the decision maker, customer organization, or public; advises the decision maker; helps generate or examine options; provides expert analysis or opinion; provides information and may provide some funding; may support the customer during or after the purchase	■ Meets organizational and end-user needs and requirements ■ Maximizes value and minimizes risk to the organization or a particular constituency ■ Satisfies legal, financial, political, or other requirements or concerns ■ Increases or reinforces the value of the external person or group to the organization

These roles may change from time to time and purchase to purchase, although your sponsors, by definition, remain loyal and supportive toward you as long as you maintain good relationships with them and they value what you represent. Table 10-1 summarizes how each of these types of people is involved in the buying decision and what organizational issues or concerns they typically have.

Identifying the people who typically make or influence the buying decisions for your products is crucial because they are the people with whom you need to build relationships. You identify them based on the cumulative experiences of you and others in your organization during past projects, previous bids (successful or not), and hours of walking the hallways in the customer organization. Who participates in their buying decisions? Who do they want you to meet? Who comes to the meetings when you present your products? Who attends the industry conferences? When you talk to customers, who do they suggest you also speak to? Over time, you learn the formal and informal networks of communication, responsibility, and influence that govern how they make buying decisions and who is involved. These networks are constantly in flux as relationships and responsibilities within their organization evolve, so you must always be relearning how they work and developing relationships with new people or building on old ones. When you analyze the account, which occurs at fixed points in time, you should take a snapshot, so to speak, of the current state of your relationships with the key people in their organization. There are many ways to classify those relationships, but I like the simple scheme here:

- *Positive.* You know these people well and have good relationships with them. They feel positive about your company and its products, although they are not necessarily your sponsors.
- *Neutral.* You know these people but the relationship is neutral. They are not biased toward or against you.
- *Negative.* You know these people but do not have good relationships with them. They either are hostile toward you or favor one of your competitors. They may act as blockers.
- *None.* You know who these people are, but you haven't made contact with them, and they don't know you.

Knowing where you stand with each key person is critical. In fact, one litmus test of an account manager's effectiveness is looking at the aggregate profile of these key relationships. If the majority of decision makers and advisors are negative or neutral toward you, then the account clearly is in trouble. It's even worse if the majority of key people have no relationship with you at all. Of course, the account manager does not have to maintain all these relationships personally. In a healthy key account, there are multiple relationships between your people and the customer's people at all

Figure 10-2. Key Person Relationship Matrix

Customer	Title	Role	Quality	Relationship with
Deena Marx	President	Decision maker	Neutral	Bob Roe, CEO Jerry Thomas, Ops
Rick Teeter	VP, Manufacturing	Decision maker	Positive	Jerry Thomas, Ops Maria Templin, R&D George Waltz, Transport
Don Shorewood	VP, Eastern Region Sales	Advisor	Neutral	Linda Betts, Sales John Oates, Sales
Landis Bach	Plant Manager Carbondale	Operator	Positive (sponsor)	Jerry Thomas, Ops John Oates, Sales Janna Piersen, Ops
Karen McHale	Plant Manager Rockville	Operator	Negative	John Oates, Sales
Jean Summers	Plant Ops Carbondale	Operator	Neutral	Janna Piersen, Ops John Oates, Sales Terry Walsh, Ops
Lavon Roberts	Purchasing Manager	Gatekeeper	Neutral	John Oates, Sales Susan Davies, Contracts
Mike Nelson	CFO	Advisor	Negative (blocker)	None

levels. In the parlance of account management, this is called *zippering*. In a zippered account, the people at all levels of your organization have solid relationships with their counterparts—your chief executive with the customer's chief executive, your vice presidents with their vice presidents, your engineers with their engineers, and so on. The account manager ensures that these relationships exist and manages the degree of interface between the two organizations, but it's neither possible nor desirable for the account manager alone to have all the key relationships. In the account plan, there should be a matrix showing the customer's key people and their relationships with your organization. Figure 10-2 offers an example.

Personal Profiles of Key People

In addition to a relationship matrix such as the one shown in Figure 10-2, account plans often include personal profiles of the customer's key people.

These profiles usually describe each person's background, experience, and interests and may include the types of items shown here (with examples):

- Name and nickname (if any): *Mark Hanson*
- Date and place of birth/home state or home town: *Born May 8, 1952 in Greensboro, NC*
- Educational level and institutions (where graduated?): *M.S. in Electrical Engineering from MIT; B.S. in Engineering from University of North Carolina*
- Professional associations: *SPE (Society of Professional Engineers)*
- Employment history or background: *Electrical engineer, Grumman Aerospace, 1976–1982; Manager, Component Design, Lockheed, 1982–1985; Manager, Power Systems, NASA, 1985–1989; Vice President, Engineering, Avalon Aerospace, 1990–present*
- Hobbies/sports interests: *Follows Tarheels basketball; season ticket holder for L.A. Lakers; drives race cars in his spare time*
- Professional Journals: reads *Aerospace Weekly, Fortune, Defense News*
- Family: *Married to Joanne; two sons, Robert and James; one daughter, Kathryn. Robert is a graduate of U.S. Air Force Academy, Class of 1992*

In addition to this kind of basic information, key person profiles often include honors and awards; military service; speeches or publications; religious affiliations; political affiliations; group memberships; personality or style; medical conditions or history, if relevant; favorite restaurants or types of food; favorite books or movies; and other aspects of people's personal preferences. As Harvey Mackay explains in his book, *Swim with the Sharks without Being Eaten Alive*,[7] the purpose of this kind of profile is to find ways to connect with these key people by knowing and sharing their interests (where that's possible). Mackay advocates keeping even more detailed information on customers, including their business concerns, opinions of others, and personal habits. He calls his list the Mackay 66, and he uses it to make personal connections. For example, if your key customer contact likes sushi, you could suggest going to a Japanese restaurant when you meet. If the person is a Tarheels fan, you can clip articles about the Tarheels to send. Obviously, you can't make these kinds of personal connections if you don't know anything personal about your customers, and these kinds of connections can make a difference.

Recording this kind of information in an account plan can be dangerous, however. Beware that many people are sensitive about having files maintained on them and could be offended if they learned that you had a written profile of their likes and dislikes. In Great Britain, it's illegal for anyone to retain this kind of information electronically. Consequently, many account managers keep personal notes on customers in their little

---

7. Harvey Mackay, *Swim with the Sharks without Being Eaten Alive* (New York: Ivy Books, 1988, pp. 28–34.

black books, but this information doesn't make its way into their account plans. Sensitive personal information probably doesn't belong in a plan that is widely circulated, although you might want to keep it in a private file with limited access.

Your Customer's Buying Process

A final important factor in the customer's structure and management is how they typically make buying decisions for your types of products. Here I am referring not to the people but to the systems, rules, procedures, and traditions surrounding their selection decisions. These vary so widely from organization to organization that it would be impossible to cite a typical case. Some customers are rigid and formal in their purchasing. They release RFPs (request for proposals) and have strict procedures for evaluating the bids. Some limit access to key people during the bid evaluation period. Others are loose and informal, sealing deals with a handshake and ignoring the formal processes imposed by headquarters. If you're in an alliance or partnership with a customer, the rules they impose on others probably won't apply to you. Sometimes the buying process depends on how critical the product is to them, whether it's a commodity, the size of the contract, or political factors, such as whether there are different factions that support different suppliers. The federal government has a comprehensive set of laws and regulations governing procurement, but even in federal contracting the formal and informal rules vary from agency to agency. The questions you should ask include:

- How do they typically buy your products or services?
- How is the need for your product identified and formalized?
- How are the requirements and specifications determined? Syndicated for approval within their organization? Communicated to potential suppliers?
- Who has the authority to make the buying decision? How broad is that authority? Can buyers decide unilaterally to select a particular supplier or are there formal or informal requirements for others to review decisions before they become final?
- Do they have a process for soliciting and evaluating bids? How does that process work?
- What guidelines do they have for selecting suppliers? What legal or compliance requirements do they follow or impose? What hoops do you have to jump through? What do the gatekeepers of the process look for?
- What factors are most important in their selection decisions? What are they typically most concerned about? How will they evaluate competing offers? How important is price? How do they evaluate it? How responsive are they to incentives, such as discounts, bulk pricing, or guarantees?
- How do they ensure that they are getting the best solution? The best deal?

- Does their process allow access to key people early in the decision cycle? Can you influence the requirements? Presell your solution?
- What role do partnerships or relationships typically play? Despite the formal rules in place, how does it work informally? What is the *real* process?

If you can develop strong enough relationships with your key account, you often can circumvent their formal buying procedures. Vendors are subject to all the formal rules, but customers usually make exceptions for preferred suppliers. Because they know you well, you won't have the same scrutiny from their contract managers or materials inspectors. They may bend the rules to give you sole-source contracts, or they may attach new work to existing contracts. With partners and strategic allies, customers often rewrite the rules entirely. In fact, there may not even be a formal buying process.

Each part of your customer analysis has a simple goal. In analyzing their industry and markets, you are exploring the arena in which they operate. In effect, your analysis says, "Here's what's happening in their arena and how they are likely to respond to it." In your analysis of their structure and management, you are saying, "This is who they are and how they work." In the next part of your analysis, the customer's performance, you are saying, "This is how they've been doing."

Your Customer's Performance

Much of their performance may not be relevant to your products and services, but you should know how their organization as a whole has been performing. Are they meeting their goals? Are they growing? Are they shipping product as planned? Are they experiencing performance problems that could impact them negatively in the future? It's important to examine not only their operations but also their financial performance, value-added tactics, and marketing tactics. These areas will give you insight on how their performance could impact their need for your products and your potential for adding more value to them in the future. The kinds of questions you might ask include:

- What are their operational or performance goals? Are they achieving them?
- How do they measure performance? What do those measures show?
- What are the gaps in their performance? Where are they failing to reach goal and why? What need do they have for improving their operations or manufacturing? Are there any leverage points for your products? In other words, can your products or any of your related services help them achieve these improvements?
- How are they performing financially? What are their trends in sales, earnings, capital spending, depreciation, operating margin, taxes, working capital, debt, return on equity, capacity utilization, or economic value added?

Not all these measures will be appropriate for your customer, but you should know which ones are. How do they measure their financial performance, and what do those measures indicate?

- What are their tactics for creating value added? (I use the term tactics here to differentiate between performance-related choices they have about how they design, make, or sell their products as opposed to the broader, strategic choices they have about which products to make.)
- What are their core competencies as an organization? What core competencies give them strategic advantage? Which competencies do they intend to maintain? Which ones are they outsourcing and why? What are the implications for you?
- How are they using technology to differentiate themselves in their products, distribution systems, or marketing? How is their technology evolving? What technologies are they researching or developing, and what impact will those technologies have? Technology can fundamentally change an industry. Does that potential exist here? What will the future look like and how are they preparing for it? What are the potential impacts on you?
- Finally, what choices are they making about marketing their products? How do they price, promote, and distribute their products? Can your products provide marketing leverage for them in some way?

If your customer is a large, complex organization with thousands of products serving global markets, then a complete performance analysis may be well beyond the scope of what's necessary in your customer profile. You have to be sensible about the amount of effort you put into it. A good customer profile has no more information than is necessary to help readers appreciate who the customer is, how they are performing, and what they need—but it should also have no less information than is necessary for readers to gain important insights into the customer. Including just the right amount of information requires experience and good judgment.

The Customer's Need for Your Products

The final part of a customer profile describes the customer's evolving need for your products. If the profile contains nothing else it should describe what customer needs your products fulfill, how your products are used, and how their needs are changing. Essentially, you want to describe the past, present, and future. How long have they been buying your type of product? How much of it do they buy from you, and how much from other suppliers? What has the volume been during each of the past 5 or 10 years? How has their demand changed, and what's driving those changes? How much are they buying now, this year? What are your projections for next year and even longer into the future? Your projections will probably factor into the sales manager's forecasts, so projecting demand accurately is important. Where demand has fluctuated widely or where it's been difficult to gauge, the profile should include a confidence percentage. You might estimate, for example, that the customer will buy 4,000 units next year, plus or minus 400 units (or 4,000 units with a 90 percent degree of confidence). It's even more helpful if you can break down sales projections by locations or buying units within the customer organization.

The Implications of Customer Intelligence

In and of itself, the intelligence in a customer profile has only marginal value unless you show how it impacts you and your business potential with the customer. The fact that the customer is opening a new office in Bolivia, for example, may be interesting to other people in your organization who read your account plan, but what they really need to know is how that development impacts you. *It's essential to identify the implications of every piece of information you include in your customer profile.* In effect, the implications answer the question, "So what?" Your customer is opening an office in Bolivia. So what? They're targeting the fastest-growing small cities in the Midwest. So what? Because of two contract disputes with suppliers last year, they are instituting more formal buying procedures. So what? If you don't have an insightful answer to the question "So what?," then the information probably is meaningless and should be removed from the profile. Remember that the primary reasons for profiling the customer are to understand what's happening in their business and to anticipate how those changes will impact you and your ability to serve their needs.

Table 10-2 provides some examples of customer profile intelligence and the possible implications for the account manager's organization. I've taken these examples randomly from different customer profiles, so they are not related.

Doing a Customer SWOT Analysis

One of the tools I've found to be helpful in thinking about customers is the SWOT analysis, which stands for strengths, weaknesses, opportunities, and threats. I'm not sure where this tool originated, but it's become a fairly standard way of analyzing an organization's competitive position. A SWOT analysis usually appears as a four-box matrix, and it's a useful way to summarize the customer's position. It's not an indispensable part of a customer profile, but many of the account plans I've seen include one, so it's worth showing how the tool might be helpful.

Table 10-2.   Implications of Customer Intelligence

Customer Profile Section	Intelligence (What did I learn about the customer?)	Implications (So what? What are the implications for us?)
Industry and Market Analysis	The industry is consolidating rapidly. Smaller firms are being acquired or are merging with each other at an accelerating rate. Analysis estimate that in ten years five or six major players will dominate the industry	The customer is seeking economies of scale by acquiring smaller firms. They will be seeking the best acquisition targets and will be looking for ways to find synergies with potential partners. Because we know many of those smaller firms, we cna help them find the right fit
	Consumer demand is increasing faster than supply. The customer is riding a rising wave, and competitors will not catch up for at least five years	If we can consolidate our relationship with this customer, we can ride the wave with them, but we must anticipate the consumers needs for increasing product sophistication through our own proactive research and development efforts and joint development with our customer
Customer Strategies, Plans, and Synergies	Because of the rising cost of fuel, the customer plans to reorganize into eight regions and to create a hub-and-spoke system that will decrease transportation costs and increase their access to customers	Given their history, they will favor local suppliers. Our central location will become a handicap and we will lose share with this customer unless we can develop regional presence of offer discounts that mitigate the increased cost of shipping
Structure and Management	Buying decisions are delegated to plant managers but the director of purchasing analyzes all expenditures and provides annual guidance to plant managers that they must follow on future purchases	Not having a good relationship with the purchasing director will be detrimental to us in the long run. Our relationships with the plant managers remain important, but the guidelines they receive from purchasing could limit their ability to choose us unless those guidelines are favorable toward us
Performance	Despite a highly visible campaign to increase productivity, the customer's before-tax revenues have continued to shrink, largely due to rising labor and raw materials costs, which cannot be passed on to consumers because of competitive pressures in the industry	They will be looking for cost-saving measures, and they may be more open to outsourcing some functions than they have been in the past. Our business will be at risk unless we can help them achieve some economies
Product Needs	Demand for our product has steadily declined in the past three years as the customer has met its needs and built an adequate base of our products	Their emphasis is shifting from product installation to training, support, maintenance, and upgrading. If we are viewed purely as a product supplier, then our value to them will continue to decline

To develop a SWOT analysis on your customer, gather and analyze all the information discussed previously in this chapter. Then identify the areas where your customer is strong or weak and where they have opportunities or face threats. Strengths and weaknesses consist of the *internal* factors that make a company strong or weak, including such things as cash position, core competencies (or lack thereof), systems, leadership and management, resources, product quality, manufacturing systems, brand image, distribution systems, and culture. Opportunities and threats are the *external* factors that are favorable or unfavorable toward the company, including changes in the marketplace, increasing or decreasing demand, price pressures, governmental actions, competitor actions, economic changes, and changes in consumer behavior.

In pursuing their business, all companies must capitalize on their strengths, mitigate their weaknesses, exploit their opportunities, and defend against their threats, so examining your customer's SWOT is an excellent way to develop insight into their corporate strategies and the decisions they are making. The following lists describe what might fall into each category in the SWOT, and Figure 10-3 shows an example of a customer SWOT.

Figure 10-3. Example of a Customer SWOT Analysis

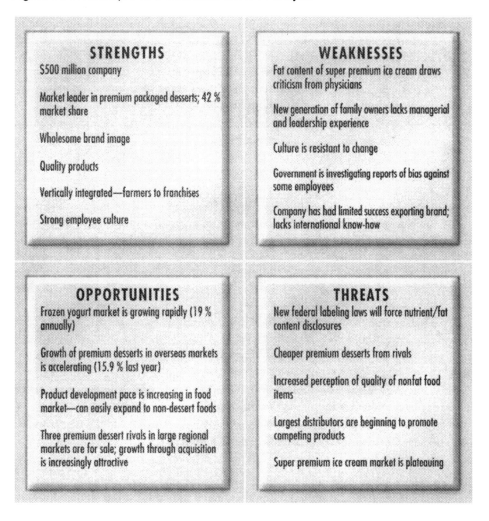

STRENGTHS

$500 million company

Market leader in premium packaged desserts; 42 % market share

Wholesome brand image

Quality products

Vertically integrated—farmers to franchises

Strong employee culture

WEAKNESSES

Fat content of super premium ice cream draws criticism from physicians

New generation of family owners lacks managerial and leadership experience

Culture is resistant to change

Government is investigating reports of bias against some employees

Company has had limited success exporting brand; lacks international know-how

OPPORTUNITIES

Frozen yogurt market is growing rapidly (19 % annually)

Growth of premium desserts in overseas markets is accelerating (15.9 % last year)

Product development pace is increasing in food market—can easily expand to non-dessert foods

Three premium dessert rivals in large regional markets are for sale; growth through acquisition is increasingly attractive

THREATS

New federal labeling laws will force nutrient/fat content disclosures

Cheaper premium desserts from rivals

Increased perception of quality of nonfat food items

Largest distributors are beginning to promote competing products

Super premium ice cream market is plateauing

Customer strengths occur when:

- They excel at meeting the needs or solving the problems in their markets.
- Their products or services are positively differentiated from their competitors' products because they have distinct advantages in people, resources, management, experience, location, distribution, marketing, packaging, service capability, manufacturing efficiencies, financing, price, technology, or access to customers.
- They are the preferred choice in their industry.
- They have so strong a brand that it creates a virtual monopoly (e.g., Intel, Microsoft, Coca-Cola, General Electric).
- They have strong, multilevel relationships outside their organization, and their people are highly regarded (e.g., Bechtel, which has long had a strategy of hiring very influential directors such as Fred Gluck, ex–Managing Director of McKinsey & Company).
- They have strong formal or informal partnering relationships or alliances with their customers (e.g., Fluor Daniel and Duke Power Corporation).
- They have proprietary or legally protected products or technology (e.g., the Viagra patent for Pfizer).
- They have no competitors or their competitors are weak or poorly positioned to compete with them (e.g, Microsoft).
- They have a strong and powerful image or reputation that biases their customers to choose them (e.g., Mercedes-Benz).
- They have a large installed base of their products that creates switching costs for customers (e.g., Microsoft Office).

Customer weaknesses occur when:

- They are out of sync with changes and trends in their marketplace (e.g, Woolworth's, which has failed to respond aggressively to Wal-Mart).
- Demand for their products is shrinking (e.g., General Dynamics after the end of the cold war).
- Internal cultural or system problems are impacting their ability to perform.
- They lack the resources or time to meet demand or solve their customers' problems.
- Their competitors have better technology or more resources.
- They are poorly perceived in their marketplace, perhaps because of legal problems or product failures (e.g., Apple's Newton).
- Their cost structure prevents competitive pricing.
- They have ineffective management or lack the leadership necessary to turn themselves around (e.g., IBM under John Akers).
- They have had to downsize drastically and no longer have the resources to invest as much in the future as they once did.

Customer opportunities occur when:

- Their capabilities position them well for future projects in their markets (e.g, General Electric).
- They are financially sound and face key investment opportunities (e.g, Microsoft, Berkshire Hathaway, Goldman Sachs).
- Demand for their products and services is growing (e.g., Intel, Motorola, Microsoft, Dell).
- An incumbent competitor has fallen out of favor, and your customer's customer is searching for an alternative supplier to meet their needs.
- Attractive market segments exist that your customer can serve but hasn't expanded into yet.
- Your customer is well positioned to cut costs, enhance productivity, or increase efficiency.
- They have emerging technologies that will advance the state of the art in their field.
- They have enlightened leadership that is opening new directions for them and energizing their organization (e.g., General Electric under Jack Welch; Coca-Cola under Roberto Giozueta).
- There are alliance opportunities for them that could expand greatly their scope and their business (e.g., AT&T and TCI).

Customer threats occur when:

- They face new, strong, vibrant competitors with deep pockets for investing or buying market share (e.g., General Motors facing the Chrysler–Mercedes-Benz merger).
- Their competitors are well positioned in the market and have very strong relationships or are developing alliances with key customers (e.g., Phillips Petroleum looking at the U.S. downstream alliance of Shell and Texaco).
- They have projects on the brink of failure.
- External market factors, such as rising interest rates, could impact their sales or margins.
- They risk losing key people, especially to competitors (this is a problem AT&T has been facing).
- A competitor is about to introduce a new technology that could make your customer's products inferior or too costly.

— 11 —

Analyzing Your Competitors

In his *Instructions to His Generals*, Frederick the Great wrote, "A general in all of his projects should not think so much about what he wishes to do as what his enemy will do; that he should never underestimate this enemy, but he should put himself in his place to appreciate difficulties and hindrances the enemy could interpose; that his plans will be deranged at the slightest event if he has not foreseen everything and if he has not devised means with which to surmount the obstacles."[1] Knowing your enemy has long been a maxim of military leaders, and the most effective account managers I know have the same mind-set.

Several years ago I worked on a major opportunity for an aerospace firm. As we analyzed the situation and pondered our strategy, we realized that we didn't know enough about our competitors' strengths and weaknesses or their likely courses of action. So we called our market research group, who sent a representative to our next meeting. We listed everything we wanted to know, and it was an imposing list, really more of a wish list than an honest expectation because it seemed impossible that anyone could uncover everything we asked for. Four days later, however, our intrepid researcher reappeared with answers to all our questions, including such arcane information as the size and disposition of a competitor's maintenance capabilities in the Far East. I was impressed not only with the extent of the information she provided but also with her ability to put the information into perspective and deliver accurate and timely intelligence. The strategies we developed as a consequence were instrumental in winning the contract. As Sun Tzu advised in *The Art of War*, "Compare your government to that of the enemy; compare your military leadership to that of the enemy; compare your logistics to that of your enemy; compare your ground to that of your enemy. Having established these comparisons, you will have a preview of superiorities and inferiorities, weaknesses and strengths; this will enable you to prevail every time in subsequent military operations."[2]

---

1. Quoted in Robert Debs Heinl, Jr., *Dictionary of Military and Naval Quotations* (Annapolis: United States Naval Institute, 1966), p. 102.
2. Sun Tzu, *The Art of War*, trans. Thomas Cleary (Boston: Shambhala Publications, 1988), pp. 82–83.

Most of the account plans I've read, however, show very little knowledge of the competition. Likewise, the competitor databases in most companies are notoriously empty, inaccurate, and unhelpful, which is surprising given the enormous potential value of the intelligence and the availability of information. There are some sophisticated exceptions, like the on-line system maintained by one of America's leading telecommunications companies. Representatives of this company can log onto the system, validate themselves, and then ask questions about their competitors. If they know, for instance, that they are competing with competitor A on the installation of a telephone system, they can receive up-to-date information on competitor A's likely technical approach, products, system configuration, service policies, guarantees, discounts, and pricing. The researchers who maintain this system watch their competitors closely. They follow their competitors' bids; solicit information from the field on their competitors' performance; and scan all four levels of information to ensure that they always are current on their competitors' business practices, strategies, strengths, and weaknesses. The proposals they create are much more focused because they can target their competitors' vulnerabilities and try to neutralize their strengths.

Gathering Competitor Intelligence

In companies with the kinds of market research systems and databases I've described, account managers have a ready source of information on competitors, and as the account managers learn more about the competition they become sources of information for the market researchers. If you don't have market research or an established competitor database, remember that there are numerous sources of public and deep public information, such as those I discussed in chapter 9. A number of books have been published about developing competitor intelligence,[3] and they are an excellent departure point if you are beginning to gather intelligence on competitors.

In addition to the sources of public and deep public information, you may have sources of private information within your own organization. Anyone who has served the customer, for example, may have learned something useful about the competition, and there may be people in your company who used to work for a competitor. In the major corporations I've worked for, one of my first tasks in developing strategies or account plans has been to identify the people in our company who have worked for my key

---

3. Leonard M. Fuld's *The New Competitor Intelligence* (New York: John Wiley & Sons, 1995) is considered one of the best sources. See also Larry Kahaner's *Competitive Intelligence* (New York: Simon & Schuster, 1996) and Kirk W.M. Tyson's *The Complete Guide to Competitive Intelligence* (Chicago: Kirk Tyson International, 1998).

competitors. Interviewing them is always enlightening. Other sources of private information include third-party suppliers, such as equipment manufacturers or raw materials suppliers, and industry consultants. Finally, your customer often is an excellent source of intelligence, particularly if you have sponsors or other people in the organization who are friendly and don't mind telling you what they know and think about your rivals.

Of course, the competitors you care most about are the ones who are the greatest threat to your position with your key account. There may be other major players in your industry, but if they aren't actively pursuing business with your key customer, then for your purposes they don't matter. The competitors who are active in your account may include incumbent suppliers with established relationships, an installed base of products, and experience in the customer's organization. They also may include competitors who currently are not serving the account but are working hard to try to penetrate it.

In gathering competitor intelligence, you should be concerned primarily with answering these questions: What are your competitors' current business activities with the customer? What are their capabilities and resources? Their strategies with the account? Their strengths and weaknesses? Your customer's perceptions of them? Later in this chapter, I'll introduce a useful device for analyzing this information called the Four Pillars of Position. For now, let's concentrate on the type of information you should gather.

Current Relationship and Business Activities

Your account plan should describe your competitors' current relationship with the customer and the business activities they are engaged in.

- Which competitors are involved in the account? What products or services are they providing? Which projects do they have? How long have they been involved in the account? What is their history with the customer?
- Do any competitors have incumbent projects or an installed base? How strong is their position? How high are the switching costs for the customer?
- How much volume are your competitors doing now? How much customer share do they have?
- Whom do your competitors know in the customer organization? Who are their key contacts? Which customer representatives are biased toward them and why? Who are your competitors' sponsors? How well connected are they at the senior or most influential levels in the customer's organization?
- What type of relationship do your competitors have with the customer: vendor, preferred supplier, partner, strategic ally?

Remember that, by itself, this information is not useful. For each piece of information you include in the account plan, you should answer the question, "So what?" What are the implications for you?

Capabilities and Resources

- What are your competitors' capabilities or limitations?
- Are they capable of expanding in the account? Are they capable of providing a broader range of products and services? Can they offer a total solution that is beyond what they currently are providing? What is their breadth and depth?
- What resources can they bring to bear in this account? Where are they resource constrained? What are they capable of doing in this account?

Competitive Strategies

- What are their apparent strategies in the account?
- How do they try to leverage their strengths and mitigate their weaknesses?
- What direction do they seem to be taking? What stories are they telling? What is their public relations effort focusing on? What does their marketing literature say?
- How are they positioning themselves to expand their business? Who are they meeting with and what are they proposing?

Strengths and Weaknesses

- How well (or poorly) are they performing?
- What do they do exceptionally well? What differentiates them from other competitors and us? In what ways does the customer consider them to be distinctive?
- What customer needs do they fulfill? How satisfied is the customer with them?
- Conversely, what are their weaknesses? What differentiates us from them? In what ways is the customer not impressed with them?
- What performance problems have they had with the customer? Where have they fallen? What deliveries were missed? Promises not met? Projects stalled? What issues does the customer have with them?

Customer Perceptions

- Finally, what does the customer think of them? In aggregate, what does all this mean? Customers may have an emotional attachment to a competitor despite the latter's poor performance. Or they may dislike the competitor despite superb performance. What is the customer's bottom-line impression of each competitor?

In a good account plan, the information just outlined would appear as a narrative or bulleted list that summarizes the relevant facts about each key competitor. In addition, you need to analyze the information to determine the implications of those facts for your company. Some account managers synthesize this data in a SWOT (strengths, weaknesses, opportunities, and threats) analysis on each competitor, but I think it's difficult to acquire accurate information on your competitors' opportunities and threats, and I'm not sure that knowing them would help you anyway. What you really care about is how well positioned your competitors are in the account and where and how they are vulnerable. Consequently, the analytical tool I prefer to use in diagnosing competitors is the Four Pillars of Position.

The Four Pillars of Position

Position is the degree of preference a buyer has for a seller. When you are well positioned with a buyer, you are much more likely to get the business because the buyer prefers you. Virtually all sales and marketing activities are intended to improve your position with your customers, including your promotions and advertising, location or methods of distribution, packaging, product fit, customization, pricing, discounting or other incentives, and relationship building.

Consequently, one way to analyze the degree of preference your customer has toward your competitors is to analyze the factors that contribute to their position with the customer. The four contributing factors are *strength, strategy, staff,* and *support,* and these are shown as the pillars of position in Figure 11-1. It's easy to imagine that a seller's position with a buyer is like a temple (account managers who've spent years building their position with a strategic account treat their customers with appropriate reverence). Supporting the structure are four pillars, each of which is crucial. If one pillar falls, it can bring down the whole building. Similarly, position with a customer depends on the four key elements of strength, strategy, staff, and support. Competitors need all four to maintain good standing and to be preferred by the customer.

As you'll see, these pillars include much of the information I discussed earlier in this chapter and that you've already gathered about your competitors. The four pillars tool is not a different means of gathering information; it's just a useful way to look at competitor intelligence so you can better understand the degree of preference your customers have for your competitors. Understanding how your competitors are positioned and where they are vulnerable will help you develop more effective strategies for competing with them for the account.

The Pillar of Strength

The first pillar consists of your competitor's strengths, the factors that give them advantage because of their technologies, experience, history, capabil-

Figure 11-1. The Four Pillars of Position

ities, and capacity to satisfy the customer's needs. The information relevant here includes their core competencies, key technologies, patents or trademarks, brand image, incumbent position, installed base, ongoing service relationships, key contracts, and so on. What makes them strong? What does the customer like about them or their products? What differentiates them in the eyes of the customer? For their pillar of strength to remain up-right, their strengths must be matched with the customer's primary needs. They must be the yin to the customer's yang.

The Pillar of Strategy

This pillar consists of their purpose and goals, directions, vision with the customer, and strategies for building and sustaining their competitive advantage. What is their vision for this account? What are their goals? What value-added dimensions do they emphasize? What are their key selling messages or themes? Lowest price? Lowest life cycle cost? Ease of operation, maintenance, or service? Quick response time? Lower risk? Higher quality? Understanding their strategies helps you know where they consider themselves vulnerable or where they admit to no differentiation. For their pillar of strategy to remain strong, their strategies must complement the customer's priorities and they must be moving in the same direction as the customer's evolving needs.

The Pillar of Staff

The third pillar consists of the staff of people the competitor assigns to the account—their executives, account manager, project managers, and others who serve the customer. A sure sign of a competitor's dedication to the customer (or lack thereof) is whom they assign to the account and how highly visible the customer is in their organization. This pillar will crumble if none of their senior executives bothers to build relationships with their customer counterparts or if the competitor assigns a new account manager every 2 years. A revolving-door approach with their account managers means they don't place value on building long-term relationships, so look at whom they have assigned to manage this relationship. How long do their account managers remain in place? How many people work the account full time? How often do they meet with the customer and at what level? Have they assigned a high-level executive sponsor? Does their CEO meet with the customer's CEO? How much importance does the competitor seem to be placing on this account?

The Pillar of Support

The fourth pillar—in many ways the most important one—is the degree of support your competitor receives from the customer. How high is your competitor's reach in the customer organization? How long and strong are their relationships? How deep is the trust? Are bid decisions biased in their favor? If so, how well placed are their sponsors? Are there any formal or informal partnering arrangements? How many sole-source awards or contract add-ons does the competitor get?

Competitors with four strong pillars in place are tough to beat. If their strengths match the customer's needs, if their strategies reflect the customer's priorities, if they've shown their commitment by assigning key people to the account, and if they're strongly supported in the customer's organization, their position may be unassailable. Competing with them may be like trying to run up Devil's Tower. Before you decide whether or how to compete, it's essential that you know how well positioned your competitors are.

As Jim Matassoni analyzed his principal competitor, Omni Hospital Supply (OHS), he discovered that they were better positioned than he'd realized. It was disheartening, because he needed a substantial increase in revenue from his strategic account, Hartman HealthCare Corporation (HHC), in order to meet his goals. However, it didn't appear that any gains were feasible; he might even lose ground. OHS looked solid on all four pillars of position. They were among the world leaders in laboratory analysis equipment, and they had a large installed base in Hartman hospitals, so the customer's lab technicians were comfortable with the equipment and knew how to use it. OHS's strategy was to continually reduce the average cost of analysis, which was a key metric for HHC. OHS's account manager for HHC, Doreen Stevens, had built the relationship over 7 years and was practically a fixture in Hartman's executive suite. Finally, OHS enjoyed considerable support from Hartman's decision makers and key executive influencers, including the purchasing director, Mark Nogata.

As Jim scrutinized OHS's position, however, he learned some interesting things. First, a confidential source inside HHC informed him that Nogata had just been offered and had accepted a position with American Hospital Supply and that his position would likely be filled by Audry D'Souza, who Jim knew had been critical of the virtual monopoly OHS had enjoyed inside Hartman. D'Souza was likely to be much more receptive to alternatives and was definitely not in Stevens' pocket. Also, recent technological improvements in his company's equipment had now made their products much more competitive with OHS's equipment. They couldn't claim an advantage, but they could neutralize one of OHS's traditional strengths. Finally, although it appeared that OHS's low-cost-of-analysis strategy was solid, they were not focusing on another message that Jim had been hearing from the Hartman lab technicians he'd been visiting—the need for greater speed and accuracy in analysis. At this point, nearly 15 percent of lab tests had to be redone because the results did not meet accuracy standards, so Jim felt that if their solutions could deliver higher speed and accuracy, they might have the leverage needed to increase customer share. The challenge, he knew, was to ensure that Hartman's executives were aware of the change in priority from their field laboratory people.

continued

His account strategy, then, had three major components designed to exploit the cracks in his competitor's positional foundation: (1) to be aggressive in developing a better relationship with Audry D'Souza and in particular to stress to her the advantages of having more than one strong supplier; (2) to neutralize OHS's traditional product strengths by showing that his company's equipment was now on par with theirs; and (3) to provide a solution that focused on the speed and accuracy of lab tests and ensure that Hartman's executives were aware of the field's growing concern with those two issues and gave priority to meeting those needs.

Cracks in the Foundation—Competitor Vulnerabilities

Equally important as knowing how well your competitors are positioned is knowing where they are vulnerable. Where are the cracks in their foundation? Where are their pillars being undermined? As Figure 11-2 shows, you can examine their vulnerabilities using the same four pillars.

Toppling the Pillar of Strength

- Have they had recent performance problems?
- Are their strengths no longer aligned with the customer's needs?
- Have they become arrogant and unresponsive?
- Are they taking the customer for granted? Failing to innovate? Losing ground to new technologies?
- Is their installed base losing its currency? No longer state of the art? Are the switching costs now low?
- Have their costs increased?

Toppling the Pillar of Strategy

- Are their strategies out of sync with the customer's priorities? For example, are they emphasizing low installed cost, while the customer has become more concerned with quality?
- Are they losing differentiation and failing to rebuild it? Are you or other rivals now at par with them?
- Are they failing to keep pace with the customer's growth and changes in direction?

Toppling the Pillar of Staff

- Has their assignment of account manager recently changed? Do they have someone new in the role who lacks the relationships his or her predecessor had?

Figure 11-2. Cracks in the Foundation

- Are their senior executives lackluster in maintaining key customer relationships?
- Do they convey, through their behavior, that they are not fully committed to the customer?
- Do they fail to stretch when the customer needs them to stretch? Do they fail to give the customer the highest priority on service?

Toppling the Pillar of Support

- Is their support mainly at lower levels?
- Have senior customers who were biased toward your competitor departed? Have your competitor's sponsors moved on?
- Have people who are either neutral or biased toward you been promoted to influential positions in the customer organization?
- Have partnering relationships been dissolved?
- Has something happened to erode the trust that once existed between the customer and the competitor?
- Are sole-source awards to the competitor now prohibited because of a change in customer policy?

Any of the four pillars of position can have cracks in their foundations. Discovering where your competitors are vulnerable is crucial to developing an effective account strategy, so this part of your account plan should highlight the areas of opportunity for you. It's generally not necessary to stipulate every weakness your competitors have but only to discover the three or four in which they are most vulnerable. Attack them there. The key is to know your competitors' strengths and weaknesses as well as you know your own. Finally, remember that the purpose of profiling competitors is not merely to help other people in your company learn about the competition, it is to gain sufficient insight to know where and how to neutralize their strengths and exploit their weaknesses.

― 12 ―

Analyzing Your Position

In his classic book, *The Art of War*, Sun Tzu observed, "If you know others and know yourself, you will not be imperiled in a hundred battles; if you do not know others but know yourself, you will win one and lose one; if you do not know others and do not know yourself, you will be imperiled in every single battle."[1] Knowing your own capabilities and analyzing your own position is a crucial part of account planning. Although this would seem to be one of the easiest parts of the planning process, it's often the most difficult, largely because you can be too close to the subject to see it clearly. The primary purpose of your self-analysis is not to discern what *you* think of yourself but what *your customer* thinks, and it's wise to remember, as Gerald Simmons observes, that "we don't live in a world of reality; we live in a world of perceptions."[2]

It's easy to be deceived about your company on two counts. First, we tend to exaggerate our weaknesses and see blemishes as fatal flaws. As we work day to day, we focus on our operational problems, fret about them, assign committees to fix them, and devote so much energy to them that they loom large in our imagination. So it's hard to believe that customers aren't as aware of and worried about our weaknesses as we are. Conversely, it's easy for us to be deceived about our strengths. We're proud of them, develop them, promote them in our marketing literature, and congratulate ourselves on them so often we imagine everyone is as enthralled with our strengths as we are. The fact is, customers usually have very different perceptions of our strengths and weaknesses than we do, and what matters in account planning and strategy development is what *they* think.

So it behooves you to begin analyzing your own position by talking to your customer. Ask, What is your perception of us? How would you describe us and our products to others? What do you see as our strengths? Our weaknesses? How would you describe our relationship with you and your company? What problems are we helping you solve? What needs are

---

1. Sun Tzu, *The Art of War*, trans. Thomas Cleary (Boston: Shambhala Publications, 1988), p. 82.
2. Gerald J. Simmons, quoted in Ted Goodman, ed., *The Forbes Book of Business Quotations* (New York: Black Dog & Leventhal Publishers, 1997).

we meeting? How would you rank us as suppliers or partners compared to your other suppliers or partners? Gathering information on customers' perceptions of you is a useful reality check, and it can highlight areas of strength or weakness you hadn't focused on and should explore further. If you conduct regular customer surveys, you should use the survey results as primary information sources. Other sources include project reviews, customer testimonials, customer service reports, complaint forms, and feedback the customer's given to anyone in your organization who meets with or talks to customers.

The information you gather from customers is an important baseline for analyzing your position. Next, it's important to have an accurate picture of where you've been with the customer and what the history of your relationship reveals.

In 1994, Travis Engelmann was hired by Kassner-Evers Field Services (KEFS), an oil field supply company. Because of Travis' experience in the industry, he was appointed as a vice president and given the responsibility to develop business in the southwestern U.S., where KEFS traditionally had not been a major player, although they had supplied some products to the American Oil Company over a 10-year period.

For the next 2 years, Engelmann worked the territory and brought in some new sales, but he spent most of his time developing long-term relationships with other major oil producers in the territory, most of whom had not worked with KEFS previously. Then, abruptly, he quit and joined one of KEFS's competitors. Recognizing the magnitude of their problem, KEFS's sales director, Mike Abasolo, asked to see Engelmann's files for the past 2 years and discovered that there weren't any. Engelmann was the type of salesperson who "keeps it all in his head," so, except for some names and phone numbers, the kind of paper trail Mike would have liked simply did not exist. Engelmann's secretary was able to reconstruct some information from copies of correspondence, but personal notes, account histories, strategies, and other documents that might provide a coherent picture of Engelmann's activities were unavailable.

A month later, Stella Chen was hired to take over Engelmann's responsibilities, and she learned that the problem was even greater than she'd been told. As she began to rebuild the territory, she could not find a coherent picture of KEFS's business with *any* customers, much less the ones in her area. Individual salespeople briefed her on their accounts, and she could discover what was being sold to all customers throughout the U.S. by looking at the sales reports nationwide. But she could not find out what had been sold in the past, what customers had been served historically, and what the patterns of activity had been for the key customers in her territory. Consequently, she found it difficult to tell a compelling story to the prospects she was contacting. Her first break came when one prospect sent her a request for quotation. As she scanned the customer's requirements, her heart sank because KEFS did not have the required experience and apparently was unable to meet the customer's technological requirements. Nonetheless, she gave it her best shot and submitted a bid. After being notified that the award had gone to another supplier, she complained to a colleague, John Fairbanks, and learned that KEFS did, in fact, have the requisite experience and would have been able to provide the technology. She just hadn't talked to the right person.

Over the next 6 months, Stella was able to rebuild the territory, but it was far more of a struggle than it should have been. She wasn't surprised, then, when Mike Abasolo started requiring strategic account reps to document their strategies and activities with customers and purchased the software necessary to start building a database on sales and customer history. The initiative came too late for her, however, and by then she estimates the company had already lost several million dollars in opportunity cost.

Building a History of Your Relationship

The companies that are most effective at strategic account management maintain comprehensive, accessible records of their relationships with key customers. Fluor Daniel, for example, has created a worldwide database of project information that constitutes a history of their work with clients on many different types of projects. This database is accessible to Fluor Daniel employees anywhere in the world. Other companies have historical files filled with details of product deliveries, customer contacts, and service records. Unfortunately, in some organizations this information is not readily available and often exists only as a kind of oral history—kept in the heads of a few old-timers and accessible, when you can track them down, through anecdotes and war stories, which may be interesting but is woefully inadequate as a diagnostic tool. Having a history of your relationship with your strategic accounts is important for a number of reasons:

- It helps educate people who need to know what the history has been, including new account team members as well as customers who aren't familiar with the history.
- It shows what customer needs you have satisfied in the past; therefore, it sheds light on how the customer's needs are evolving.
- It documents what you have done for the customer or promised to the customer.
- It provides some of the data needed to analyze account management effectiveness, including revenue growth, profitability, and customer share.
- It can highlight problems and opportunities in the account.
- If you track customer service calls, it can enable you to spot problem trends and apply corrective action before they become more serious.
- It provides valuable information for bid and proposal writers, including corporate and project experience, proofs of effectiveness and customer satisfaction, names of project managers and customer contacts, and so on.

- It provides the basis for identifying such trends as penetration of business units, international growth, product evolution, and cost and margin changes.
- It helps create institutional memory of the account relationship, so people who don't follow it day by day can be reminded of the business relationship that has existed with the customer. Also, if the strategic account manager suddenly departs, someone can take his or her place without losing too much momentum.

Customer histories should be maintained in a relational database such as Microsoft Access, Lotus Approach, FileMaker Pro, Act!, or Goldmine. These programs allow you to relate different databases through index fields, which means that you can search on virtually any field and find the information you want. Historical databases typically include customer names, addresses and locations, key customer contacts, titles, telephone numbers, fax numbers, e-mail addresses, types and amounts of products purchased, date of purchases, key internal contacts, and product or project descriptions. Obviously, whatever information is important to you can be stored in a database and can be accessible to authorized users throughout the world if you can store the database on the Internet or through an Intranet accessible through modem connections. The primary purpose of such a database is to answer these questions:

- Which customers have we served? What have we done for them? What products sold? Services delivered? Projects completed?
- When? Where? What? How much?
- Who are our contacts and their contacts? Who knows about these projects or shipments and could provide more information?
- What were the results? Success stories? Problems overcome? Proofs of superior service or customer impact?

These databases also might include fields for describing the customer's needs, their key issues and concerns, feedback you've received from them, and testimonials. Beware, however, of making databases too comprehensive. It's best to keep them simple. There is an inverse relationship between the size and complexity of a customer database and its functionality and life expectancy. The more complex these databases become, the less likely people are to maintain them. Keeping the information current is the most difficult challenge in managing historical databases. Although everyone wants a comprehensive tool at their disposal, it's often impossible to get them to enter the data on their projects, and an incomplete database is almost worse than none at all. Consequently, on major sales or sales to strategic accounts, the sales task should not be considered finished until the database has been updated.

In some companies, such as my own, an office management system is in place to ensure that all relevant data is entered. None of the salespeople receives credit for sales until the information is in the computer and is linked to a historical database. In others companies, such as Dell Computer, the database plays so prominent a role in sales that it would be unthinkable not to maintain it thoroughly. Dell is widely regarded as having the most comprehensive customer database in the world—in any industry. They can track anything related to any computer they've ever sold including order date and form, configuration, upgrades, returns, problems, troubleshooting, shipping, and billing. Consequently, they're able to offer very responsive customer service, and much of this information is available to their corporate customers over the Internet.

Analyzing Your Position

We've discussed two important sources of information on how well you are positioned with the customer: the customer's perceptions and your own history of the relationship, which should be maintained in a database. Table 12-1 lists other important sources of information and what these sources should be able to give you.

Before trying to make sense of the information, you should be sure that you're taking a 360-degree view of your organization. Gather views from the customer, particularly your deep private sources. If it's feasible, talk to everyone in your company who interacts with or serves the customer in some capacity. Talk to the industry analysts and explore the media. You'll recognize patterns in what you're hearing, and these patterns can help shape your analysis. In analyzing your position, you should ask the same kinds of questions you asked of your competitors when you analyzed them:

Your Current Relationship and Business Activities

- What is our history in the account? What products or services have we provided in the past and what are we supplying now?
- Do we have any incumbent projects or an installed base of products? How high are the switching costs for the customer?
- How much volume are we doing now? How much customer share do we have?
- Whom do we know in the customer organization? Who is biased toward us and why? Who are our sponsors? How well connected are we at the senior or most influential levels in the customer's organization?
- What type of relationship do we have with the customer: vendor, preferred supplier, partner, ally?

Capabilities and Resources

- What are our capabilities and limitations?
- Can we grow in the account? Are we capable of providing a broader range of products and services? Can we offer a total solution beyond what we currently are providing? What is our breadth and depth?

Table 12-1.   Internal Sources of Information on Your Direction and Capabilities

Source	Relevant Information
Mission Statement	Your direction and purpose as an organization; your focus; the boundaries of your business
Strategic Plan	Your long-term strategic direction; the core competencies your organization has and will seek to capitalize on; the strategic programs your company is committing to; the products, services, and regions to focus on; the overall strategic objectives of your organization
Sales Plan	The sales strategies in place; the products or services to emphasize; the projections for volume and income; the goals for your account and other accounts; the resources available
Other Account Reps	Intelligence on competitors' capabilities compared to your own; industry knowledge; changes in needs and requirements; early warning on trends that may affect your account; how your company and products are perceived in the marketplace
Marketing	Promotions; marketing communication campaigns; pricing information; information on distributors or channels; product comparisons; value-added differentiation from major competitors
Operational Managers	Operational changes and improvements; best practices in product design and delivery; how operations is meeting customer needs; ongoing intelligence from customers on what they want; operational problems and solutions; intelligence on competitors' capabilities compared to your own
Customer Service	The level of customer satisfaction; the numbers and types of problems experienced with your account; typical problems and solutions
Engineering/R&D	Product design changes; technical performance specifications; product differentiation; customization needs and approaches; emerging technologies; new products and solutions; technology comparisons with competitors
Manufacturing	Production capability; delivery schedules; shipment and installation; quality standards; customization capability
Finance	Financial analysis of your products and services; margin expectations; performance of your account
Legal	Legal or contractual issues and concerns; agreements with your customer

- What resources can we apply to this account? Where are we resource constrained?

Competitive Strategies

- What are our current account strategies? How successful have they been?
- How do we leverage our strengths and mitigate our weaknesses?
- What opportunities have we pursued? How successfully?
- How have we been positioning ourselves to expand the business?

Strengths and Weaknesses

- How well (or poorly) are we performing?
- What do we do exceptionally well? What differentiates us from our competitors? In what ways does the customer consider us to be distinctive?
- What customer needs do we fulfill? How satisfied is the customer with us?
- Conversely, what are our weaknesses? How do our competitors provide more value? In what ways is the customer not impressed with us?
- What performance problems have we had with the customer? Where have we fallen? What deliveries were missed? Promises unkept? Projects stalled? What issues does the customer have with us?

Customer's Perceptions

- Finally, what does the customer think of us? How do they think of us? Are we important to them?
- Does the customer imagine us growing in business volume? Do they see us playing a larger role? Or in their minds do we have a limited role? Where could they imagine this relationship going?

An account plan that merely answered these questions probably would not tell a coherent story, so it's important to synthesize the information; ask the "So what?" question about every important fact; and then craft a narrative that describes the history of the relationship, your current status, and the strengths and weaknesses of your position. At a minimum, an account plan should include this narrative.

The Four Pillars tool that I discussed in chapter 11 also might be useful, particularly if you used it to analyze your competitors. Like them, your position depends on the efficacy of your strengths, the appropriateness of your strategy, and the strength of your staff and support from the customer. It's not uncommon to do a Four Pillars analysis on your company and discover that several of your pillars are weak. The weakest, in my experience, is the staff pillar. It's rare for companies to assign enough of the right people to key accounts to have the kind of impact with customers that can lead to partnerships and strategic alliances. In most companies, the biggest deficit is the absence of senior executive support or sponsorship for strategic accounts. I talk more about this in chapter 14.

The Relationship Life Cycle

In analyzing your position with an account, you should think about where you are in the life of your relationship with the customer, an analysis I refer to as the relationship life cycle. All sales relationships invariably follow a "birth, growth, and death" pattern from the initial sale to the final sale. The length of time between the initial and final sale varies considerably, but inevitably the relationship will die as companies come and go, needs change, and products become obsolete. Because of the size and longevity of most strategic accounts, the life cycle pattern typically is more complex, having the seven predictable phases shown in Figure 12-1.

In the beginning, you penetrate the account by making that initial sale. An initial delivery or installation usually is risky, however, because clients don't know you and don't know whether they can trust you or your products. So following penetration you have to consolidate your foothold in the account—meeting the initial need and delivering quality, bridging into other buying units, and building more relationships. Until you are well consolidated, your position with the account is vulnerable. You're being watched and evaluated. If you pass muster, you can establish a stronger presence; if not, you lose ground from the initial sale and have to penetrate the account again. Penetration and consolidation are like the opening stages of a marine assault on an island. They find an undefended beach, the initial point of attack. While the landing is in progress, they are most vulnerable. But if they can survive the initial penetration, they can drive further inland, establishing a larger beachhead, building defended positions, and ferrying in supplies.

You know you've succeeded in consolidating your position when you receive follow-on contracts or make initial sales to other buying units. They've begun to accept you as a trusted supplier, and your presence is growing. In the best of circumstances, your consolidated position leads to a long period of growth, when you are selling more product to the initial buyer, expanding into other divisions or regions of the customer's organization, and cross selling other products and services. Relationship building dominates this phase of the life cycle. You're still learning about each other, learning what's possible and how each organization works. You may be customizing your products, developing a shared sense of what's possible, and building mutually beneficial strategies for working together. In the military metaphor I introduced, this phase is like the marines capturing the rest of the island. When they're done, there's no more growth possible, and this is the point of maximum customer share.

Now you enter the harvest phase, delivering maximum value to the customer and receiving maximum value in return. The harvest phase is equivalent to Boston Consulting Group's concept of the star customer or cash cow. It's the premium position because you're at the point of maximum trust, value provided to the customer, and return for your company. A harvest position attracts competitors who are jealous of your position, and they attack—often by undercutting your prices or offering benefits or deals you haven't provided. You respond to the attack and fall into a defensive posture as you try to maintain your position and customer share. You may lose some sales to buyers who listen to your competitors' promises or are lured by their discounts. In the worst of cases, you may have become complacent and your performance may be slipping. Responding to poor quality, the customer starts looking elsewhere and invites promising com-

Figure 12-1. The Relationship Life Cycle

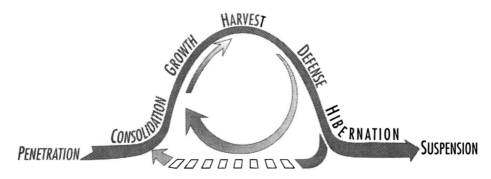

petitors. If you can counterattack successfully, you will be able to reenter the growth phase and rebuild the harvest position you enjoyed previously.

In some cases, through no fault of your own, the customer's needs diminish to the point where maintaining a strong, active position in the account simply is not cost effective. This happens in the construction industry, for example, when an owner builds a factory or a municipality builds a school. Once the factory or school is built, they may not need your services again for 10 years or more. Companies that provide high-cost services, such as engineering and construction, often have customers whose needs can span decades. In this flood-and-drought business environment, some strategic accounts may enter a hibernation phase, where you maintain minimal activity in the account until another need surfaces. When activity in the account resumes, you may return to the consolidation phase, as shown in Figure 12-1.

At the end of the cycle is suspension. This phase occurs when it is no longer profitable for you to serve the account. Suspension is rare, but it can happen when customers decline and their economics no longer support the margins you need to work with them. When they are no longer attractive to you, you need to exit in a graceful and effective way, after which you have no activity in the account. When customers reach this point, they usually lose many of their best people anyway, and it's best to maintain the relationships with those people and follow them to their new organizations. In hibernation, you seek a low activity level and monitor the account periodically; in suspension, you cease activity altogether. Both types of actions are done at your discretion and should be part of your overall sales strategy. The relationship life cycle is a key concept in strategic account management, so I will discuss each of the phases in more depth.

Penetration

Penetration often is the most difficult phase in a customer relationship. By some estimates, the cost of establishing a presence in an account is four times higher than the cost of getting repeat business from existing customers. Before you penetrate the account, the customers don't know you. No trust has been established. If you have a strong brand or a local presence, they may be aware of you, but there are far more unknowns than knowns in this phase. Giving you that initial nod requires a leap of faith on their part.

By the time many accounts achieve strategic account status, you are well past the penetration phase, so the problems encountered here are less important to account managers than the problems experienced in other phases. Occasionally, however, a prospect is deemed a strategic account because of its attractiveness or potential, and the account manager has to make the initial sale. Clearly, if you're in this phase of the relationship, your account strategies are designed to build a knowledge base through public and private sources, find and cultivate relationships with customer decision makers, analyze your competitors' positions (particularly the ones established in the account), develop strategies to build trust and credibility, and find ways to topple the pillars supporting your competitors' positions. The single most important goal of this phase is to get the first sale.

Consolidation

The consolidation phase is critically important to your ability to grow the account into profitable strategic status. The customer will be more forgiving later, when the switching costs are higher, but at this point any stumbling on your part can destroy your beachhead. So excellence in execution is paramount—and it's not always assured. Because at this point the customer has a very low profile among your operations people, your operations managers may treat it as *business as usual* and may assign some of their least experienced people to handle it (their most experienced people already are working on the existing major accounts and high-profile opportunities or shipments). Account managers typically have to work hard during this phase to consolidate the relationship both in the customer's organization *and in their own*. The technical and customer service reps who later will champion the account are likely to resist giving special attention to the account at this phase. So mustering support and convincing them to go the extra mile are essential and not particularly easy.

The primary goal during consolidation is sterling delivery of the product and total customer satisfaction. In fact, if you can go beyond satisfaction and *delight* the customer, you are leagues ahead. You want this initial delivery to generate substantial positive word of mouth, to create buzz throughout the customer's organization about you and your capabilities. The results you deliver will open doors for you and enable you to meet the people who were stonewalling you before. Your success in the initial delivery validates you and establishes your credibility far beyond the initial buying unit.

The consolidation phase is complete when any of the following is true: (1) you are awarded more contracts with the same buyer and have gained an advantage because of your superior performance on the first contract; (2) you develop a sponsor in the initial buying unit who enthusiastically endorses you to others throughout the organization, which generates more demand for "face time" with you; or (3) you are awarded a sole-source contract for follow-on deliveries or projects. Now you've started building a history in the customer organization. You're on the inside learning track, which is supplied by private and deep private information. For some customers, it means you've achieved "approved vendor" status or something similar, which a number of organizations require before they can contract with you for major pieces of business.

Growth

The growth phase obviously is one of the most desirable positions to have with key customers. You've consolidated your position and are building customer share by providing an increasing range of products and services to an expanding number of buying units and locations. During this phase, you are trying to maximize your company's value to the account while maximizing the value of the account to your company. This is a mutually satisfying phase as both you and the customer strive to find more ways to satisfy their needs.

The growth phase ends when you have reached the *maximum available customer share* or maximum account potential. As Figure 12-2 shows, customer share represents the customer's total need for your types of products or services—whether they buy them from you or others. Your customer share (slice A) is the percentage of their total need that you currently are satisfying. Available share (slice B) is the total amount of need that is unsatisfied now, is emerging as new needs, or is being met by competitors whose positions are weak. Through your selling efforts, this business is available to you, and you can potentially grow into this slice of total share. Unavailable share (slice C) is not available to you for any number of reasons (but is available to other suppliers). Well-entrenched competitors may have locked up the business through long-term contracts or excellent customer relationships. Or the customer may have decided that no supplier should meet more than X percent of their needs and so prohibits you from growing further share, no matter how well you're serving them. The maximum available customer share for you is the sum of slices A and B. When your relationship with customers is as a vendor or even preferred supplier, you fight for share and usually have some upside potential. However, if you're a partner or strategic ally, there may be no unavailable share because they've made a strategic decision to trust you to meet *all* their needs. Coca-Cola's contract with McDonald's Corporation is an example.

Figure 12-2. Customer Share

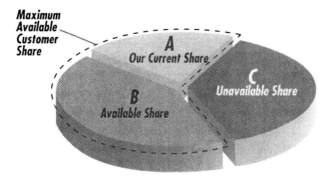

Harvest

When you've achieved harvest status with a strategic account, you have reached the maximum available customer share point. Pursuing growth within the account probably is not feasible, but there is a rich relationship to maintain and perhaps a bountiful harvest to enjoy. The harvest phase typically is the most profitable for both you and the customer, because your sales cost should decline, you should be finding economies in product or service delivery, and you should be working closely together to reduce costs. So it's an attractive position for customers as well. Formal or informal partnering becomes more feasible at this point, and, as Neil Rackham et al. observe in *Getting Partnering Right*, this is a point where both organizations can achieve a greater degree of intimacy and can focus on impact.[3]

In the harvest phase, the principal activities are managing quality, managing relationships, resolving problems, and seeking opportunities for continuous improvement and cost reduction. This is the time to be less transaction based and more business based. To manage the harvest, you have to work vigorously with customers to provide increasing value to them through ongoing business improvements. For example, you might form a joint task force to identify and implement product quality or business process improvements. You might try to streamline ordering and billing processes. Or you might assign some of your engineers to work with them on redesigning their products for greater efficiency. Remember that when you're in harvest, the winter is not far behind. The greatest danger when you're in the harvest mode is benign neglect. It's better to remain on the offensive and to continually improve your products and your relationships with the customer. Otherwise, you'll be forced into the defensive mode.

---

3. Neil Rackham, Lawrence Friedman, and Richard Ruff, *Getting Partnering Right* (New York: McGraw-Hall, 1996), p. 61.

Defense

Regardless of your relationship with a key customer, your position will come under attack at some point. The attack may be prompted by competitors attempting to gain customer share, and their tactics generally are to introduce significant price pressure or new technologies that leapfrog your products in capability or business impact. Sometimes, a key customer decision maker leaves and is replaced by someone you don't know or someone whose allegiances are with a competitor. Or perhaps economic or regulatory conditions change, which prompts the customer to reexamine their relationship with you or need for your products. In the 1980s, Intel's position in the memory chip market came under attack from predatory Japanese semiconductor firms whose strategy was to undercut Intel's prices by 10 percent, no matter to what level Intel reduced its prices. Intel's defense was to abandon memory chip production (which became commoditized under intense industry rivalry) and to focus instead on the processor chips that drive most personal computers today.

However, attacks on your position in an account also may be prompted by your own negligence if your product or service quality has slipped or if you're neglecting the relationship. One of the world's leading engineering and construction firms experienced this problem with an oil refinery project in the Midwest. When the project started going over budget, the firm told the client that it would cost millions more to complete the job. The client disagreed and took over the project—completing it on time and within the original budget. The black eye resulting from this project damaged the firm's relationship with this client for nearly a decade. Sometimes the problem is complacency, which can be thought of as the "high blood pressure" ailment of account management—it's a hidden killer. After a key account relationship has been established, the people who built it move on to conquer other mountains, and those who are left to manage the relationship are less engaged and feel less of a sense of urgency about maintaining it. If you aren't constantly vigilant, you'll find yourself scrambling and on the defensive.

Attacks can occur at any time, not just while you're in a harvest mode. When you go on the defense, your strategies become focused on rebuilding relationships and paying extraordinary attention to quality and service concerns. The defensive mode usually saps energy and profit because you have to invest more to regain lost ground. If you're successful, you may reenter the growth phase, and you could conceivably return to the harvest mode.

Hibernation

Hibernation occurs when the customer temporarily has no need for your type of product or service but will need them later. Like bears in the winter, they take a long sleep and awaken, much later, hungry and in need. While they're hibernating, you can't afford to sustain a high level of account activity, but you need to maintain enough presence to be well positioned when their needs resurface. At the very least, a good hibernation strategy keeps them informed of your capabilities and developments, maintains the relationships at some level, and keeps you informed of their status. Your goal should be to maintain your sponsors' good will and to remain a credible and reliable supplier in their eyes, responsive to their questions and concerns and interested in their business. They should see you making a long-term but sensible investment in them. The best way to do this is to ensure that the account manager who's been serving them continues to do so, even if the elapsed time between needs is 10 years. Old friends dropping by will be welcome, but newcomers asking questions will be viewed with suspicion.

The danger in the hibernation mode is what customers sometimes refer to as the "jack-in-the-box effect," where salespeople only pop up when they hear of a new opportunity or at the end of a quarter when they're desperate to meet their quotas. In one of Dell Computer's surveys of customers, Dell learned that what customers hated most were jack-in-the-box salespeople. "Where were they the other 11 weeks of the quarter?" customers asked. So even in the hibernation mode, it's important to maintain contact on an ongoing basis, and some contacts should be purely social. There should be no strings attached.

Suspension

Finally, the terminal point in an account relationship is suspension. As I noted earlier, you decide to suspend an account relationship when it is no longer profitable for you to serve the customer or if serving them no longer serves your strategic interests. The typical strategy is to exit with grace and good will, telling them openly why you can no longer serve them, and to maintain cordial relations with their key people. If their economics are dire enough for you to suspend the relationship, then they are likely to be losing good people, and you want those good people to take you with them to their new organizations.

Suspending a customer relationship is very difficult for some account managers and companies. It seems like admitting failure, and you keep hoping the situation can be revived. One company, whom I'll call AJAX Teleservices, is a case in point. They had an extremely challenging, demanding, and disagreeable customer for whom nothing was ever good enough. This customer chewed through six account managers in 2 years. Everyone groaned when this customer's name was mentioned. Being assigned to the account was like being sent into battle. Finally, after 2 years of misery and unprofitability, AJAX terminated the relationship. Why did it take so long? On the surface, the account looked profitable, and AJAX sales executives assumed that their problems were a matter of chemistry. Finding the right account manager for this customer might solve the problem, they thought. But when they examined the account and added up all the resources expended fighting fires, meeting demands, and bending over backward to satisfy this customer, they discovered that they were losing money hand over fist. In effect, they were *paying* the customer to drag them through hell. No matter how great the potential, some customer relationships aren't worth it, and you should suspend them.

There are obvious correlations between the relationship life cycle phase and the types of customer relationships I discussed in chapter 3. When you're in the penetration and consolidation phases, the customer is likely to treat you as a vendor. As you grow your presence in the account and build trust and credibility throughout the customer's organization, your status should shift to preferred supplier. In the best of circumstances, during the late growth and harvest phases, you may achieve partner or strategic ally status. In an industry with intense rivalry among suppliers, you may be forced into a defensive mode no matter what your relationship status is, but partnerships and alliances are formidable, and competitor assaults are more likely to fail than to succeed.

As Figure 12-3 shows, there is also a typical correlation among relationship life cycle, customer share, and account profitability.[4] From penetration to consolidation, your margins probably will decline although share increases, because the costs for servicing the account and ensuring a quality installation will rise as you give special attention to the account. Share and profit should escalate during the growth phase and reach their zenith during harvest. The harvest phase should be the point of maximum value for you and the customer as your cost of sales declines, you achieve operational efficiencies, and you find mutual cost-reduction opportunities. When you come under attack, your margins will decline to some degree because of the increased cost of the defense and because you may be forced to reduce prices.

Using the relationship life cycle in analyzing your position helps you determine what information is important; what you should be concerned about; and, as we'll see in chapter 13, what your account strategies should be.

Identifying and Prioritizing Your SWOTs

The goal in analyzing your own position in a strategic account is to determine where you are strong and weak, where you have opportunities, and where you face threats. These insights drive your account strategy, so an

---

4. My thanks to Horst Kayser of Siemens A.G. for suggesting these relationships.

Figure 12-3. Life Cycle, Customer Share, and Account Profitability

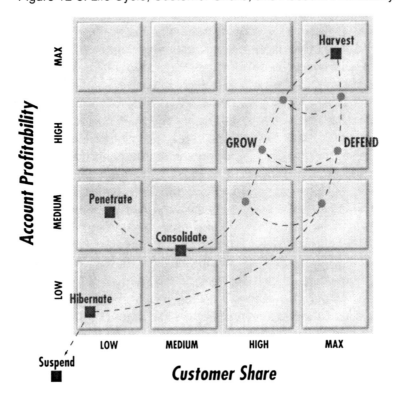

appropriate tool for organizing the information gathered here is the SWOT (strengths, weaknesses, opportunities, and threats) analysis. The SWOT analysis is a helpful way to organize the intelligence you've gathered, to put it into a framework that facilitates strategy creation. If you also used the Four Pillars tool, then much of the information you gathered there will be relevant in the strengths and weaknesses portion of your SWOT analysis. Remember that what is important is how the customer perceives you, so your SWOT analysis should reflect the customer's point of view. The items that might fall under each category are listed in the following, and Figure 12-4 is an example.

Your Strengths

- Your product and service features and benefits match your customer's primary needs and requirements, and you are meeting their needs and solving their problems.
- Your customer sees you as uniquely different and better than your competitors.
- Your customer considers you a preferred supplier, partner, or strategic ally. Consequently, you work at the business level with them and participate in joint problem-solving or opportunity-developing initiatives.

Figure 12-4. Example of a Self-SWOT Analysis

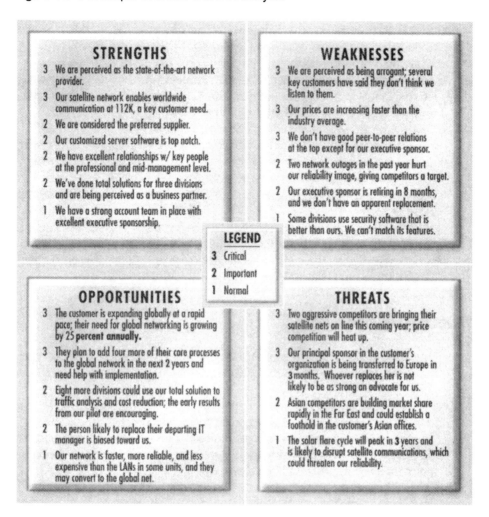

STRENGTHS

3 We are perceived as the state-of-the-art network provider.

3 Our satellite network enables worldwide communication at 112K, a key customer need.

2 We are considered the preferred supplier.

2 Our customized server software is top notch.

2 We have excellent relationships w/ key people at the professional and mid-management level.

2 We've done total solutions for three divisions and are being perceived as a business partner.

1 We have a strong account team in place with excellent executive sponsorship.

WEAKNESSES

3 We are perceived as being arrogant; several key customers have said they don't think we listen to them.

3 Our prices are increasing faster than the industry average.

3 We don't have good peer-to-peer relations at the top except for our executive sponsor.

2 Two network outages in the past year hurt our reliability image, giving competitors a target.

2 Our executive sponsor is retiring in 8 months, and we don't have an apparent replacement.

1 Some divisions use security software that is better than ours. We can't match its features.

LEGEND

3 Critical
2 Important
1 Normal

OPPORTUNITIES

3 The customer is expanding globally at a rapid pace; their need for global networking is growing by 25 **percent annually.**

3 They plan to add four more of their core processes to the global network in the next 2 years and need help with implementation.

2 Eight more divisions could use our total solution to traffic analysis and cost reduction; the early results from our pilot are encouraging.

2 The person likely to replace their departing IT manager is biased toward us.

1 Our network is faster, more reliable, and less expensive than the LANs in some units, and they may convert to the global net.

THREATS

3 Two aggressive competitors are bringing their satellite nets on line this coming year; price competition will heat up.

3 Our principal sponsor in the customer's organization is being transferred to Europe in 3 months. Whoever replaces her is not likely to be as strong an advocate for us.

2 Asian competitors are building market share rapidly in the Far East and could establish a foothold in the customer's Asian offices.

1 The solar flare cycle will peak in 3 years and is likely to disrupt satellite communications, which could threaten our reliability.

- You engage in joint planning with your customer or in continuous process or quality initiatives that result in cost reductions or customized solutions, which increase the customer's switching costs and increase their loyalty to you.
- You have excellent relationships with your customer's key people, particularly at the top but also at the mid-management and professional levels where their future leaders are being groomed.
- You are in the growth or harvest phase of the relationship life cycle.
- You have sponsors in key positions in your customer's organization.
- You have excellent sources of private and deep private information.
- You are colocated with your customer or have substantial distribution advantages.
- Your company has assigned a powerful executive sponsor to the account, and you have key top-to-top relationships between organizations.

Your Weaknesses

- Your product and service features and benefits no longer match your customer's primary needs and requirements, which have changed.
- Your customer considers you a vendor.
- Competitive pressures or performance problems have forced you into a defensive mode and you are under pressure to reduce prices or to introduce new technologies, which you don't have.
- You are in the penetration or consolidation phase of the relationship.
- Your customer can't satisfactorily differentiate you from your competitors.
- You have limited relationships with your customer's key people; you face significant blockers or have no sponsors in key positions.
- You have limited sources of private information and no sources of deep private information.
- A performance problem has caused your customer to lose trust in you, find you less credible, or question your ability to deliver as promised.
- Your organization is unwilling to assign a key executive sponsor to the account or adequate resources to grow the account.

Your Opportunities

- Your customer is growing in ways that increase their need for your types of products. In other words, the maximum available customer share is expanding.
- You are in the growth phase of the relationship life cycle, and there are products, buying units, or locations you haven't tapped yet.
- An incumbent competitor has experienced a performance problem or otherwise has fallen out of favor with your customer; one of their key sponsors in the customer organization has departed.
- Your sponsors in your customer organization have been promoted or moved into more powerful positions; or the customer has hired a key executive who favors you.
- Your customer has decided to outsource something your company can provide.
- Your customer has decided to work with you on a business basis instead of a transactional basis, and there are clear opportunities for process improvements or cost reduction that could expand your presence or enable you to provide increased value.
- Your customer's SWOT analysis reveals areas where you can help them highlight their strengths, mitigate their weaknesses, or defend against their threats so they can capitalize on their opportunities.

Your Threats

- Your customer's business is declining or changing in some way that shrinks the maximum available customer share, or they are experiencing performance problems that impact their need for your products.

- Your customer is forming a partnership or alliance with one of your competitors, or an aggressive competitor is outperforming you and is becoming the preferred supplier.
- Changes in the economic, political, or legal environment in which you or your customer operate are creating an unfavorable climate.
- Your technologies are falling behind.
- Your customer has decided to build its internal capabilities in your area.
- For various reasons, you enter the defense phase in the relationship life cycle.
- One of your key customer sponsors is nearing retirement, and the most probable replacement is neutral toward you or biased against you.

It should be clear that as you do a SWOT analysis on your company, you will be considering not only the information you've gathered on your company during your self-analysis but also the intelligence you generated on your customer and key competitors. In particular, it's not feasible to develop a full appreciation of your opportunities and threats without knowing what's happening externally. To some extent, you control your strengths and weaknesses, although remember that it's the customer's perception that matters, not reality. If you have strengths the customer isn't aware of, then they aren't strengths. If you have weaknesses the customer doesn't know about, they aren't weaknesses (but you might consider them threats because the customer could learn of them through your competitors' positioning efforts as they try to undermine your position).[5]

Prioritizing Your SWOT Analysis

Most self-SWOT analyses have too many items to be helpful unless you discriminate between the merely interesting bits of information and the truly important bits. If you're working on a large, strategic account with whom you've had a long-standing relationship, your list of SWOTs is likely to be many pages long. Making sense of that information necessitates that you prioritize the items so you and others can act on the most critical insights you've developed.

A useful way to prioritize is to review your list of SWOTs and assign a rating to each item depending on how much it could impact you (see Figure 12-4). The simplest rating scheme is 3 (highest impact) to 1 (lowest impact), according to the following criteria:

---

5. Dr. David Pugh, an expert on business development, suggests that you should create a self-SWOT based on your perceptions of yourself and then do a "reality SWOT" that factors in your customer's perceptions and reveals how their perceptions differ from the facts. He argues that this approach forces you to see the "reality" of your position and thus minimizes self-deception.

Strengths

3   A substantial advantage; a perfect match between the customer's needs and our products or capabilities; leverages our relationship in exclusive ways

2   Advantageous for us but insufficient by itself to be compelling

1   Offers us some advantage but can be copied by competitors

Weaknesses

3   A substantial weakness; could be a fatal flaw

2   An important weakness; could be debilitating if not mitigated

1   An annoying weakness but can be overcome

Opportunities

3   A must-win opportunity; has the most potential to help us achieve our strategic vision for the account and our goals

2   A key opportunity that should be pursued, but its loss would not be critical

1   An interesting opportunity that may be more critical in the long term

Threats

3   A significant threat; poses the greatest danger and would have substantial negative impact on us; demands strong action on our part

2   A serious threat that cannot be dismissed

1   A remote threat; we need to beware but should not worry inordinately about it

By applying these criteria, you should develop a clear sense of what's critically important to your position and what you need to attend to as you develop strategy. As I said earlier, it's easy to be deceived about your own position, and the tools discussed in this chapter will help you formulate a more objective view of the strengths and weaknesses of your position with your strategic account. Together with your customer profile and competitor profiles, your position assessment establishes the foundation of intelligence and analysis necessary to build effective account strategies, which is the subject of the next chapter.

— 13 —

Developing Account Strategy

The primary purpose of account planning is to determine where you want to go with the account and how you are going to get there. As Basil Walsh observed, "An intelligent plan is the first step to success. The man who plans knows where he is going, knows what progress he is making, and has a pretty good idea when he will arrive. Planning is the open road to your destination. If you don't know where you are going, how can you expect to get there?"[1] Establishing clarity of purpose, which culminates in action, is the raison d'être of planning. All your preceding efforts in the planning process—gathering information, profiling the customer and competitors, and analyzing your own position—come to closure as you use the insights you developed to set a vision, define your objectives, and identify the actions necessary to accomplish your purpose. In short,

Account strategy = vision + account objectives + action plans

The last part of the equation, action plans, is critically important. Strategy must be actionable. Otherwise, it sits on the shelf and gathers dust, which is the fate of account plans whose strategies have no action component. But if your account strategy includes not only your objectives but also *the means to achieve them*, then you create a link between your ambitions and your daily, weekly, and monthly activities inside your company and with your customer. When an account strategy is done well, the step beyond it is filling in your "to do"s and appointments on your schedule planner—and then updating both your strategy and your action plans as events unfold and conditions change. The best account strategies, as shown in Figure 13-1, are dynamic. They evolve continually as you work the strategy, evaluate the results, and respond to unforeseen opportunities and threats. Your strategy shapes your actions; your actions produce results, which in turn provide feedback on the efficacy of the strategy. You respond by modifying the strategy accordingly, which suggests a new set

---

1. Basil Walsh, quoted in Ted Goodman, ed., *The Forbes Book of Business Quotations* (New York: Black Dog & Leventhal Publishers, 1997), p. 653.

Figure 13-1. The Dynamic Planning Cycle

of actions, and so on. This process loop, whose *plan-act-learn-respond* cycle is evocative of Deming's quality process, *is* the heart of account management.

Before discussing how to develop an account strategy, I want to address a common piece of advice for account managers—being totally open with your customer and sharing your account objectives with them. In their book, *Successful Large Account Management*, Robert B. Miller and Stephen E. Heiman argue that the customer "should understand in general terms what you are about, and specifically they should be able to endorse your Goal, your Objectives, and your sales and support programs."[2] They also suggest that you present your account plans to the customer, reasoning that "when you are positioned effectively at an account, you should have no hesitancy in sharing with the firm's decision makers the substance of your plans."[3] Although this is sound advice when you have a partnership or strategic alliance with the customer, it can backfire on you earlier in the relationship before sufficient trust has been developed. On a first date, it's probably best not to announce your intentions so explicitly ("By the end of the evening, I want to kiss you and then set up another date"). Once you've moved beyond the vendor stage, have developed deep relationships, have learned enough about them, and vice versa—then it makes

---

2. Robert B. Miller and Stephen E. Heiman, *Successful Large Account Management* (New York: Henry Holt & Company, 1991), p. 188.
3. Ibid.

sense not only to share your objectives with them but to develop at least some of those objectives jointly. The customer–supplier relationship will always be a little delicate, even under the best of circumstances, because some of your goals inherently are at cross purposes with your customer's goals: they are driven to reduce costs and you are driven to increase volume and margins; they want multiple suppliers to stimulate price competition and technical improvements, whereas you strive to find economies and maximize customer share.

Clearly, the sweet spot occurs where these inherent tensions in the relationship are addressed jointly and made to work for both of you. This occurs when trust is highest; when there is broad sharing of information, including the more closely held secrets; when their need to reduce cost is matched by your need to find economies; and when you and they have each other's best interests at heart. Developing relationships of this richness and complexity takes years and considerable experience with one another. Yes, you should strive to share many of your objectives with your strategic account customers, but first be certain that your trust levels are high enough.[4] Otherwise, you may find them pushing back at your objectives and resisting what might otherwise be the right course of action for them.

Developing a Vision

The dictionary defines vision as the ability to foresee what's going to happen, or "a mental image created by the imagination."[5] A vision is an imaginary look into the future, as though you're a fortune teller gazing into your crystal ball. It differs from a wish, as in "I wish we were their preferred supplier." When you create a vision, you imagine that the wish has already been realized, as in "I envision us as their preferred supplier."

A useful way to create a vision is to find a quiet place to reflect, close your eyes, put your head in your hands, and relax. Imagine that it's 2 years

---

4. Let me offer a personal anecdote on this point. In working with a strategic account some years ago, I developed a close relationship with one key manager. I shared a number of our objectives with him, and together we formed a joint plan for serving them that met their needs very well and satisfied our account objectives. Given the context of the relationship it seemed feasible to be open, too, about our growth objectives in the account—where we felt we could serve them even more. He responded well in our meeting, but months later, during a joint planning session with other customer representatives, he was almost hostile toward any thought that we do more for them than we currently were. Instead of an ally, he'd become a blocker. I asked him about this later, and he said he didn't like the idea that we had revenue targets for our business with them, although he acknowledged that it was reasonable to do so. He said it felt manipulative to him, although he understood it was part of business. Whether his reaction was reasonable or not, it highlighted for me the dangers of sharing your business goals before the relationship is ready for that.

5. *Webster's II New Riverside Dictionary*, Rev. ed. (New York: Houghton Mifflin Company, 1996).

hence. You've achieved all your goals with the customer. You're in the best possible position with them and are serving them in ways you and they couldn't have imagined. The relationship is very tight, your business is growing, and you are their preferred supplier. Imagine what that would be like. Imagine yourself in their offices, talking to their CEO, making calls jointly with your senior executives. In your mind's eye, put yourself in that place. See it, hear it, touch it. The more concrete it is, the more animating the vision and the more real and compelling it is for other people. Your account vision is that picture of the future, the end state you see yourself reaching within a set period of time. Having a vision of the account is crucial because it's the organizing principle for your strategy and thus for all your account efforts. The vision says, in effect, "Here's where we're going. This is the destination." An effective vision is simple and concrete:

> Our vision is to be Genexco's preferred provider of laser dental equipment nationwide in 3 years and to jointly develop and promote the technology to improve the safety, comfort, speed, and effectiveness of dental surgery.

> Our vision is to help York Pharmaceuticals improve the quality and efficiency of their product distribution through improved packaging and shipping systems and in doing so to become the dominant supplier of the nation's fastest-growing drug company.

Setting Account Objectives

How will you realize your vision for the account? Getting from here to there generally means that you must achieve certain intermediate goals or objectives. Those objectives either take you toward the vision or remove the obstacles in your path. One objective might be to develop stronger relationships with key customer executives. Another might be to satisfy particular customer needs or to find creative ways to add more value to the customer, perhaps through customizing your products, providing a total solution to their needs, or developing new technologies. You might need to capture particular opportunities or defend against certain threats. A workable account strategy includes between five to seven *major* objectives. If you have more than that, you probably aren't focused enough and may have trouble achieving them all within the scope of the plan. In a plan that you revise annually, five to seven *major* objectives is about the maximum number that can reasonably be accomplished within the year.

The obvious question at this point is, "How do you determine what your objectives should be?" Fortunately, you already laid the groundwork for answering that question when you analyzed the situation and determined your SWOTs (strengths, weaknesses, opportunities, and threats). The answer depends on where you are strong and weak and where you have prime opportunities or serious threats. The fundamental strategy for every account is based on how you *respond* to those SWOTs.

Fundamental Strategy

Common sense dictates that you should capitalize on your strengths. Where you're strong, you have the greatest chance of success. This is as true in account strategy as it is in sports, games, and war. As von Clausewitz said, "The first rule is to enter the field with an army as strong as possible."[6] Conversely, you must find ways to mitigate your weaknesses, particularly those that can erode your position or give your rivals leverage against you. You may not be able to overcome your weaknesses, but it may be possible for you to compensate for them or render them unimportant. Similarly, it makes sense to take advantage of the prime opportunities facing you. In many situations the prime opportunities are must-wins, because they represent sizable customer share, would enable you to establish an installed base, or would position you for future prime opportunities. Finally, you must defend against or eliminate the threats to your position, to the extent possible.

> ### Fundamental Strategy
>
> Capitalize on your strengths
> Mitigate your weaknesses
> Exploit your opportunities
> Defend against your threats

At the end of chapter 12, I suggested that you prioritize your SWOTs. Doing so provides a practical and commonsense way to identify and set your objectives. Clearly, the high-priority elements have the most positive or negative impact on your position, so your objectives should indicate how you will capitalize on your primary strengths, mitigate your primary weaknesses, take advantage of the prime opportunities, and defend against any serious threats. Based on the SWOT example shown in Figure 12-4, then, you might have the following kinds of objectives:

- Our objective is to use our state-of-the-art network technology to provide, within 12 months, a superior, value-added, nationwide network to Genexco that surpasses their network quality and functionality requirements by no less than 15 percent while reducing their operational and administrative costs by at least 10 percent. *(capitalizing on a strength)*

---

6. Karl von Clausewitz, quoted in Robert Debs Heinl, Jr., *Dictionary of Military and Naval Quotations* (Annapolis: United States Naval Institute, 1966), p. 312.

- Our objective is to broaden our base of support in the customer's organization and to position ourselves to render higher value service to them by broadening and deepening our peer-to-peer executive relationships. Within the next year, we want to develop sustained, high-trust relationships with at least four senior customer executives up to and including the CEO. *(mitigating a weakness)*
- Our objective is to facilitate Genexco's rapid global expansion and help them realize their goals by providing a total global network solution that meets all their global needs within the next year. *(taking advantage of an opportunity)*
- Our objective is to defend our position by seeking system efficiencies and reducing Genexco's operating costs by at least $20,000 per month before competitors can offer discounted pricing. We must accomplish this by the start of the third quarter. *(defending against a threat)*

Note that the S (strength) and O (opportunity) objectives are very customer oriented. They focus on how your capabilities and solutions benefit the customer. Objectives based on strengths and opportunities reflect your aspirations for helping the customer and enhancing the relationship. In contrast, the W (weakness) and T (threat) objectives are more focused on real or potential problems you might have. These objectives reflect your concerns and are more defensive in nature.

How many objectives of each kind should you have? There is no simple rule of thumb. It depends on the nature of your relationship with the customer and the relative importance of each element of the SWOT. That's why prioritizing your SWOT is a good preliminary step to developing account objectives. At the very least, you should set objectives for addressing all your highest priority SWOTs. Your account strategy should be based on the most critical factors facing you in the account, and this depends in part on where you are in the relationship life cycle. If you're in the growth or harvest phase with the customer, then S and O factors are likely to dominate your objectives; if you're defending your position, then W and T factors may be more important, particularly if you're working to overcome an execution or quality problem.

Kaz Ohbura had known that his harvest position with Ewens-Burak (EB) was too good to last, but he hadn't expected the bottom to fall out so quickly. Kaz was a senior account manager for Hollings, Anderson & Pierce (HAP), a Chicago-based advertising agency, and his client was a builders' supply conglomerate with regional chains throughout the U.S. and Canada. EB had been using HAP for all its advertising needs, although it ran regional, rather than national, ad campaigns based on demographic differences between regions. However, at the insistence of EB's newly appointed chief operating officer (COO), the six regions of EB were now free to contract for their own advertising needs so long as they followed certain minimal guidelines from corporate.

Where Kaz previously had one major client, he now had six buying units to contend with. He thought his relationships with all the regional managers were

continued

solid, but the manager of the northwest U.S. region unexpectedly signed with a rival agency located in Seattle, a blow that instantly cost Kaz $14 million in expected revenue. Finally, the results of HAP's latest television campaign in the northeast U.S. had just arrived, and they were not good. Focus groups and in-store surveys showed that potential buyers were not responding well to the ads, and EB's regional manager in Boston had called to cancel the campaign. "Call me ASAP," said the angry message he left on Kaz's voice mail.

"Fine," Kaz thought, irreverently, "And what do I do after calling you a sap?"

After his shock wore off, Kaz reflected on the crisis facing him. He was now suddenly on the defensive, and the account objectives he'd previously had in place were no longer relevant—conditions had changed so quickly. Because of EB's own growth, he'd expected their advertising needs and budget to increase by 14 percent next year. Now he was certain of a decline in customer share as well as profitability, because of the need to compete in six locations instead of one and the price pressure that invariably would occur as other competitors jumped on the bandwagon.

Accordingly, he reanalyzed the situation and developed an updated set of SWOTs on HAP. Not surprisingly, his list of strengths and opportunities had decreased while his list of weaknesses and threats grew larger. This suggested that he needed to set some defensive objectives, the first of which would be to problem solve and correct the ad situation in EB's northeast region. He couldn't allow any further erosion of their position, and solving Boston's problem was therefore his primary immediate objective. Another short-term objective was to prevent the defection of any other region, and he intended to do this by expanding his presence in those regional offices and asking his managing director to accompany him on some of those trips. A final objective was to recapture the lost northwest region account. Knowing that time was of the essence on that objective, he put it at the top of his list and made the flight to Seattle that afternoon.

He wasn't able to win back the account on that trip, but he did have an excellent meeting with the regional manager and got her to agree to recompete the business in 12 months. Meanwhile, prompt attention to the problem in Boston restored the client's confidence, and he was able to hang on to the other four regions. Today, he's still in a defensive mode, but his account objectives are now more long-term focused and based on the vision, which he shares with his clients at every opportunity, of being EB's sole agency again and helping them achieve their growth ambitions.

The majority of account objectives are aspirational and have one or more of three intentions: (1) to improve your position with the customer, (2) to strengthen the value you add to the customer and thus increase your differentiation, and/or (3) to satisfy the customer's needs. For example, your objective might be to advance from vendor to preferred supplier, an improvement in your position. You might try to do this by building stronger relationships with their top executives or by emphasizing the importance of some features and benefits of your product that your competitor's product lacks. Value-added objectives typically focus on ways in which you can augment or customize your products, or offer new or advanced technologies that make you uniquely capable of meeting the customer's needs. These objectives increase your differentiation and build competitive advantage—at least until your competitors catch up. Finally, some account objectives focus on your goals for satisfying the customer's needs:

> Our objective is to achieve the highest rating among all suppliers during the customer's semiannual satisfaction survey to be conducted next March.

An effective account strategy is not intended to level the playing field with your competitors. You don't want a level playing field. As rogue warrior Richard Marcinko argues, the last thing you want is a fair fight: "Your fights should be *fixed*. The deck should be *stacked*. Every rule in the book should favor you and hamper your opponent."[7] Sometimes, an objective is intended to exploit a competitor's weaknesses, often by highlighting your solution or technology advantages at your competitors' expense:

> Our objective is to strengthen our position as the preferred network systems provider prior to the customer's September planning meeting by promoting our highly reliable redundant-node network technology and ghosting our competitor's network system failures during the past 6 months.

These kinds of objectives are built on your key strengths or opportunities. When you need to mitigate weaknesses or defend against threats, your objectives would probably focus more on increasing customer satisfaction or resolving problems. Account strategies also may be built around two special kinds of objectives—relationship objectives and revenue/profitability objectives.

Relationship objectives. These specify your goals for building key relationships between your company and the customer's organization. They usually focus on specific customer executives and indicate what you would like those relationships to be:

> Our objective is to develop stronger relationships with each member of the Genexco's executive committee by the end of next year and to establish a preferred position with at least four members, including Jim Hawkes.

Setting a relationship objective removes the element of chance from your relationship building, and it provides guidance for your account team and senior executives on what you expect the relationship-building efforts to accomplish. It's unwise to trust that the right relationships will be built at the right levels unless you set goals and target the customer representatives with whom you most want to have better relationships. Also, as we'll see later, it enables you to make the right contacts for developing the intelligence you need and for keeping the customer informed about your capabilities and intentions in a timely and efficient manner.

---

7. Richard Marcinko, *The Rogue Warrior's Strategy for Success* (New York: Pocket Books, 1997), p. 30.

Relationship objectives prompt a particular type of action plan—the contact plan—which I discuss later in this chapter.

Revenue/profitability objectives. These specify your fiscal targets for the account and may include revenue goals, margins, product sales volumes, and growth targets for expanding into other product or service lines or into other units or locations. Revenue/profitability objectives are always quantitative. They establish some of your key performance metrics for the account. The revenue and profitability numbers are especially important for forecasting, and in complex accounts with multiple product lines these objectives help your manufacturing or service groups determine product demand or resource needs.

Revenue/profitability objectives are set largely by projecting demand for the year or years ahead, based on customer intelligence, and by examining the previous years' numbers and trends. To the extent possible, projections should be based on identified needs or contracts already in place rather than on speculation about what the customer might need. The best account managers know the account well enough to have a fairly realistic view of the business potential in the account. Obviously, it's easier to forecast when you're in the growth or harvest phase of the relationship.

Objectives grow out of your vision, and they are based on your most critical SWOTs. They show what you must do to improve your position, provide value-added service to your customer, satisfy your customer's needs, or build the relationship. Revenue/profitability objectives establish your performance targets and indicate how you will measure success. But what makes a good objective?

SMART Objectives

Good objectives have five characteristics that are easily remembered because they form the mnemonic SMART: *specific, measurable, attainable, relevant*, and *timely*.[8] Writing objectives with these characteristics ensures that they are focused and actionable.

- *Specific.* The objective should clearly state what you expect to accomplish: *expansion into Japan and Korea* is preferable to *international expansion; 15 percent project growth in the southeast region* is better than *increasing domestic sales*. The more specific the objective, the easier it is for people to clearly understand what results you want—and therefore what they must do to achieve those results.
- *Measurable.* The objective should be quantifiable or otherwise indicate how you will know when you've achieved it: *12 percent return* or *winning three of seven major projects (>$5 million each) in the next calendar year*. It's easy when

---

8. I would cite whoever created this mnemonic, but I don't know who it was. It's widely used in the field at this point, so it appears to have entered the public domain. I use it with apologies to its now-anonymous inventor.

the goals are inherently quantifiable. The challenge is to make qualitative objectives measurable: *Our objective is to improve our relationships with their senior executives.* The problem is, how will you know when that's been done? To answer the question, determine what will be different when it's accomplished. Improved relations could mean improved access to their senior executives, regular CEO–CEO meetings, partnering opportunities, and demonstrated positive bias toward you in bids. Make those kinds of results your objective: *Our objective is to establish an average of twelve senior executive, quality contacts per year and to receive at least one partnering proposal from a Genexco executive in the next fiscal year.* So long as "quality contacts" is defined, this is a good, measurable objective.

- *Attainable.* The objective should be realistic and attainable within the designated time frame. Avoid the temptation to set account objectives higher than you or your organization can reasonably achieve. Stretch targets are desirable, but it's disheartening and deflating to set objectives that can't possibly be achieved.
- *Relevant.* The objective should be tied to your vision for the account and be based on your highest priority SWOTs. If it's based on good analysis and reflects your business purpose, then it probably will be relevant. The key question is, would accomplishing this objective help you achieve your vision for the account? If the answer is "no" or "well, indirectly," then the objective probably is not relevant. There should be direct links among objective, SWOT element, and vision.

Account Objectives Should Be:

Specific
Measureable
Attainable
Relevant
Timely

- *Timely.* The objective should indicate when you expect it to be attained. Establishing a time frame for achievement is critical. You can specify in your plan that all objectives are expected to be accomplished within the next year, or you can establish a time frame for each objective.

Once you have drafted your account objectives, you should consider sharing them with your high-trust customer contacts, particularly your high-level sponsors. Are they realistic? Achievable? Are they consistent with the customer's goals and vision? Will they advance the relationship and enhance your capability to serve the customer's needs? From the customer's viewpoint, would any other objectives be more relevant or compelling than the ones you drafted? At this point in planning, the objectives should be syndicated with a number of people inside your own organization as well, including account team members (who may have helped create the objectives), senior executives, relevant managers, and other stakeholders whose participation in the account is crucial to your and its success. It's important to reach consensus on the account vision and objectives before you move to the more tactical level of action planning.

Creating Action Plans

Action planning is where the rubber meets the road, as they say. Plans that are not actionable are virtually worthless, so completing this final step in account planning is essential. Action plans are the tactical derivatives of your strategic vision and objectives. They specify what tasks must be completed, by whom, and within what time frames, for the objectives to be met. There are three types of action plans: the basic plan for achieving objectives and two special plans based on relationship and revenue/profitability objectives.

Basic Action Plans

An action plan that you might write for most objectives is shown in Figure 13-2. The objective is stated at the top of the plan, and it is followed by a table showing the tasks or steps necessary to achieve the objective, the person in your company responsible for completing the task, and the deadline for completion. A final column is often included for checking off completed tasks. I like this feature because it shows that the action plan is a work in progress. You can consider the plan itself complete when the task list includes everything necessary to achieve the objective, although as conditions change you probably will need to add or modify tasks later. Initial action plans are a loose blueprint for a very dynamic process. Most account managers update their action plans frequently as events unfold and they gain new insights on what they should be doing to achieve their objectives.

The primary purpose of action plans is to turn your vision into reality. They're like a master "to do" list in that they enable you to identify what's required, assign responsibility for action, set deadlines, track progress, and dynamically recreate the plan as you go.

Relationship Action Plans

One of the aims of account management is to develop systematically the network of relationships between your key people—at all levels in your

Figure 13-2. Action Plan

Objective: Consolidate our postion in National General's Western Division by winning at least five major projects that exceed $40 million each and achieving a 20% customer share in two years.

Action Plan

Actions	Who	Start	End	Done?
Complete Larson Hills project on time and under budget	E. Hayes	4/97	9/98	✔
Conduct an awareness-building campaign with NG's West Division management on our offshore capabilities and design services	Jan Martin	2/98	10/98	✔
Build key relationships between S. Anatone and R. Keeley and NG's T. Johnson and H. Chavez	R. Crisp	2/98	2/99	✔
Host capability demos with NG execs at 6/98 Expo in Garden City	R. Crisp	3/98	6/98	✔
Follow up on Expo with intensive series of on-site meetings in San Francisco, San Diego, and Los Angeles offices of NG	R. Crisp	6/98	1/99	✔
Establish "early warning" system for responding to NG opportunities; quick reaction and proposal teams	Donnelly & J.T. Hornug	6/98	10/98	
Establish office in Santa Monica; move TEOPS capability there	B. Tees & J. Farley	7/98	2/99	
Develop and implement pursuit strategy for Montgomery-Laxman offshore project	R. Crisp	9/98	4/99	
Develop and implement pursuit strategy for LA County project; define specs with T. Hammond and B. Sparks	R. Crisp & J. Jones	11/98	6/99	
Participate in joint planning session with NG on fiscal 99/00	R. Crisp & S. Anatone	11/98	12/98	
Initiate Broadmoor R&D project to reduce time-to-production on green field process plants; have proof of concept by 3/99; have preliminary designs by 7/99	B. Munoz, F. Bolger, I. Yoshita	1/99	7/99	

company—and the customer's key people in comparable positions (e.g., CEO to CEO, vice president to vice president, and engineering manager to engineering manager). I referred to this earlier as creating *zippered* relationships between the two organizations. Given the importance of systematic relationship management, account managers often include a relationship objective in their account plans. The related action plan, which is sometimes called a contact plan, is shown in Figure 13-3. Contact plans are a means of managing this network of personal relationships between your company and the customer organization.

Figure 13-3. Contact Plan

Objective: Establish a preferred supplier relationship with Sirex Corporation by the beginning of their next fiscal year by increasing our frequency of contact, improving some problem relationships, and leveraging our sponsor relationships so we can broaden our network within the customer's organization.

Contact Plan

Our Key People	Customer's Key People			
	C. Barnes CEO	**H. McKay** VP, Ops	**O. Leclerc** Mgr., East Region	**T. Cheung** Mgr., Platt River Plant
S. Ryan CEO	No current relationship; introduce at Expo and build social ties; golfing at Pinehurst; 2x goal	No current relationship; invite him for site visit and lunch w/Ryen; 2x goal	None	None
T. Woxen VP, Sales	Excellent relationship from previous company; leverage to create stronger ties with other senior executives; 4x goal	Okay relationship; could be a chemistry problem; explore with Woxen—but not a critical tie; 2x goal	None	None
M. Bonvini Mgr., Engineering	None	Limited current relationship; goal is to build this crucial tie for future business; introduce at Expo; 6x goal	Good current professional relationship; strengthen through co-authorship of article on safety; seek joint speaking engagement; 6x goal	None; goal is to introduce and build a professional relationship as strong as that with Leclerc; 4x goal
W. Gold Mgr., Design Services	None; need to build ties due to Barnes' interest in design; leverage through Woxen; 2x goal	Negative current relationship; goal is to turn around by Oct.; 4x goal	None	None
C. Spaans Acct. Mgr.	Limited contact to date; need to build trust thru links with Ryen and more frequent contacts; 4x goal	Good current relationship, but he perceives me as a salesperson; need to create business relationship and trust; 6x goal	Excellent relationship; initial penetration of account here; goal is to sustain at current level and build social ties; 12x goal	Okay current relationship but need to build much stronger ties; focus on professional contacts in SPE; 12x goal
N. Bhatia Mgr., Customer Service	None	None	Negative perception due to customer service delays; goal is to solve problems and create positive relationship ASAP; 6x goal	None currently; need to establish ties; schedule joint meetings and problem-solving sessions; 6x goal
T. Dietrich Project Mgr.	None	Positive relationship; 12x goal	Sponsor relationship; broaden social ties and ask for referrals; consolidate through introductions through-out region; continuous contact goal	Positive relationship; goal is to work more closely w/Cheung to extend current contract; continuous contact goal

As Figure 13-3 shows, contact plans usually consist of a matrix showing the network of relationships you want to build between your key people and the customer's key people. They also might list some of the activities you've identified for building those relationships, as well as the frequency of desired contact. For example, as shown in Figure 13-3, a frequency goal of "6×" means your goal is to schedule six prime contacts per year. As you work this type of plan, you use the matrix to schedule customer contacts, provide information to the people in your company who are making those contacts, and debrief them afterwards. Managing contacts helps ensure that you're achieving the frequency you want, at each level of the customer's organization, and it enables you to manage the information flow to and from the customer. I discuss relationship management more in chapter 15. Suffice it to say here that, given the enormous value of systematic relationship management, it's difficult to imagine an account strategy that doesn't contain a contact plan.

Revenue Action Plans

The most self-focused of your objectives is the one identifying your revenue and profitability targets. Like the contact plan, it's hard to imagine an account strategy without a revenue plan, because this plan establishes your performance targets and identifies the metrics you will use to evaluate the success of your account strategy.

Figure 13-4 shows a typical revenue action plan. This plan sets revenue targets, usually by product or service line and sometimes by customer buying units or locations as well. This is what you expect to sell in the account during the next year (or whatever the time frame is for your account planning). Note that revenue is shown as a "projected" amount, which is the expected level of demand for each product line. The "Get %" is the probability that you will receive the order. Lower get percentages occur under the following kinds of conditions:

- Low price is the dominant factor in buying decisions, and you face price competition.
- Your rivals are active in the account, and you are competing intensively for share.
- Some competitors have an installed base or existing contracts for some items.
- You have performed poorly in some way, and the customer is shopping.
- Something else has occurred that reduces your confidence that you'll receive 100 percent of the volume, such as a change in the customer's buying process or people.

Figure 13-4. Revenue Plan

Objective: Generate $4,250,000 in revenue from this account during the next fiscal year at an average margin of 4%. This represents a revenue increase of 13.9% and a margin increase of 0.3%

Revenue Plan

Product	Projected	Get%	Outcome	Probable Margin	Profit	Comment
T-400 tape drives	50,000	70	35,000	2.7%	945	50% of orders already in
T-600 tape drives	34,000	90	30,600	2.1%	642	All in Far East
SX-586 chips	1,700,000	100	1,700,000	5%	85,000	Could exceed $1.7M
SF-486 chips	560,000	50	280,000	4.5%	12,600	Some orders may cancel
Modular desks	800,000	90	720,000	3%	21,600	Demand is increasing
GH com controls	450,000	75	337,500	2.3%	7,763	Three will close soon
R104 monitors	78,000	100	78,000	1.8%	1,404	Order pending
R204 monitors	230,000	80	184,000	6.1%	11,224	Waiting field test
Power servers	1,500,000	80	1,200,000	4.9%	58,800	Hottest item going
Total			**$4,565,100**		**$199,978**	

My probable outcome exceeds the revenue goal by 7.5%, which provides some cushion.

Margins should also exceed the goal because the power servers and SX-586 chips, which are more than half the projected revenue, are two of our highest margin products. Estimates of margin for the products and revenues listed above = 4.3%.

Actions:
Most revenue generated will occur through normal, ongoing sales efforts. But the following actions will also be taken:

To Be Continued

Multiplying the projected volume by the get percentage yields the probable "outcome" or volume you can reasonably anticipate from the account. The "probable margin" is your expected profit for each product line and typically is based on historical margins. Multiplying the outcome by this factor yields the expected profit. The cumulative figures for all product lines or customer locations represents a sales forecast for this account, which obviously is of great interest to the sales manager.

Taken together, the action plans, objectives, and vision constitute your account strategy. This is what you envision for the account, what you must do to realize that vision, and what is required to accomplish each objective. Whereas the vision and objectives show your strategic intent, the action plans establish your tactics. Once you create and distribute your action plans, however, they begin to lose their currency because they are static while the customer and the environment are dynamic. Consequently, you should consider the action plans changeable. The most effective account managers work their action plans daily. They copy their tasks into their daily, weekly, and monthly schedules, and they revise their action plans as conditions in the account change, as they achieve intermediate goals, and as new information becomes available.

After you draft your plan, you should syndicate it with all the relevant stakeholders, including your sponsors and allies in the customer organization. When you've received and responded to their comments, put the plan into effect. From this point, you are managing the plan and working the account, which is the subject of the next part of the book. Each quarter, typically, you sit down to formally review the account and each year you start the account planning cycle again.

Summary of Part III

Account planning is the strategic level of account management. Periodically, usually once a year, you have to step back and take stock of the situation—analyzing and profiling the customer, profiling your major competitors, and examining the four pillars of *their* position with the customer, then analyzing *your own* company and *your* position. The intelligence you gather and the scrutiny you subject it to should yield insights about where you are strong and weak in the account and where you face opportunities and threats. Prioritizing these SWOTs helps you know what's possible in the account. From these insights you create a vision for your work with the customer and then set objectives that will help you attain that vision. Finally, you create action plans designed to implement your strategy day by day. These plans are the dynamic and actionable components of your account strategy—the pieces you use to establish, schedule, and track not only your activities in the account but also those of your executive sponsor or other senior executives and other members of the account team.

The account planning process helps you identify the conditions of the account when the plan was developed, but the situation in the marketplace and with customers is dynamic, so it's crucial that your plan be a guide and not a straitjacket. You should modify it continually as conditions change. The most effective account plans are evolutionary. Finally, it's important to syndicate your plans with the stakeholders in your own company who must support it, as well as with your sponsors and allies in the customer's organization. The better your relationship with the customer, the more you should share your plans with them. They obviously are the biggest stakeholders in the process, and their support of your plans will be reflected in a stronger, better, and more profitable business relationship for both of you.

— PART IV —
Implementing the
Account Plan

Everything to this point in the book has been preparatory. This is the main event. *Planning* to manage a strategic account is not the same as *managing* the account. Managing the account means rolling up your sleeves; walking the hallways in the customer's organization; and plunging into the white water of daily circumstances as initiatives are undertaken, meetings are held, bids are released, and opportunities and threats surface. Your account plan helped you analyze the situation and establish your intentions and goals, but in the daily, weekly, and monthly struggle to manage the account, what exactly do you manage?

First, you manage syndication and implementation of the plan (chapter 14). This means bringing the stakeholders on board, aligning them with the vision and objectives, gaining their support and commitment, finding the resources you need, and engaging the other people in various divisions throughout your company whose cooperation is crucial to giving your strategic customer preferential treatment. It means enlisting executive sponsors who will run interference for you, be the standard bearers for the customer within your own organization, and work the hallways with you to build peer-to-peer relationships with key senior customer executives. Finally, it means dogging the plan—monitoring the tasks people committed to in your action plans, following through, responding to developments and solving problems, seizing opportunities when they arise, and modifying the action plans as necessary to keep them current.

Implementing the plan also means managing relationship building, extending your own personal network inside your company and throughout the customer's organization, and weaving a network of relationships among other key people in both organizations (chapter 15). Relationship building is too important to be left to chance; you must manage the network of contacts so that it maximizes your penetration of the account and the customer's concomitant penetration of your company. The closer, more extensive, and more vibrant that network of relationships, the greater the switching costs for the customer and the more value you can provide them. Without discounting the other important aspects of ongoing account management, it is safe to say that relationship management is the most important of an account manager's daily responsibilities.

However, communication may be the most visible of your ongoing activities, and managing the flow of information to and from the customer organization is an important aspect of implementing your account plan (chapter 16). It's essential to develop your private and deep private sources within the customer's organization and to ensure that the channels are open to the key people in your company. Because people have different communication styles, you have to manage what information goes to the customer and how it goes there. Conversely, you have to ensure that the right people in your company have the right customer information at the right time. In selling, what matters are the customer's *perceptions*, not reality, so information management in its most complex form is really impression management.

Clearly, one of the primary impressions you have to manage is the customer's degree of satisfaction with your company and products. Today, however, it's not enough to merely satisfy customers; you must go beyond satisfaction and *delight* them by exceeding their expectations (chapter 17). Reactive tasks, such as surfacing and resolving problems and handling complaints, are often an important part of that role, but you also need to be proactive in assessing customer delight and keeping your finger on the pulse of the relationship. Harvard's Ted Levitt argues that customers are never entirely satisfied and that the absence of complaints actually may be problematic. In any healthy relationship, there will be moments of discord, but they must be heard, addressed, and resolved if the relationship is going to remain strong.

Implementing the plan and managing the account continuously mean managing momentum (chapter 18). To borrow an image from basketball, you can't sustain a full-court press throughout the entire game. It takes too much energy. In most strategic accounts, there are peaks and valleys—periods of more intense activity and less intense activity, periods of high opportunity when you must bring many of your company's resources to bear and periods when those resources can be focused on other things. You have to know when to bring in the big guns, so to speak, and when to let things subside. Most account managers have built up a "favor bank" with the people in their company whose support they need. When account activity increases, they need to withdraw from that favor bank and get help; when activity decreases, they need to ease off and make deposits back into the account. Managing timing and energy levels in response to events in the account is a subtle but very important aspect of implementing the plan and managing the account on a daily basis.

Finally, managing the account and implementing your strategy mean managing opportunities when they arise. This business development function is usually the most visible of an account manager's activities because it is the one that leads directly to new sales. However, not all opportunities are worth pursuing, so you have to assess each one and make a thoughtful pursuit decision. If you decide to pursue the contract, then you must develop an opportunity strategy and position your company to win. Most bids are won before any proposals are written, so managing opportunity pursuits is a crucial part of strategic account management, and doing it well demands all of an account manager's skills and resources. It also requires flexibility because, although many opportunities are predictable, a good number are not. They may arise throughout the year from sudden and unexpected quarters.

As Maurice Hulst observes, "Things almost always turn out otherwise than one anticipates."[1] Account planning is a critical part of managing an account, but you can't allow it to become a straitjacket. In the white water of daily account management you have to be responsive to what's happening in the moment. This part of the book discusses how to do that.

---

1. Maurice Hulst, quoted in Rolf B. White, ed., *The Great Business Quotations* (New York: Dell Publishing Company, 1986), p. 182.

— 14 —

Building Internal Support

Baseball great Lou Gehrig said that you don't get the breaks unless you play with the team instead of against it. This is particularly true in strategic account management, which—if carried to its logical extreme—has the capacity to fundamentally change the way you do business because of your extraordinary customer responsiveness. Further, as Catherine Pardo argues, "The creation of a key account management program implies a new form of coordination between the supplier and the key account but also for the supplier himself, a sort of integration of different departments of the firm.... This is the reason why key account management imposes changes in working habits and is rarely without opposition."[1]

Because of their importance to you and your company, strategic accounts expect and deserve preferential treatment. Every employee in your company must be willing to go the extra mile for your account. You must motivate other employees—even those who don't report to you—to avoid doing *business as usual* when working with your account. Because your request is extraordinary and different than their normal mode of operating, it will engender resistance, as Pardo notes. So it's imperative that you build support, not only for your plan but also for routinely giving your account preferential handling. Further, you can't wait until after your plan is written to build internal support; it must be built continuously from the moment you are assigned the account to the moment you hand it over to someone else.

To build the level of support you need, you should syndicate your account plan with the various people in your company who will be supporting it, serving or interacting with the customer, providing resources, or otherwise contributing to the success of the account relationship. They should be aligned with you on the account vision and objectives and should be committed to the account's success. In most companies, gaining support means overcoming resistance as people struggle with multiple,

1. Catherine Pardo, "Key Account Management in the Business to Business Field: The Key Account's Point of View," *Journal of Personal Selling & Sales Management* XVII (1997):25.

conflicting priorities and full schedules. In business today, everyone has some form of attention deficit disorder—there's simply too much to do and too many masters to serve. So a key skill in account management today is influencing others to gain their support and cooperation, especially a senior executive in your company who will agree to be the executive sponsor of the account. Finally, you will need to form an actual or virtual account team—a network of supporters who assist you in managing the account and accomplishing the tasks in your action plans.

It seems ironic, but the National Account Management Association's surveys of account managers in the United States show that the single biggest obstacle most account managers face isn't building stronger relationships with key customers, it's building *internal* support.

Syndicating Your Account Plan

It's best to begin syndicating the plan before the plan is finalized so you can incorporate people's ideas and suggestions into it. People buy into a plan most when they've contributed to it and feel some ownership of it. If the plan comes across as a fait accompli, you are more likely to create resistance than consent. So, by definition, syndication should occur when the plan is still being formed and when you are actively soliciting and are open to other people's ideas on account strategy. Here are some best practices for syndication:

- First, identify the core group of people who need to be involved in the account planning and implementation process. This core group includes everyone with a stake in the account as well as the key people whose support of the account is essential, including account team members, relevant sales and operations managers, project managers, and customer service managers. Clearly, you have to make some choices about whom you involve, because in large corporations the number of people who interact with a strategic customer is potentially enormous. The core group should include only those people in critical positions who acknowledge the importance of the customer to them and their functions and who are willing to commit time to the account.
- Before developing the plan, involve all the core group members as well as your executive sponsors. It's imperative that they be, and feel part of, the process of developing the account plan.
- Syndicate the plan with other people whose support is necessary well before the plan is final. The plan should first appear to them as an early work in progress, and you should solicit their ideas and suggestions, acknowledge them, and then incorporate them if possible. People respond best when they are consulted about the plan well ahead of its final stages, they feel listened to, and they see that you've built their ideas into the plan.

- Try to develop a broad, multifunctional view of the plan, but don't get distracted by narrow, tactical issues or concerns. Keep your early focus at the strategic level (but record any tactical issues and return to them later).
- Remain open to other people's ideas and perspectives. If your syndication of the plan is a rubber-stamp exercise, they will know it and treat it cynically. Your quest for buy-in and your willingness to rework the plan with them must be genuine.
- Be specific about what you are asking people to do as they review the plan. Clarify the type of feedback or input you want (e.g., Are your objectives aligned with the corporate strategic plan? Does your SWOT [strengths, weaknesses, opportunities, and threats] analysis reflect their perception of the customer and situation? Are your work plans feasible?).
- Identify the resource needs—and resource providers—necessary for each action plan and be explicit to the resource providers about your need for their approval and commitment. The time to gain resource commitments is when you're developing the plan and syndicating it with your key people.
- In conveying your plan to people, paint a strong business case for serving the customer the way you are proposing. Show the tangible, bottom-line benefits to your company and the value-added benefits to the customer. Make it a compelling case and be sure it can stand up to the scrutiny of the least supportive internal managers.
- Remember to syndicate the draft with your sponsors in the customer's organization as well. They are your litmus test for how well the plan addresses the customer's needs, how realistic the plan is, and how receptive the customer is likely to be to your strategies.

You are finished syndicating the plan when all the major players have reviewed it, offered their comments, agreed on the revisions, and committed to the final product. This typically is an ongoing process and may take considerable time in large organizations.

Gaining Internal Alignment

One of the major challenges in syndicating a plan is gaining alignment on the account vision and objectives, and this challenge deserves some special attention. Alignment occurs when the stakeholders in the account concur with your analysis of the account and the vision and direction you've set; when they agree on the facts of the case, draw the same conclusions from them, and agree that the strategies that have been set are the right ones; and finally when they concur with the level of investment required and are willing to make the resource commitments that are within their purview.

Alignment is essentially the process of opening a dialogue, exploring diverse points of view, and achieving a synthesis of ideas that everyone will support. The principal skills required are the ability to listen, manage disagreement, distinguish what's essential from what's merely important, and identify alternatives that incorporate the salient elements of divergent points of view. Appreciating each stakeholder's broader perspective is essential because at the tactical level the stakeholders' arguments and opinions often seem idiosyncratic and unhelpful, but within the context of their experience and functional mandates their views usually are sensible. To get a diverse group of people enrolled in your vision, you have to hear their perspectives and satisfy their need to impact the outcome. That's why finding a way—any way—to incorporate at least some of their ideas goes a long way toward getting them aligned. Some stakeholders will be dogmatic about what they believe about the customer and will insist that you adopt their perspective wholesale. If that's not feasible for you, then you have to find a way to work around them, but most stakeholders are more reasonable. They can't support your account plan (and shouldn't!) if they don't believe it will produce the results they and your company need, but most will work with you, and if you are flexible they will support the plan.

You should seek alignment on your overall account vision first. Be sure people agree with your assessment of the situation and are aligned on your essential purpose. In essence, they should say, "Yes, that's where I want to see the account go. I can buy into that vision. That's what I envision, too."

Next, you want alignment on the account objectives. This typically is more difficult because the objectives are based on priorities, and various stakeholders may have a different sense of the priorities than you do—precisely because they look at the account from their functional perspective and do have a stake in the matter. Aligning on objectives often takes some negotiation and compromise.

"It shouldn't be this difficult to serve a national account well," thought Jana Valluri. She'd been Edwards Pharmaceuticals' strategic account manager for Pharm-Aide for 3 years and had grown the account from $14 million 3 years ago to $35 million today. She felt the account had considerably more potential, but as its size grew so did the customer's expectations. To achieve the next quantum leap in growth, her company would have to modify its packaging and agree to a just-in-time inventory management system that enabled Pharm-Aide stores nationwide to have stocks replenished on 2 days' notice—a virtual impossibility given Edwards' existing distribution system.

Jana needed help from two key stakeholders inside Edwards: Ellen Christiansen, the marketing director, and Sebastian Kapsner, the transportation manager. Christiansen initially was appalled at Pharm-Aide's request that all Edwards' products be relabeled as a Pharm-Aide brand. The cost of changing the labels would add about 2 cents to every product. Worse, Christiansen feared losing some of Edwards' brand value because consumers wouldn't associate their products with the Edwards name. Lately, she'd been warming to the idea but would still need convincing.

The bigger problem was Kapsner. He insisted that fulfilling just-in-time or-

continued

ders in 2 days simply was not feasible with their current systems. Most stock re-orders took 10 days to fulfill, and he wasn't willing to completely overhaul their systems for one finicky customer—never mind that that customer produced 8.2 percent of Edwards' revenues and 11.3 percent of its profits. "If I did what every customer wanted done differently," he said, "my department would be in chaos. This is a well-oiled machine. It works flawlessly because we've worked out the bugs over a long period of time. The last thing I want to do is mess with it."

His attitude made sense given his incentive package, Jana realized. His objective was to run an error-free shipping department. He was paid to make no mistakes, so changing his system and striving for a fivefold reduction in shipping times represented considerable risk.

Still, if she couldn't meet Pharm-Aide's needs, she was likely to lose a lot of potential business and perhaps existing business as well. Her executive sponsor, vice president David Reynolds, would not agree to step in on her behalf and pressure Kapsner to comply. Instead, he advised that she write a business case and show how reducing shipping time would benefit Kapsner's group and the rest of the company.

So she investigated the options and put some numbers on paper. It turned out that other retail pharmacy chains also were looking into just-in-time systems and were interested in much shorter reorder times. Also, reducing the length of shipment times reduced total shipping costs. In her business case, she showed that using distributors in some of the more remote areas helped spread Edwards' risk and did not increase the likelihood of distribution errors—quite the opposite. When she showed her projections to Reynolds, he was immediately enthusiastic about them and met spontaneously with Kapsner, Christiansen, and other managers to discuss the possibilities. When they recognized the benefits, they agreed that not only did the approach have merit but that other customers might support the same approach, and they'd find another solid way to differentiate themselves from their competitors.

Within 2 years, Edwards' revenues from Pharm-Aide had grown another 40 percent, and Jana was looking for further ways to strengthen the relationship and grow the account. A key lesson for her was that creating a business case and communicating the rationale for doing business differently are fundamental to gaining alignment. People like Kapsner aren't being unreasonably stubborn, but they may lack the imagination to see the possibilities by themselves. Sometimes you have to show them.

You'll also need alignment at the tactical level of the action plans, particularly because you'll be asking many of the stakeholders to commit time, budget, or other resources to these plans. They may have other ideas about how to achieve the objectives, and it's wise to listen carefully at this point because they often have better ideas than you do. They're closer to the ground and may have tried many of these approaches and ideas before. A great way to gain alignment is to consult with them on the actions necessary to achieve the objectives and, in essence, let them write the action plans.

Gaining alignment is a process, not an event. Persistence and patience usually are necessary, especially in the political landscape of most organizations. An account manager is often like a political campaign manager—working behind the scenes; forming coalitions; extracting favors; and pulling people with diverse priorities, interests, and viewpoints together in a common cause. In the ideal world, alignment should come naturally because everyone understands the importance of the customer and the mission. In the real world you have to work tirelessly in a shifting political landscape to achieve your goals, not because the people whose cooperation you seek act malignantly but because they have their own goals, needs, interests, and priorities.

Overcoming Resistance

According to one pundit, "If you find a path with no obstacles, it probably doesn't lead anywhere."[2] Resistance is natural and can even be beneficial. The most productive way to handle resistance is to treat it as an opportunity to explore your ideas from another perspective. It often means there is a legitimate and helpful contrary viewpoint that, when considered, leads to a better solution. However, if you consider the objection and still disagree with it, you can present your case using the facts and logic that led you to your conclusion. The facts should stand on their own merit. If they don't, maybe your idea is not so good.

Of course, some resistance occurs because people and the bureaucracies they serve in large organizations don't like change. As Eric Hoffer noted in *The Ordeal of Change*, the idea of change itself is disturbing.[3] Some people will resist a new approach because it's risky and unfamiliar and they're uncertain of the outcome. You often can enlist these people by discovering what's in it for them. How does it make their job easier? How does it further their goals? How do they benefit from taking a few extra steps for this key customer? Afterward, give them credit for the successes, and it will be much easier to work with them in the future.

The most difficult resistance will come when you are truly asking your company to stretch or when serving this customer will have negative short-term impacts (such as lower margins during an investment period) that reflect on the person whose support you need rather than on you. Then they have something personally at stake and should pause while they contemplate the possible outcomes. If they're at risk, then see if your executive sponsor will agree to provide air cover for them. Resistance sometimes occurs because people don't understand the facts or they disagree with the priorities. It also occurs because what you're asking is different, and the

---

2. Frank A. Clark, quoted in Ted Goodman, ed., *The Forbes Book of Business Quotations* (New York: Black Dog & Leventhal Publishers, Inc., 1997), p. 618.
3. Eric Hoffer, *The Ordeal of Change* (New York: Buccaneer Books, 1976).

risks to them or their division might be high. In the former case, provide the facts and discuss the priorities; in the latter, find ways to mitigate the risk.

Finding an Executive Sponsor

Up to this point, I've assumed that you have an executive sponsor, but that may not be the case. If you don't have an executive sponsor, a key to implementing the account plan and achieving your objectives is finding and enrolling a key executive in your company to sponsor the account. In most organizations with established strategic account programs, executive sponsorship of key accounts is a fact of life. Xerox calls them "focus executives" and has a formal program for selecting, training, and assessing the focus executives for their major accounts. In Praxair, Fluor Daniel, and other large corporations with strategic or global account programs, executive sponsors include the highest ranking executives, such as the chief executive officer, chief operating officer, and chief financial officer. Here are some suggestions for bringing an executive sponsor on board and using your sponsor effectively:

- *Set clear expectations up front.* They and you should know where and how they can add value and what role you expect them to play. Don't hesitate to be frank with them about what you need. If you can't be straightforward and peerlike with your own executives, you signal that you can't work at the higher levels of the customer organization either. You may need to negotiate how and to what extent they are involved. At the end, you want to have a set of shared expectations and agreements about what you are going to do for them and how they are going to support you and the account strategy and team.
- *Select the right sponsor.* Try to choose an executive who cares about the customer and whose role makes him or her a natural for this relationship. The executive should speak the customer's language, know and care about the industry, and want to be involved in the account. If sponsoring the account is a chore, it will come across that way to the customer. You can't fake genuine interest, and genuine interest in the customer's business is about 90 percent of what it takes to succeed as a sponsor. The best executive sponsors are people who have "skin in the game." It has to matter to them, and they need to be willing to commit themselves and take some risks. If they don't have this level of commitment to the account, then choose someone else.
- *Know how your senior executives think and what their priorities are.* Know what keeps them up at night and what's on their calendar throughout a typical day. Know how to communicate best with them. Most executives are too busy to wade through volumes of information, so you have to distill it to its essence and be crisp and timely in your communications. In short, you should treat your own executive sponsors the way you'd treat a customer's senior executive.

- *Be willing to take both the long- and short-term views simultaneously, as senior executives must.* Every day they have to focus on short-term results while also taking the long-term view of the business. This paradox forces them to make tough choices now and then, for example, to sacrifice a short-term gain in order to make a long-term investment. If you don't understand this, you will be frustrated with some of their decisions, which may seem contrary to the customer's best interests, and they will see you as acting simplistically or being shortsighted.

- *Frame most account information as a business case.* Know the business issues and present customer facts, trends, concerns, and strategies as part of the business picture. Talk in terms of commitments, agreements, options, benefits, costs, schedules, and margins. Bring everything to the bottom line and think in terms of impacts.

- *Facilitate peer contacts.* Most senior executives thrive on high-level, peer-to-peer personal contacts with their counterparts in the customer's organization. Your executives have reached positions of power and prestige in your company, and for most of them it's a thrill to mix with other people of high stature. So orchestrate those contacts for them. Similarly, you may need to ask your sponsor to act as a matchmaker with other senior people, such as introducing your CEO to the customer's CEO.

- *Keep them informed.* No matter how much your executive sponsor knows about the customer, he or she will rely on you as a source of privileged information. So keep your executive sponsors informed. Send them insights on the customer's industry, products, technology developments, trends, and so on. Write briefings now and then that summarize key insights they can share with their customer counterparts or other internal executives at their level.

- *Coach them on their role.* Before every meeting or event in which you need something specific from your sponsors, communicate your expectations and the customer's needs. Set up meetings by briefing them on who's attending, what the issues are, what needs to be resolved, what our position should be, and so on. Brief them prior to account team meetings, conferences, telephone calls with customer executives, site visits, and other events. Remember that they can't take time to familiarize themselves with the details of every situation, and they have many other priorities. In part, your job as account manager is to help make them successful in their role as executive sponsor. The more they succeed, the more you do, so don't hesitate to provide clear, explicit guidance. Most executives appreciate it.

- *Don't hesitate to ask for help.* If the customer's needs are not being met and you are experiencing unreasonable resistance from a manager and/or department and can't persuade them to cooperate any other way, then call on your executive sponsor for help. Ask initially for advice, but you also may need your sponsor to intervene. One key role your sponsor should play is being the customer's high-level advocate in your company, and the activist part of that advocacy is applying pressure where necessary to provide stretch for the customer. If you're in a bureaucratic organization, then high-level pressure is often the only way to get extraordinary things done.

What do you do if your executive sponsor isn't providing what you need, is too busy or distracted to provide much help, isn't committed to the account, or is ineffective at building strong relationships with peers in the customer organization? This is a difficult and politically sensitive situation, but not getting the high-level support you need is unacceptable. One course of action is to be explicit with the executive about what you're not getting. Feedback may work, particularly if the executive is committed to the account and agreed to the expectations you established up front. But in the worst case the person may be intransigent and you may need, in essence, to fire him or her. In Xerox's Focus Executive program, there are guidelines for who can become a focus executive, and candidates are interviewed and selected. It's prestigious to be a focus executive, but it's also acknowledged that not everyone can do it well, and there are provisions for excusing from the program executives who aren't successful.

What if none of the senior executives in your company feel the heat? It's difficult to imagine an established strategic account management program without executive sponsors in place. Companies that institute strategic account management programs realize, sooner or later, the value of this part of the program and create executive sponsors. However, if yours is a less-developed program, you may not have reached that stage. The best advice is to lobby for executive sponsors, beginning with the sales manager but going quickly to the CEO. The extent of the resistance you encounter is a measure of how much your company is more internally focused than externally focused. The companies who are best in class in sales or business development are very customer focused, and the strongest evidence of their external focus is the extent to which their senior executives are committed to, interact with, and advocate key customers.

Creating a Virtual Account Team

Account managers sometimes work in account teams, where people from relevant departments are assigned to the team and therefore have a vested interest in supporting customer initiatives and achieving the account objectives. Even when that is true—and always when it isn't—a key function of account management is building a network of people throughout the company who will do whatever it takes to meet the customer's needs. Because of their role, strategic account managers are uniquely suited to building these kinds of virtual teams. As Lisa Napolitano notes, "Perhaps more than anyone in an organization, NAMs [national account managers] know their company's core skills and competencies and the people who can make it happen in every department—from research and development to manufacturing and marketing. Those who can put these people together with the same kind of people in customer organizations [are] treasured resources."[4]

Virtual teams are particularly important when you have to stretch for the customer—when problems must be resolved quickly, when the schedule must be accelerated, when quality must exceed the normal standards, when something must be customized, and so on. If you haven't built a virtual team of people who are ready and willing to respond to extraordinary customer needs or requests, then you won't be providing added value to the relationship, and the customer will have no reason to consider you special.

> Kevin Bucklin realized that his first order of business was building an internal network that would support his efforts to build the Wilkes Process Manufacturing (WPM) account. WPM was a nationwide producer of paints and varnishes, and Kevin's new company, BaseAir, provided carbon dioxide and other industrial gases to a few of WPM's locations. The account potential was enormous and more so now because of BaseAir's recent acquisition of another gas manufacturer, which gave them the capability for simpler and cheaper nationwide distribution.
>
> However, BaseAir was relatively new to strategic account management and had no protocols or traditions for supporting strategic sales efforts. Kevin was the only salesperson with strategic account experience, and he had been on the job less than 2 months. He knew that he had little chance of getting an account team formally assigned. In his brief discussions with functional managers, he'd already seen resistance to the idea and felt that pushing for it now was unlikely to succeed. So he decided to form a virtual support team.
>
> He began by working his way through the company, ostensibly as an orientation to learn about the different functions and how they were serving WPM. But his primary goal was to get the lay of the land—to see who was responsive to his questions, who knew the most about the customer, and who seemed to care about and be most committed to serving the account. He asked about times when they had to do something extraordinary for customers, and he asked for their ideas on improving customer service. Some people had good ideas; others had nothing insightful to offer. In effect, he was interviewing each of them for a "job" on his virtual team.
>
> When he returned to his office, he made a list of the people he wanted on his virtual team, and then he began his proselytizing effort. He created a virtual e-mail group and sent thanks to each of his virtual team members, along with a simple fact sheet he put together on WPM. Over the next few months, he sent a regular series of e-mails to the people on his list. Each e-mail provided information about BaseAir's capabilities or history with WPM, asked for ideas, or informed team members about developments in WPM. The initial responses to his e-mails were spotty, but as his communication campaign continued, he began to
>
> *continued*

4. Lisa Napolitano, "Customer-Supplier Partnering: A Strategy Whose Time Has Come," *Journal of Personal Selling & Sales Management* XVII (1997):3.

notice more and more responses to his messages. Some people now were initiating contact with him and were proposing meetings to talk over customer service issues or ideas. The buzz in the hallways grew, and he began to attract attention from some senior executives. As he developed his account strategies for WPM, he solicited ideas from everyone on his virtual team and was delighted with the responses he got. Whether they contributed ideas or not, Kevin met with everyone on the team individually and discussed his proposed objectives and action plans. By the time he finished, everyone on his list had some hand in creating the account strategy.

Six months into his campaign, Kevin scraped together enough money from the sales budget to commission a local artist to create an impressionistic mural of the gas injection part of WPM's manufacturing process—not sexy maybe, but it was done with WPM spray paints. His contacts at WPM were pleased with the result, and he encouraged them to cosponsor an unveiling ceremony in their auditorium. Kevin invited all his virtual team members, along with BaseAir's executive group, and many were present when BaseAir's CEO gave the mural to WPM's CEO. Kevin's name wasn't mentioned during the ceremony, and that was okay with him. As he looked around the room and saw the mingling of BaseAir and WPM representatives, he knew that he'd already received his reward. There was interest here. Excitement about the product and the "partnership" between the two companies. And there was something more—he had a team.

The best practice for creating a virtual team is to find people in the relevant departments and positions who are already enthusiastic about serving customers' needs, who are willing to go the extra mile when necessary, and who want to be engaged in the company's mission beyond their current job. In short, not everyone qualifies. You have to work the hallways, get to know people, build your internal network, and find the people throughout the company who meet these criteria. Trying to build an effective team from a mass of nonbelievers is bound to be frustrating, and life is too short for that. So begin with a cadre of people who are already invested in serving customers well and have proven it in previous situations in which they had to stretch for a customer. Let someone else work with those whose attitude is "It's not my job," or "You have to go through channels." Virtual teams provide stretch.

Here are some other tips:

- Don't demand that virtual team members consider themselves part of a team or regularly set aside hours to work on team issues, although they might do this. A virtual team is a cooperative network of individuals, some of whom might not know each other. The only person who considers it a team is you.
- The glue that holds the virtual team together is communication. Provide plenty of it. Develop a distribution network, e-mail group, or newsletter list, and communicate often about customer events, needs, upcoming opportu-

nities, and so on. Initially, you will need to drive outgoing communication to virtual team members. Eventually, the spirit will move other team members to initiate communication with the team.

- Now and then, create focus groups composed of virtual team members to discuss particular customer service issues. Communicate the results of focus group discussions to everyone on the virtual team.

- Create a web site for the virtual team. Include discussion threads so you can hold online discussions of problems, concerns, and solutions. This is particularly useful if virtual team members are located in different sites around the country or the world.

- Now and then, solicit lessons learned or best practice ideas from virtual team members and then syndicate the assembled ideas to everyone. Be sure to attribute credit to the people who contributed the ideas. However, never blow your own horn.

- Develop and circulate success stories and case studies to the team. Early on, focus on quick wins; later, focus on the success of various account strategies and major bids.

- Be open about failures, but never assign blame. Use failures as opportunities to learn and grow, and solicit people's ideas on how to avoid a recurrence.

- Where feasible, facilitate contacts between virtual team members and their customer counterparts. It makes them feel more engaged in the account, strengthens the relationship with the customer, helps develop information, and improves customer service. There's no appreciable downside to doing this.

- Involve your executive sponsor on the virtual team. If possible, arrange for the executive sponsor to recognize virtual team members for their contributions to the customer.

- Involve virtual team members in the account planning process. Invite their ideas, suggestions, and reviews of drafts.

- Invite their contributions at other times as well. Then use as much of what they contribute as possible. Nothing engages people more than feeling listened to and having some ownership of the outcome.

- Periodically, write and circulate white papers on the customer; summaries of account activity; profiles of the customer and competitors; updates on changes in customer personnel; and notices about other significant events, including new opportunities or initiatives the customer is undertaking that could impact your company.

- Similarly, act as the clipping service for the virtual team. Do the Internet searches and clip articles on the customer from *Forbes, Fortune, Business Week,* the *Wall Street Journal,* and other public sources.

- If feasible, conduct briefings on the customer for virtual team members. Do a formal briefing to present the completed account plan, as well as periodic account status update briefings throughout the year, and invite all virtual team members along with key executives. Further, consider scheduling training seminars or workshops on the customer, the customer's needs, and how your company customizes its products or services to meet the customer's needs. If such training helps virtual team members do their jobs better, they will see the value in it for them and will attend. Or schedule a dog-

and-pony show for virtual team members that features the customer's new and interesting technologies or future directions. Most people are fascinated by that and will be interested in attending.

As I noted earlier, virtual team members have their own jobs and priorities and won't necessarily consider themselves part of your team. But if you can engage them in the account and motivate them to cooperate in providing stretch when needed, you will have a highly functioning virtual team. You have to put energy into the team. That's your investment in them. The return to you is their engagement, support, and commitment to the customer.

Building internal support is fundamental to your success as a strategic account manager. Without it, you have little chance of serving the customer as well as you'll need to, to maintain that customer's loyalty and commitment to you as a preferred supplier, partner, or ally. Building support is a complex, ongoing process and requires considerable skill in listening, facilitating, motivating, influencing, and negotiating.

— 15 —

Managing Relationships

In *The Marketing Imagination*, Ted Levitt notes that the relationship between buyer and seller seldom ends when the sale is made. "The sale merely consummates the courtship. Then the marriage begins. How good the marriage is depends on how well the relationship is managed by the seller. That determines whether there will be continued or expanded business or troubles and divorce, and whether costs or profits increase."[1] Relationship management is one of a strategic account manager's most important responsibilities. You are expected to be the *single point of contact* between the two organizations, the one person anyone in your company can and should call to discuss the customer and the one person any customer representative can call to discuss your company and its products.

Indeed, one measure of the effectiveness of your strategic account management program is whether the account manager is considered the single point of contact between the two organizations and whether everyone, particularly your senior executives, respects that fact. This is not to say that there shouldn't be a web of relationships among people at all levels in both organizations. There should be. But the account manager should be the focal point of contact between organizations and should be brought into any significant dialogues or interactions. As Catherine Pardo argues, "As a facilitator, [the account manager] is not a substitute for existing relationships, as there will always be equipment installed on sites by specialists, maintenance carried out by other specialists, provision of services to different customer locations and representatives responsible for local relations, tasks the key account manager is not able to do by himself or herself."[2]

Perhaps it's best to think of the account manager as the hub of a vast, interconnected set of wheels, each wheel representing the network of people in your company and in the customer's organization. The account manager should map the ideal sets of relationships between the two organiza-

---

1. Theodore Levitt, *The Marketing Imagination* (New York: The Free Press, 1983), p. 111.
2. Catherine Pardo, "Key Account Management in the Business to Business Field: The Key Account's Point of View," *Journal of Personal Selling & Sales Management* XVII (1997):24.

tions and identify who should know whom and which groups should be sharing ideas. The account manager must ensure that those connections are made frequently enough to build and sustain a high level of trust and preference. The closer those relationships, the more responsive the people in your company are likely to be and, thus, the greater service the customer gets and the more value you provide to them. In their study of switching costs in key account relationships, Sanjit Sengupta et al. discovered that "the biggest factor that gives rise to customer switching costs is customer investment in relationship-specific assets."[3] So one of the aims of relationship management is to build those relationship-specific assets—the solutions and benefits customers receive only if they do business with you.

To build strong relationships with customers you must establish a deep and abiding trust between you and your company and them and their organization, and this occurs on three levels: needs satisfaction, personal, and institutional. Further, you have to manage relationship building in a deliberate and self-conscious way because the network of relationships you need is unlikely to occur by happenstance.

Building Needs-Satisfaction Trust

Needs-satisfaction trust occurs at the basic level of interaction between buyers and sellers, and it's the first gate you must pass through. If you succeed, you can go on to build deeper trust. If not, you won't be doing more business together. As Jane Helsing observes, "Trust in a supplier begins to develop out of a series of successful deliveries, thus leading the customer to believe that the supplier is reliable when it comes to providing its products or services. Reliability encompasses quality of the deliverable, timeliness, appropriateness, and completeness."[4] This kind of trust involves meeting the customer's expectations in the fundamental exchange of value that the sales transaction represents. Ask yourself:

- Do you understand the buyer's needs?
- Do your products or services satisfy those needs? Are you willing to modify them if necessary to suit the buyer's specific requirements?
- Are your products or services of acceptable quality? Do they perform as promised? Do they last?
- Are you responsive to the buyer's questions and concerns? Do you address them in a straightforward manner?

---

3. Sanjit Sengupta, Robert E. Krapfel, and Michael A. Pusateri, "Switching Costs in Key Account Relationships," *Journal of Personal Selling & Sales Management* XVII (1997):15.
4. Jane Helsing, "What is Trust?" in *The Trust Imperative* (Chicago: National Account Management Association, 1998), p. 23.

- Is your price competitive with the marketplace? Is it fair given the value of the product and services received?
- Do you deliver the product on time? Do you meet your other obligations?
- Do you quickly and satisfactorily resolve complaints and problems?
- Do you ask for reasonable terms and conditions in your contracts?

These factors are the basic conditions for doing business. If you can't meet them, then you have no basis for building closer relationships. You need to attend to these factors assiduously, particularly during the penetration and consolidation phases of your relationship when transactional trust is being established (and evaluated by the customer). However, there's really never a point where these factors aren't important. A company's failure to meet needs-satisfaction requirements is a tremendous source of headaches for account managers who've worked hard to build trust and confidence only to see them eroded when a shipment is delayed, a motor arrives with the wrong mounts, or the customer service department doesn't return phone calls promptly.

Needs-satisfaction trust is a necessary but insufficient condition for building sustained relationships with customers. To put it another way:

Relationships based purely on needs satisfaction cannot be sustained.

The marketplace plays no favorites. If your rivals are competent, they will be able to establish needs-satisfaction trust, too. At this level of trust you are establishing your right to be a credible but undifferentiated supplier, no better than comparable suppliers who also can satisfy the customer's needs. In short, you are a common or commodity vendor. To build thriving strategic account relationships you have to go far beyond this.

Building Personal Trust

Assuming that you have met the needs-satisfaction requirements, the next level of trust occurs on the personal level between you (and others in your company) and people in the customer's organization. Personal trust concerns the interpersonal relationship you establish between one human being and another, and it exists when customers can favorably answer the questions shown in the box following. Are you trustworthy? Dependable? Respectful? Fair? Do you exercise good judgment? Are you discreet? Obviously, these issues are fundamental to good interpersonal relationships, and they transcend the essentially transactional nature of buyer–seller interactions. If you treat customers as marks and think of them as objects of manipulation, then you can't possibly build good personal relationships because no one wants to be treated that way.

Do I Trust You?

✓ Are you credible? Do you know what you're talking about?
✓ Do you always do what you say you'll do? Do you keep your commitments?
✓ Can I believe what you tell me? Are you candid and honest?
✓ Do you own up to your company's problems and your own mistakes? (or do you blame others and try to hide problems?)
✓ Do you care about me as a person? (or am I just a "customer" to you?)
✓ Do you respect me and my work?
✓ Do you have my organization's best interests at heart? (or are you acting purely out of self-interest?)
✓ Are you willing to go the extra mile for me and my organization?
✓ Do you use good judgment? Do you know when to push and when not to? Do you know when not to ask for or about something?
✓ Are you fair? Do you treat others with respect and equanimity? (or do you joke about them behind their backs?)
✓ Do I enjoy being with you and working with you?
✓ Can (and do) I share personal information with you? Are you discreet with that information?
✓ Likewise, do you disclose personal information to me?
✓ Are you willing to do favors for me?
✓ Am I willing to do favors for you in return?

To be sure, there are purely transactional buyer–seller interactions. In these, the buyers are tough negotiators, view all sellers with suspicion, try to get as much as they can for free (and consider it a victory when they do), beat up suppliers on price, and share sellers' solutions with their competitors so they can level the playing field and then select the lowest bid. The sellers, being equally suspicious—for good reason—withhold vital technical information so competitors won't receive it, are coy about their costs, offer discounts and other incentives to bribe buyers into selecting them, and deliberately low-ball their bids while expecting to make their margin on change orders. In this transactional atmosphere, there can be no personal trust and no sustainable relationships, because everyone is out for himself or herself and relationships are reduced to the lowest common denominator of tit for tat.

So the first prerequisite for building personal trust is that you care about someone other than yourself—namely, your customers. You must care about them as people and treat them respectfully and sensitively. As I write this I realize how much it sounds like a platitude from a "let's hold hands and get along together" book, but it's remarkable how many account managers aren't able to build personal trust with their customers and don't understand why they can't. (It's because they have a transactional attitude toward these relationships.)

Is socializing necessary in order to build personal trust? The answer is, it depends. I said earlier that the first prerequisite is that you care about your customers as people. The second is that you be genuine. If you are naturally a social person, then socializing can help build personal trust; if not, then most customers will understand (they have home lives, too, and may not want to spend another night away from the family). It's unwise to socialize if your heart's not really in it, and you shouldn't let socializing become a transactional ploy (e.g., "I'll take you to the Mets game if you'll give me the order"). If you enjoy playing golf and one of your customer contacts enjoys it as well, then playing golf together is a great way to strengthen the relationship. Just don't force this kind of bonding, and don't talk shop during social activities unless the customer brings it up.

Relationship building is not about being cordial, or taking people fishing, or sending them cards on their birthday, although if such things are natural to you and don't seem unnatural to your customers there's no reason not to do them. What's far more important is knowing what your customer worries about, what keeps him or her up at night; knowing how the person solves problems and makes decisions; and knowing when to raise issues and when not to. What's important is caring about them as people and being genuine yourself.

Clearly, the "hard sell" is incompatible with trust-based relationships. Whenever customers start to feel manipulated, personal trust is destroyed. And this raises a critical but paradoxical point: customers need to feel that you are more concerned about meeting their needs than meeting your own—that you put their interests first. This creates a paradox, because customers know that your goal is to develop business, that you are paid to sell, and that your incentives are based on achieving certain levels of revenue and income. So when you say to them, "Your interests come first," they realize the inherent conflict of interest, and some will be suspicious of it. Yet in strategic account selling, you must, in fact, place their interests first, even if this means turning away opportunities because you know they're not right for you or the customer. If you can consistently do what's best for the customer, regardless of the impact on your goals, then you will build substantial personal trust.

There's one final prerequisite for building personal trust: it must be reciprocated. Personal trust cannot exist unless it goes both ways. You have to trust that they are forthright, dependable, respectful, and fair. The personal-trust questions I cited earlier also apply to your customers:

- Are they credible? Do they know what they're talking about?
- Do they always do what they say they'll do? Do they keep their commitments?

- Can you believe what they tell you? Are they candid and honest?
- Are they willing to admit when they are wrong?
- Do they care about you as a person?
- Do they respect you and your work?
- Are they willing to do favors for you?
- Are they willing to disclose information about themselves?

We've probably all been in situations where we know the customer is not telling us the truth, where a buyer accepts a dinner invitation and then brings his wife and daughter along for the free meal, where a customer demands more details on our approach to a problem than is strictly necessary to evaluate our ability to do the job (and it becomes obvious that they have no intention of signing a contract—they just want free consulting). The power that buyers have goes to some people's heads, and they use it to manipulate sellers and, frankly, to steal from you. Just as there are unscrupulous sellers, there are unscrupulous buyers. People who operate in this mode sometimes will reform over time, but some are dishonest by nature and will never change. My advice is to fire them. Yes, you can fire a customer. There are too many good customers out there to waste your time on buyers who will only work with you transactionally.

Personal trust is based on the concept of reciprocity. I trust customers to treat me fairly, and they trust me to do the same. If we can establish a good, respectful working relationship, then we can share information and insights that benefit both of us and deepen the bond between us. It can only happen if customers know that you really do place their interests first, because then you've removed the transactional obstacle to developing deeper personal relationships.

Being willing to disclose information about yourself and your company is crucial to building personal trust, and one old framework I find illuminating is the Johari window. It was invented by Joseph Luft and Harry Ingham—hence the name "Jo" + "Hari." As shown in Figure 15-1, the Johari window has four boxes based on the X and Y axes shown. The upper left quadrant is the area of shared information—in this example, information about me as a person. This is the arena, and it includes the information about myself that I've shared with the customer. The upper right quadrant is my blind spot—what the customer perceives about me that I don't perceive about myself (e.g., that I know more about his or her company than I realize, or that I seem ill-informed about the company's upcoming merger, or that my cuffs are frayed). The lower left quadrant is my façade—what I know about myself that the customer doesn't know (e.g., that I plan to call on the customer's plant in Michigan next week, or that I don't enjoy meeting with her boss because her boss smokes heavily and I'm allergic to cigarette smoke). The lower right quadrant is the unknown—things about me that neither of us is aware of. In an ideal situation, the arena of shared information is larger than any of the other areas, as shown in Figure 15-1.

Figure 15-1. The Johari Window

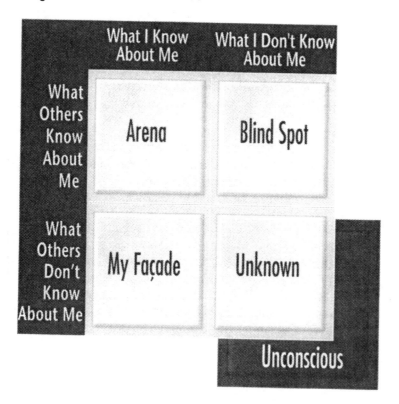

In poor personal relationships, the arena typically is small. I tell customers only what I think they need to know about me and my company, and they don't give me feedback or otherwise tell me what they really think about me or my company. Consequently, we have little basis for deeper interaction. In the best relationships, the arena is much larger. I feel comfortable disclosing information that otherwise would be part of my façade, and my customers feel comfortable giving me feedback and sharing their perceptions. So the arena grows larger. The larger the arena, the better the relationship. You can enlarge the arena primarily by disclosing what's in your façade and soliciting feedback about what's in your blind spot. Now, apart from all the jargon, what does this mean? Simply that the more you tell your customers and the more open you are to hearing their impressions of you, the stronger your relationship will grow and the higher your personal trust is likely to be. Clearly, this kind of trust takes time. If you disclose too much too quickly, you can arouse suspicion. Relationship building follows its own time line, and two of the essential skills are timing and an ability to read the signals and know when to move to the next stage of disclosure and openness. Both of these issues are cultural to some degree, so building relationships in Japan is different than building them in the United States.

A special kind of personal trust exists with customer sponsors—the people in the customer organization who want you to win. They open doors for you, make introductions, and give you deep private information. The way you create sponsors is to build deep personal trust, and it requires that your arena with them be large. Many people I've worked with are reluctant to disclose personal information about themselves, but it's the fastest way to build deeper personal trust with customers, and it's how you build sponsors.

Although Anita Hansen's company had done business with Gulf Southern Energy Corp. (GSEC) for years, her initial meetings with Roland Massenet were icy, to say the least. Having just taken over the account, she expected a warmer reception from Massenet, whom her predecessor described as a "friend of our company." But in her introductory meeting with Massenet, he said, "I don't mean to put you off, but we're very busy now, and I don't have time for salespeople. If you have a specific proposal, write it up and fax it to me. I'll take a look at it when I get a chance." Subsequent attempts to penetrate his façade were futile, although she did receive—by mail—a half dozen requests for quotation (RFQ) in the next 6 months. She responded to each with a proposal and cost estimate. Her company won two of the awards, which satisfied her sales manager, but she knew she was being treated as a common vendor and wouldn't be able to build the business relationship she wanted with GSEC until she'd established some personal trust with Massenet, whose position as procurement manager gave him the central gatekeeping role in GSEC's buying process.

She knew some of the details of Massenet's personal life but felt that trying to connect with his human side would be futile and presumptuous at this point. Instead, she decided to search for ways to add business value whether or not he asked for it. When she received the next RFQ in the mail, she went to her company's engineering group and asked if they could give her two alternatives to what GSEC was asking for—one that was just beyond what they called for and one that was radically beyond their specifications. The first one—Alternative A—proposed a maintenance solution that was somewhat more costly to implement but resulted in lower life cycle costs over the next 3 years. Alternative B suggested that they radically rethink their approach to the job and do something they hadn't tried before, an approach that could potentially cut their operating costs in half. In addition, Anita produced a proposal and bid that gave GSEC exactly what they'd asked for.

She called Massenet and asked for 15 minutes of his time so she could present their ideas. He was dubious about the need to meet but granted her request. He was predictably surprised at the fact that she'd submitted three proposals, but she explained that she was trying to find the best long-term solution for GSEC and didn't feel that what they were proposing to do would serve their long-term financial and business interests as much as the two alternatives she submitted. He thanked her for the extra effort but still looked aggravated as she left, and she wasn't surprised later to learn that they'd lost the bid. He never did comment on her alternative proposals.

continued

Two months later, she received another RFQ from GSEC and responded the same way. She didn't get that award either, but the third time she submitted three proposals, he surprised her by calling to ask if she'd be willing to set up a presentation on the radical (Alternative B) proposal to a group of their facility managers. She agreed, provided she could involve her engineering manager and the designer who'd conceived the idea. During this meeting, the opportunities and risks of this approach were presented and debated by the technical people present. The facility managers were intrigued by the concept and felt that it deserved serious study, which they agreed to fund. Meanwhile, they felt that her less radical proposal (Alternative A) was better than what they'd initially planned and asked Massenet to draw up a contract for that project.

During the next 6 months, Anita worked on building the engineer-to-engineer relationships between her company and GSEC, and she continued to provide alternative proposals where feasible. The level of contact between her and Massenet increased slowly. Then, nearly 18 months into her assignment as strategic account manager for GSEC, she had lunch with Massenet and was able to break through his cautious façade. After talking about their families for a while, he told her about GSEC's expansion plans into the western U.S. and said he wanted to get her ideas on how best to establish the production facilities they would need. Although he never would have said it explicitly, the implication was clear—he trusted her.

Sustaining Personal Relationships

The interesting thing about personal relationships is that they are never static. Invariably, they change over time—growing stronger, fainter, or disappearing altogether. How many of your high-school chums do you still have close relationships with? Personal relationships are reinvented continuously, and this is as true with customers as it is with friends. Here is what's required to sustain personal customer relationships over time:

- *The relationship must be reciprocal and mutually respectful.* Neither person can have a transactional attitude toward the relationship or the other person. There must be mutual trust.
- *You must have or develop common interests.* Without finding some commonality of outlook, attitudes, or interests, it's difficult to sustain a long-term working relationship. The commonalities I've developed with people range from mutual interest in racing cars or sports teams to a fascination with computer chess programs to professional topics such as TQM, leadership development, and supply chain management.
- *You must have problems and resolve them.* Most healthy long-term relationships take a bumpy road at times. It's probably helpful to go through some bad times and work through the issues. If you're not getting bruised now and then, you're probably not playing at it hard enough.

- *The relationship must be enjoyable and renewable.* Ultimately, the relationships we sustain are the ones we enjoy most for a variety of reasons. Further, that enjoyment has to be renewed from time to time with new experiences, new jokes, new fascinations, and new professional joys.
- *The relationship must evolve from one state to another, and it must continue to do so.* I'm thinking of my own marriage, which has evolved in 24 years from youthful fascination and exploration to sustained friendship and devotion. Professional relationships are like that, too. As you work together over the years, the relationship changes. If it doesn't evolve, it probably can't be sustained because you're not the same people now that you were then. Things change, and healthy relationships change with them.
- *There must be frequent and regular contact.* Without meaningful interactions periodically, you can't sustain personal trust because you grow too far apart and lose the commonality and mutuality on which close relationships are built. There are no rules of thumb about how frequently you should get together, but it must be frequent enough to sustain the quality of the relationship. At least some of these contacts must be quality contacts, not holiday cards or brief notes every 3 months. They must be face to face or otherwise show that you've committed time to the contact. A four-page handwritten letter, for example, is worth more than twenty brief e-mails. Quality contacts require an investment of time, which means you must prioritize the ones you make because you can't develop meaningful personal relationships with hundreds of customers.

Building Institutional Trust

Institutional trust is an emergent phenomenon, coming as it does from a series of successful interactions between two organizations over an extended period. Generally speaking, there's no single event that gives rise to institutional trust; it emerges slowly and naturally as people open up, mutual dependencies are created, and the formality of a buyer working with a supplier gives way to the familiarity of colleagues working with each other. I don't mean to imply that institutional trust is either serendipitous or easy. Quite the contrary, its development demands considerable relationship management on the supplier's part, and it often requires suppliers to adapt their culture and business practices to the culture and business practices of the buyer.

When trust between institutions is strong, both organizations have faith that the other one will treat them fairly and equitably—and you can see this in relaxed contracting standards, fewer written agreements, and more frequent communication at all levels between the organizations. There is a sense of commonality in their values, vision, and goals. Both are focused on serving the users of the customer's products, and there is considerable trust in the working relationships between the functions in each organization that coordinate with one another, including engineering, marketing, manufacturing, shipping/receiving, maintenance, accounting, sales and service, field support, and so on. This sounds like a partnership, and at this level of institutional trust it very well may be, at least informally.

The principal reason for developing institutional trust is to ensure that the trust with your customers transcends you and other people in your company, including the CEO, as well as specific individuals in the customer's organization. As Ted Levitt observes, "Clearly, relationship management requires not just the care of little things day in and day out but also the cumulative constructive management of all things large and small throughout the organization. The idea is to build bonds that last, no matter who comes and goes."[5] If trust relies solely on individual, personal-trust relationships, then the trust may be lost when those people move on. Now and then, suppliers rely on a particular sponsor in the customer's organization to give them business. It's happened to me at least half a dozen times, and when my sponsor retires or is reassigned or leaves, my connection with the customer is threatened. Strategic accounts are too important for you to rely on personal-trust relationships between individuals in the two organizations. You must build trust at the institutional level.

There are many more reasons for wanting to establish deep institutional trust. When trust is strong, customers share much more information with suppliers, including deep private information, which leads to better problem resolution, lower costs, and richer innovation. At high trust levels, the buyer's contract administration costs are lower, as are the supplier's selling costs, and problems can be resolved without involving attorneys. Hewlett-Packard's (HP) relationship with Canon is an example. Canon supplies the laser engine that powers HP printers, and HP dominates the printer market. The partnership between Canon and HP is extraordinary, even though they compete in other areas. Another example is Chrysler, which has formalized its partnering relationships with key suppliers in a program called Extended Enterprise™. Its close relationship with Becker Corporation has long been a model of buyer–supplier relations with very strong institutional trust.

How do you build strong institutional trust? It requires considerable energy from you and a strong commitment from your company's senior executives. The following list describes the key conditions:

- *Mutual need and a fair exchange of value.* A necessary condition of institutional trust is that customers and suppliers continue to need each other, that they can't fulfill their missions without the other. Mutual reliance is central to a sustained business relationship. Further, there must be a perception of a fair exchange of value. The supplier must earn a fair return for what the customer receives, and the customer must get equitable value for what the supplier charges. For this sense of equity to be maintained, the supplier's products and pricing must be in line with market forces. If you charge more than your competitors and your products, services, and intangible extras are not

---

5. Theodore Levitt, *The Marketing Imagination* (New York: The Free Press, 1983), p. 124.

demonstrably better or provide more value, then you will be misaligned with market forces and the customer eventually will lose trust in you. The market always determines equity.

- *Protection of private and deep private information.* People throughout the customer's organization must trust that you are discreet and will protect their private and deep private information, that you will maintain confidentiality agreements, but, more to the point, that you will act with their best interests at heart and will not do anything to compromise their competitive position. Professional firms have conflict-of-interest provisions to help ensure that they always act in their clients' best interests, but even if your company doesn't have such provisions it is wise to act in the best interests of your strategic account customers and to avoid serving their rivals—at least with the same people. If you want to build strong institutional trust, then you can't treat them like commodities.

- *Alignment of goals and values.* Much has been written about the need for institutional alignment of goals and values. It's possible for suppliers to serve buyers without such alignment, but it's not possible to build high institutional trust without it. In short, if you aspire to be a preferred supplier or partner with a customer, then alignment of goals and values is essential. One of the prime examples is Coca-Cola and McDonald's Corporation. They are aligned in their desire to dominate their markets, in expanding internationally, and in being ubiquitous to the consumer.

- *Care and commitment from senior executives.* You won't build institutional trust unless your senior executives care about the customer and are committed to the special caretaking you give the customer. Further, their customer advocacy must go beyond words; it must be evident in the decisions they make, the support they give, the road blocks they remove, and the personal relationships they build.

- *Senior leadership.* At least one of your senior executives must take a leadership role in advocating the customer and helping build the senior relationships. If you have an informal partnership or alliance with the customer, then this executive should devote a healthy percentage of his or her time to account development and nurturing.

- *Companywide programs committed to exceptional service.* To create strong institutional trust, customers must feel that you care enough to treat them specially, that every part of your company is committed to giving them exceptional service. Although it's easy to *say* you'll do this, in practice it means ensuring that every system in your company is organized for and committed to giving special service, and the larger and more bureaucratic the company, the more difficult this is to effect. Despite everyone's best intentions, it's hard to change large, already well-functioning systems and to permit exceptions, particularly when the company has not one strategic account but fifteen of them, which is common. Nonetheless, if you want to build strong institutional trust, you must continually stretch for the customer. Further, the account manager can't be the only person doing the stretching—it must occur throughout every function and at every level where there is customer interface or impact from operations.

- *Open information sharing.* Generally speaking, the more information you share, the deeper the personal trust, assuming both parties protect sensitive information and use it wisely. Figure 15-2 shows the Johari window as applied to organizations. In this case, the window shows the information known or unknown about the customer, but we could draw a similar diagram showing the information known or unknown about our own company. Ideally, the arena of shared knowledge is very large. As customers reduce their façade by revealing more information to you, the more insight you have about them and their needs. Conversely, the more you reveal about your company, the more insight they have about your capabilities and how you can serve their needs. As we'll see in chapter 16, managing the arena of shared information is an important aspect of strategic account management.
- *Evolutionary adaptation of your systems.* Finally, to build institutional trust, you must be flexible and adaptive. Over time, your systems must change to fit the customer's unique requirements and protocols, and you must demonstrate continuous improvement and cost reduction. Key customers won't trust you in the long term if you appear to be resting on your laurels. Today, active quality improvement programs are mandatory, and yours must produce a steady stream of innovations, process improvements, and cost reductions that help customers sustain or enhance their competitive advantage. You build relationship-specific assets and raise the switching costs

Figure 15-2. The Johari Window for My Customer

when you have an active learning organization. The ideal is to innovate with the customer, to learn together in ways that create lasting synergies between you while improving the customer's business and making heroes of the customer's people who participated. An example of this is General Electric's Work-Out program, which began as an internal problem-solving event. After some years of successful internal innovation, Jack Welch and his GE team began including customers in Work-Out sessions, where teams of GE and customer people worked intensively together to solve problems. The success of these joint problem-solving events is a testament to their power in building trust between organizations.

"Let me give you some friendly advice," Catrin Miller said. "That guy's a pain in the butt. If you want to keep doing business with us, you need to keep him the hell out of here. I don't care who he is." Chilling words. Cat Miller was a senior product line manager for Great Foods and was probably the only person willing to give Pete Samek the lowdown on why their business with this key customer had been declining. Unfortunately, the guy Cat referred to was Owen Timko, a senior vice president in Pete's company and officially the executive sponsor of the Great Foods account.

Years ago, Timko had been the salesman who landed the Great Foods account, and he'd considered it his baby ever since. But as he'd grown older and gotten more seniority, the qualities that made him a great salesman—aggressiveness, tenacity, creativity—had become a detriment. Now most people considered him arrogant, pushy, and intolerant of other people's ideas, and the worst sides of his personality showed most with subordinates and customers. Pete was aware of the damage Timko was doing but was afraid to doing anything about it until Cat Miller laid it on the line for him.

His sales manager advised Pete to tough it out and said that he'd ask Timko to tone it down, but Pete knew that wasn't a solution. To do the right thing for his company and Great Foods, he had to get Timko out of the account. The last thing he wanted to do was confront Timko, who had a reputation for eating subordinates, but he decided that was the right first step, and it was as disastrous as he'd imagined. Timko blew up and accused Pete of incompetence and stupidity. Then he stormed out. At this point, Pete decided that no matter what the consequences to him personally, he was going to do what he thought was right, so he went back to his sales manager, told him what he'd done, and then said he was going to talk to the vice president of sales, his manager's boss. His manager wanted to let the dust settle first, but Pete was already on his way, so his manager quickly joined him.

In the vice president's office, Pete swallowed the last ounce of his caution and said, "We have a problem. Firing me won't solve it, but if that's what you have to do, fine." Then he told the managers what Cat Miller had said and laid out what had been happening in the account. "If we look at this purely from the customer's standpoint," Pete said, "this isn't about pride or ownership or anything else. It's about salvaging a deteriorating relationship with one of our most important customers. I can tell you flat out that's not going to happen as long as Owen Timko is sponsoring the account. If it'll help for you to talk to Cat Miller, I'll get her on the
continued

phone." Initially, the vice president had thought it best to discuss the problem with other senior executives and try to find a face-saving way to get Timko to back away from the account. At the end of a long and sobering discussion, however, and considering Timko's volatile personality and probable resistance, the vice president decided to preempt the debate and just tell Timko that he was no longer the executive sponsor.

He scheduled a private meeting with Timko and afterward kept the details of the meeting to himself, but Timko no longer was involved with the account. To help reverse the decline in the relationship, the president devoted more time to high-level customer meetings. After several weeks of soul searching on the possibilities, the vice president found another executive to assume the role as executive sponsor. It hadn't been easy. Pete found himself shunned whenever he was in Timko's vicinity, but the problem had been resolved and the relationship with Great Foods was on the mend.

Sustaining Institutional Relationships

The key conditions I cited previously are necessary but insufficient for sustaining institutional relationships over the long term. You also must fight complacency and periodically reevaluate the relationship, no matter how well it appears to be doing on the surface. In business as well as personal relationships, people tend to become complacent once the hard work of building the relationship is over. We don't want to continually reinvest in the relationship. We'd rather assume that it will always be as good as it is now. By the time we discover that the relationship is plunging into the abyss, we're often too far down the disintegrating slope to arrest our downfall.

So perhaps one of the biggest challenges in sustaining institutional relationships is to attack complacency. You have to continually reinvent the sense of urgency and special caring that helped you create a strong relationship in the first place, and this must be done throughout your company, from the shipping clerks to the CEO. If people aren't continually sensitized to the need to treat the customer especially well, they will slip into "business as usual." Among the best practices for sensitizing people are these:

- Publicize instances of other companies whose complacency cost them a customer. Building awareness of the danger usually is quite helpful.
- Find face-saving ways to inform people about problems your own company has experienced with the customer because you'd become complacent. Or identify instances where you avoided problems because you weren't complacent.
- Conduct customer "sensitivity" briefings or workshops periodically, especially with account team members, to remind people how important it is to sustain the customer's sense of specialness.
- Hold joint problem-solving or opportunity-seeking workshops with customers so some of your people can work more directly with them.

- Build a virtual network of the people who serve the customer and communicate regularly with them about the customer's needs, your satisfaction of those needs, and any issues the customer raises.
- Use your own performance metrics and customer-satisfaction surveys to measure your sensitivity to the customer's changing needs and issues. Even the answers to simple questions such as "How well are we listening to you?" are useful.

Another best practice is to do relationship checks now and then (for further suggestions, see Chapter 17). Suffice it to say here that you should not assume that everything is all right. Even in the best of customer relationships, it's helpful to be explicit by asking the questions:

- How are we doing?
- Are we meeting your needs?
- Are we providing added value beyond our products and services?
- How satisfied are you with the way we're working together?
- How satisfied are you with the people in our company you work with most closely?
- How could we improve our working relationship?

One of the best examples of a sustained high-trust relationship between companies is that between Procter & Gamble and Wal-Mart. They maintain the relationship through a joint interface team, and the team's operating principles include guidelines on the business results and leadership focus the team wants to achieve, how the two companies will work together, and how the teams from each company will interact.[6]

Institutional relationships are sustained when your customers perceive that you care about them and are committed to their success, when you know their industry as well as your own, when you do things for them that you don't do for their rivals, when your innovations improve their competitive position, when you go to bat for them inside your company, when your senior people are committed to their success, and when you place their interests ahead of your own. Clearly, this is a tall order, but if your goal is to sustain strategic account relationships over many years, you must achieve this level of performance with those key customers.

Building a Zippered Net

I spoke earlier about the need to build relationships between key people at all levels in your company and the customer's organization. The metaphor

---

6. Tom A. Muccio, "Organization-to-Organization Trust: Procter & Gamble/Wal-Mart," in *The Trust Imperative* (Chicago: National Account Management Association, 1998), pp. 103–5.

that's often used to describe the resulting network is a zipper—with important connections occurring up and down the line. Building a zippered net is fundamentally important to managing strategic accounts effectively. If you can't do this, you can't succeed as an account manager, and it's not always easy because people aren't as cooperative you might wish. Here's the hell scenario:

> You have great relationships in the buying unit you've been serving for 4 years, but you don't know many of the decision makers and influencers in other parts of the customer's organization. In fact, you're not sure whom you should know. The operations managers working with the customer have their own contacts, but they jealously guard them and aren't forthcoming when you ask for information. You get the sense that they're protecting their turf. For instance, you don't know when your operations managers meet with their customer contacts, although they sometimes call you afterward with "oh, by the way" information. You're frequently blindsided in bids by information your own people either should have known but didn't or knew but didn't tell you. Finally, there appear to be huge gaps in your network of customer relationships, but it's difficult to orchestrate efforts to build those relationships because everyone you talk to in your company thinks it isn't part of his or her job. You would appeal to your senior management, but they don't seem to have good top-to-top relationships either, although rumor has it that your CEO met the customer's CEO once at a charity function.

I've lived this nightmare more times than I want to recall. Maybe you have, too. A challenging but critically important part of account management is constructing the right network of relationships between your company and the customer's organization. You also help the executives and professionals in your company build personal trust-based relationships with their counterparts. Over time, and through this complex net of relationships, you then build institutional trust.

Figure 15-3 illustrates what I referred to earlier in the book as zippered relationships between the two organizations. Trust-based, working relationships should exist at multiple levels between your company and the customer organization, and it's the account manager's job to ensure that these links exist at every relevant level, between every critical function, and with all the movers and shakers in both organizations. In this regard, the account manager is a matchmaker who insists that the right people know each other, interact often enough to build trust and understanding, and are motivated to *make things happen* in both organizations.

Here are some best practices for constructing a zippered network:

- *Know how your customer is wired.* Clearly, a customer's organization chart never tells the real story about how authority and influence are distributed throughout the organization. To truly understand any organization, you need to fathom its informal structure and its actual patterns of communication and influence. In *Corporate Cultures*, Terrence Deal and Allen Kennedy

Figure 15-3. A Zippered Customer–Supplier Network

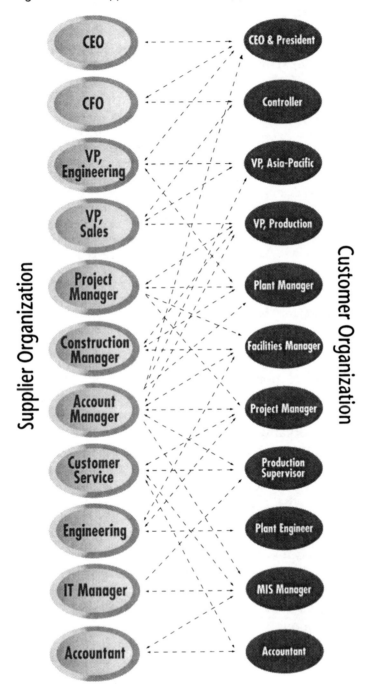

argue that "90 percent of what goes on in an organization has nothing to do with formal events. The real business goes on in the cultural netwo
real organizational life, some people are dead-ended in positions and have less actual influence than their titles imply. Some people are figureheads. Others are deemed poor managers but are influential thinkers and have considerable impact on decisions although they are not in management positions. Some are good performers but don't have the CEO's ear; others, for whatever reason, are more trusted by the CEO and other senior executives and tend to have more influence on decisions and events.

Also, every organization has its cadre of rising stars. They aren't always easy to identify because they don't yet hold critical positions. They are the ones given the most important projects. They're assigned to the task forces and are called into the critical meetings. They're on the mental waiting lists of the people who can promote them when openings become available. To be connected with the right people in a customer's organization, you have to know these rising stars, and you must be able to identify the actual patterns of power and influence. In short, you have to know how the customer's organization is *wired*. Figure 15-4 shows a "wiring diagram," which depicts the formal organizational structure with the informal structure imposed on it. Obviously, you want to have relationships with the real movers and shakers, particularly those people who are moving up in the organization. They are today's influencers and will be tomorrow's decision makers.

- *Know how your company is wired.* Your company is no different than the customer's organization. It also has an informal structure, a "cultural network." It has both current stars and rising stars, and these are the people you want to be connected with their influential counterparts in the customer's organization. A wise account manager understands how both organizations actually work and who are the real movers and shakers—and then arranges it so that these people get to know one another.
- *Identify the right functional and political connections.* Beyond the informal network I've just discussed, it's important to know which functions should be networked. If there are no movers and shakers in a critical functional area in your company or the customer's organization, then you must forge the links anyway. Certain functions must be linked no matter what. Similarly, there may be important political connections to be made, like the link between your regional vice president for South America, for instance, and the customer's country manager in Brazil. Some relationships are politically important regardless of any other considerations.
- *Determine who has the right chemistry.* A subtle but important consideration in relationship building is determining which people have the right chemistry. Here we enter the sometimes murky world of personal operating styles and interests, and there's probably more art than science to making the right match. Nonetheless, you should consider the interpersonal factors that help

---

7. Terrence E. Deal, and Allen A. Kennedy, *Corporate Cultures: The Rites and Rituals of Corporate Life* (Reading, MA: Addison-Wesley Publishing Company, 1982), p. 86.

Figure 15-4. Wiring Diagram of a Typical Customer Organization

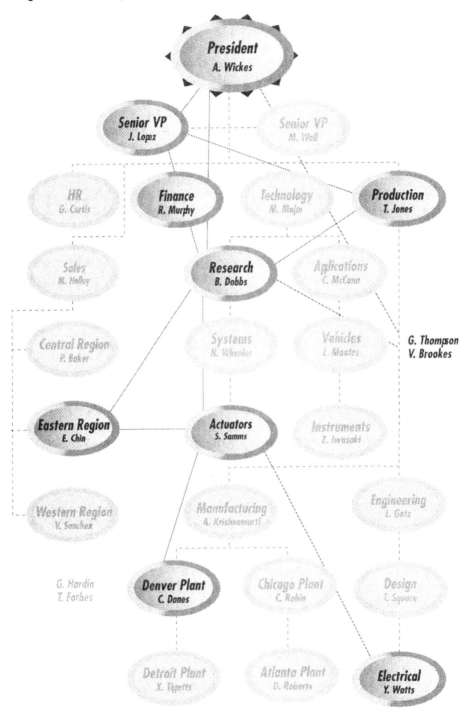

different people relate to one another and think about whether you're trying to make the right matches.

For example, if the customer's vice president is ex-military, compulsively well organized, conservative, and hard charging, you probably don't want to try to build a relationship between that person and one of your executives who is liberal, impulsive, disorganized, and laid back. It's best to match operating styles, interests, and backgrounds for the simple reason that people tend to relate better to others who are like themselves. The key questions are: Will these people like each other? Will they find a basis for relating to one another in ways that build personal trust? Do they have enough in common to forge a personal relationship?

At one point, Xerox's global account management group implemented a formal process to identify their executive's interests and styles and then match them to customer executives who had similar interests and styles.[8] They found the effort useful but difficult to keep up and eventually abandoned the formal part of that effort, although they still tried to find the right matches. However you do it, it's important to link people who have the right chemistry.

- *Identify the best relationship builders.* Some senior executives are excellent relationship builders and are naturally good with people; others have attained their positions because they have superior financial or technical skills but have no interest in people or simply lack good people skills. Obviously, it's best to have your better relationship builders involved in your customer network. If that's not always possible, then you may need to work more closely with the executives who aren't naturally talented in relationship building and coach them on their people skills—an effort that usually is difficult, to say the least, because their poor people skills makes them hard to work with.

- *Determine each customer executive's expectations.* So far in this list I've been focusing on finding the right people to link together in the relationship network you need to have. It's important also to know what customers expect from these relationships. Who in your organization does each of them want to know? And why? What do they expect to gain from their connections? Networks are inherently valuable to businesspeople because they enhance your knowledge base, capacity to solve problems, access to resources, and sense of connection with the broader business world. Networks are a source of power for people. The more extensive their network, the more reach they have. So in helping customers build their networks, you add value to them as professionals. But it's important to know what they expect from their relationships with people in your company: Information sharing? Problem-solving assistance? Thinking partnerships? Expert solutions? Industry knowledge?

- *Build bonds with both people and positions.* How many times have you had to update your address book because names, addresses, phone numbers, and

8. David A. Potter, Vice President Global Accounts Marketing, Xerox Corporation, in "How to Develop a Successful Executive Sponsor Program," speech given at the 34th Annual Conference, National Account Management Association, San Diego, California, May 4, 1998.

everything else changed? Building a complex, zippered network between your company and the customer's organization is challenging enough. What makes it even more difficult is that the situation is constantly changing. Networks are dynamic because the people in them are promoted, reassigned, transferred, fired, and die. So you have to prepare for the departures and reassignments in both organizations. An interesting way to look at it is that you have to build your network both with the current people in various positions and with the positions themselves. Let's imagine, for instance, that your customer's country manager in Spain is Rodrigo Dominguez. You need to have a relationship not only with Señor Dominguez but also with the country manager position, which means that when Dominguez leaves that role, you are poised to develop a relationship with the person taking his place. Ideally, you already know who his replacement is and have already forged a relationship with that person. One of the primary reasons for building early relationships with the customer's young rising stars is that they already know and trust you when they are promoted into power positions.

Relationship management is one of an account manager's most important roles. As you can see from this discussion, it's not a trivial matter. To simplify this discussion, I haven't mentioned your competitors, but an important concern in relationship management is how well your competitors are connected. Who do they know? How well are they networked? Who are their allies and detractors? If your competitors are smart, they will be working hard to build their customer networks with the same people you've identified as the movers and shakers in the customer organization. So you'll be competing for face time, meeting availability, interest, customer loyalty, and personal trust. You're going to need all the help you can get from the people in your own company. If they're indifferent in any way, then not only will you be caught in continuous white water, you'll be paddling upstream against powerful currents.

I began this section by describing the hell scenario. Here's the heaven scenario:

> Your company entrusts you—the account manager—to be the focal point for building the network of relationships with your strategic account, and the executives and other professionals in your company are cooperative. You've analyzed the customer's organization and have a good understanding of how they actually are wired. You know who the movers and shakers are and where and with whom you have to build relationships. Moreover, you've thought about each person's operating style and interests and have mapped out the ideal pattern of relationships between people in both organizations.
>
> Making this network a reality is challenging but you do it by arranging meetings, making introductions, doing site visits with other people in your company, and arranging for meetings and social events involving your senior executives and theirs. Your senior people are committed to building relationships with their counterparts and are adept at doing so. Although the landscape

is constantly changing, you can anticipate the personnel shifts and suffer no loss of institutional trust as these changes occur and new people are brought into your relationship net.

If only it were that easy. It's not, of course, which is why relationship management is an ongoing challenge. Done well, it helps build strong personal and institutional trust, which positions your company for the best possible type of relationship with your strategic account.

— 16 —

Managing Information

The currency in account management is information. It's your primary medium of exchange, the value you create for your company by talking to and learning about the customer, and the value you create for your customers by informing them about your capabilities and using knowledge to help solve their problems and fulfill their needs. In strategic accounts, there is a nearly constant flow of information between various people in your company and various people in the customer's organization. The account manager's job, to borrow a metaphor from Al Gore, is to direct traffic on this information highway between the two organizations.

Clearly, not all information has value. In this age of information overload, we are bombarded daily with new information, most of which is superfluous. If you're like me, you can give it only a passing glance before deciding whether it's valuable to you. By some estimates, the amount of knowledge in the world is doubling every 10 years—and the rate is accelerating. No wonder it seems impossible to keep up. If we consider the impact on customers, it becomes obvious that an account manager's mission is not to contribute to the customer's information glut but to provide just *the right amount of information at the right time*—a challenging prospect even in the best of circumstances because you are only one of many sources of information for customers and you compete for their attention.

What is the right amount of information at the right time? Information has value only if it helps customers do their jobs better, understand more about their business environment, appreciate the strengths and limitations of their plans and technologies, diagnose and solve their problems, make better decisions, and track and evaluate their results. For information to have value to them, it must be both *relevant* and *timely*. These are key concepts for account managers because most of the information customers receive fails both tests.

Relevance means that customers need the information, that they can apply it to their problems or opportunities, that it enhances their understanding of the problems or gives them more insight into their options, and that it changes the way they think or impacts their decisions. My own experience suggests that much of what salespeople tell customers is irrelevant, largely because it's not meaningful to the specific issues customers are addressing when they receive the information. The standard brochures, product descriptions, and lists of features and benefits are too unfocused. They're like blizzards. Salespeople dump everything they have on customers hoping that *something* sticks. When you're a customer, you're inundated with this stuff from numerous suppliers, and whatever isn't relevant creates noise. To make information relevant, you have to appreciate the full context in which customers are operating—their aspirations and concerns, their view of the big picture, the niggling details that are bothering them, their reactions to their current performance numbers, and so forth. Then you can select the information that truly is relevant within the context of their current thinking.

Timeliness also is crucial. Because of the information glut most businesspeople experience, information that arrives either too late *or too early* has less value. If it's too late, they obviously can't act on it; if it's too early, the information may be forgotten or taken out of context when they finally need it. Timely information has value because it arrives precisely when it's needed to solve the problem, and customers can act on it to enhance their decisions. I've known a number of account managers, however, who follow the strategic bombing approach to information management. They seem to feel that if they saturate their customers with information long enough, loud enough, and often enough, their customers can't possibly miss the message. But carpet bombing is wasteful, confusing, and noisy. The essential messages often are buried in the rubble. If you follow this approach, you're like the boy who cried wolf too often. You desensitize customers to your message, and they don't hear it when it's important that they do. It's far better to identify what's truly important for customers at the moment and then to provide just enough information in context for them to be smarter.

When Howard Weinstein was assigned the Simons account, he began by conducting what he called an "account audit." He reviewed the existing contracts; the outstanding proposals; and the account records, which, to his delight, were exhaustive and very informative. He also talked to everyone in his company (R.J. Consumer Products) who had contacts with the customer, and he met with all the key customers identified in his predecessors account plan. His audit revealed that R.J. Consumer Products was well positioned with Simons but that business had not grown significantly in the account for the past 4 years, although by Howard's estimates the account potential was much higher. He felt that his company was leaving a lot on the table and at first glance couldn't understand why they hadn't been able to grow the business.

Howard's company produced and distributed a broad range of electronic consumer products—from satellite receivers to handheld children's games. How-

continued

ever, Simons' retail outlets carried only 17.5 percent of R.J.'s total line, and they had never used any of R.J.'s innovative promotional services. Then, as Howard learned more about the account, he felt he'd discovered the cause: most of Simons' executives were unaware of the breadth of R.J.'s services for retailers and many were ignorant of R.J.'s total product line. Howard found it most disturbing that they didn't know R.J. could customize its products for Simons and create unique "signature" products that, for other retailers, had stimulated consumer interest and increased sales by as much as 22 percent.

Howard's solution was to blitz Simons' executives with information. With help from R.J.'s marketing group, he initiated a massive campaign with catalog mailings, a series of "did you know?" letters, on-site product demonstrations, and mailings of third-party product comparison charts showing all R.J.'s various products stacked up against competing products. Howard personally visited more than sixty buyers for Simons' outlets across the country and gave them comprehensive briefings on the full range of R.J. products and services.

When his efforts yielded only a modest increase in sales, Howard was puzzled. As he diagnosed the situation, however, several errors became apparent. First, his blitz coincided with the major consumer electronics show, which all the buyers attended, so they were deluged with information on competing products. He'd just added to the glut. Second, each of the buyers had different needs based on the patterns of consumer sales for their outlets. He hadn't taken that into consideration when he sent them information. Third, he'd sent so much information at once that he'd overwhelmed many of them. He found that some had filed his catalogs, promising to get back to it when they had time, and others had remembered getting the information but had passed it on to their assistants. Howard wondered if he could have done anything to create less impact.

To follow up, he profiled each of the buyers and tried to determine their information needs. He created a master calendar showing each of the annual events that impacted their purchasing decisions and determined their buying cycles. Then he planned an information campaign for each buyer, and his plans differed from one buyer to the next, sometimes considerably. A buyer in Kansas City, for instance, was methodical in examining competing products and purchasing only those lines with a proven track record. For her, Howard provided monthly and quarterly sales figures on various product lines for other retail outlets in the Missouri–Kansas region and emphasized the most successful lines for consumers in her area. By contrast, a buyer in San Francisco was always looking for innovative products and was willing to try new things. He was a self-described "gadget man," a hands-on buyer who wanted to play with the merchandise and feel the difference between competing products before buying. This buyer was excited by the prospect of customized products for his stores, so Howard flew out to meet with him. The information Howard brought included two dozen samples of customized products R.J. had created for other customers.

In the end, Howard learned that he had to have a different approach for every buyer. Each needed different information at different times, and he was most successful when he met their information needs. His master calendar became a living part of his account plan.

It's important for account managers to recognize the enormous value information has—and how it can strengthen their position with their customers. As the account manager, you are the conduit of information between the two organizations. You can connect customers with the experts and executives in your company who can help them. You know how your products work and how to apply them, fix them, customize them, and use them most effectively. You know how other organizations have used your products. You know what benefits they've received and how they've measured successful implementations of your products. The knowledge you have of your products, industry, markets, and customers is invaluable because, by and large, your customers don't know these things nearly as well as you do.

Moreover, because you talk to people in other parts of their organization (and perhaps throughout the world), you often know more about their organization than they do. It seems ironic, but if you are talking to people throughout the customer's organization (as you should be), you usually are more aware of strategies, initiatives, and problems in other parts of their organization than any local customer is.

Here is a *short* list of the information you have that can be valuable to customers:

- What your products are and how they can be modified or customized for them
- How the features of your products benefit them and meet their specific needs; how the product can be used in different situations or for other applications; how to use your product most efficiently and effectively
- How to make your products more effective or longer lasting through training, service, or additional products
- How products and services in your industry are evolving; what features and benefits will be available soon; how upcoming innovations can benefit them
- What's possible in using your products; what other customers have done; what's not possible; what the real limitations are
- What the strengths and weaknesses of your competitors' products are—and what to be cautious about in evaluating their approaches or solutions
- How your customer's competitors are changing; what products they're using; how their technologies or strategies are evolving
- What's happening in other parts of the customer's own organization; how other units in their organization have used your products and benefited from them
- What their own senior people have told your senior people
- How upcoming legislation, regulations, or other regulatory changes could impact them, their use of your products, or their consumers
- How to buy your type of product; what questions to ask; how to evaluate all suppliers and products of this type

As you can see, this is a formidable list. The information at your disposal as an account manager makes you invaluable as a consultant to your customers. When you add your capacity as a relationship builder and networker and your ability to help customers solve their business problems, you offer substantial value to customers who are open to receiving what you can provide, who are willing to disclose enough information about themselves for you to know how to help them, and who are receptive to supplier alliances or partnerships, even informally.

Of course, you first have to know what information you have, and this is no trivial matter. In large, complex corporations, it's not easy to discover what information is available inside your own company. First, you have to know the information exists. Then you have to discover who has it. Then you have to get it from them. I've known account managers who were in place for 3 years and still were surprised to learn that their company had done a particular project for the customer some years ago—and they learned that by talking to the customer! In its quest to document this kind of information, one large engineering firm created a sophisticated database for all projects. They discovered after several years of effort and much hand wringing by executives that the system was too detailed and time consuming for people to maintain, and it fell into disuse. The most they were able to do was to keep a list of projects and project managers. Then if people needed more details, they had to track down the project manager and ask questions. It ought to be easier than it is, but a fact of organizational life is that one of the most difficult things to manage is internal information.

Figure 16-1. Mutually Beneficial Information Flow

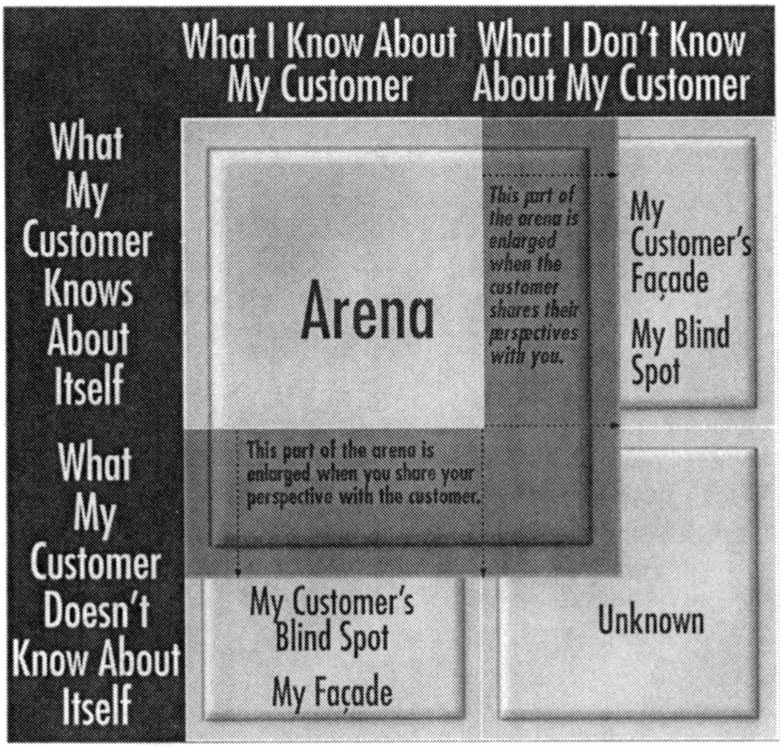

Think of yourself as the traffic director on the information highway between your company and the customer's organization. As I said earlier, you have to know what information your customers need—what's valuable to them. In the ideal information exchange, you give them deep private information on your own company and its products that educates them and helps them best determine how to meet their needs. In turn, they give you deep private information about themselves that educates you on their needs and helps you craft the most efficient, cost-effective solutions for them. This is reminiscent of the Johari window concept, which I introduced in chapter 15. As shown in Figure 16-1, the ideal exchange of information decreases *both* your blind spots and your façades and makes you better, more trusting partners.

To accomplish this, you have to help customers develop their information base while simultaneously developing your own, and you have to maintain and distribute information effectively. Account managers sometimes use an information plan to help them organize and manage this process.

Informing Customers About Your Competitors

For years now, VISA has attacked American Express through television ads, pointing out with glee the places where VISA cards are accepted and American Express cards are not. How wise is it to attack your competitors by name? Clearly, executives at VISA believe that it pays to do so because they keep running the ads. Generally, however, attacking competitors by name is risky, and in some industries and professions, it would be considered very bad form to do so.

The attitude among most buyers in large organizations is that the products and bundle of services they receive from suppliers should stand on their own merit, and a supplier who attacks competitors by name seems desperate and provincial. Would you want to do business with someone who practices those tactics? Most of us probably experience similar revulsion during election campaigns when we see the grossly negative ads being run by some candidates. It cheapens the process and reflects as badly on the attacker—if not more so—than on the target.

Consequently, there are a few basic rules for handling competitor information:

• If customers are misinformed about your capabilities and mistakenly believe that a competitor has greater capabilities, then it is appropriate to correct the impression, particularly if the customer has raised the issue and discussed your competitor's products. However, keep the focus on the product comparison.

continued

> • If you have objective, third-party product comparisons that favor your company and its products, then it is appropriate to ensure that your customers receive copies of the comparisons.
> • It's effective to help customers become better informed about product capabilities and smarter about selecting products and suppliers, so if you can educate them about what to look for and then tell them how to find the comparative product information, then you've helped them make the right decision.
> • One of the most effective ways to address your competitors' weaknesses is to *ghost* them. You ghost their weaknesses when you highlight the area of weakness and talk about how important it is to the customer (assuming that this is true). For example, if your competitor does not have a local office or experience in the country, then you could highlight the importance of having local offices and in-country experience—just don't mention that your customer doesn't have these things. By trying to elevate the importance of the issue, you make your competitors' weaknesses more apparent—and alarming—to customers.

Developing the Customer's Information Base

The first rule of information management is to keep your customers well informed. In essence, you want to build their information base so they'll make smarter, more informed decisions about your products and solutions. Keeping customers informed usually is one of your account objectives, and you may have action plans in place for accomplishing this. However, it involves more than just sending them technical bulletins and giving capability demonstrations. Developing their information base means helping them build their knowledge in your product and expertise areas and, perhaps more importantly, reducing their uncertainty about you and your products. Remember that customers are deluged with information from a variety of sources, including your competitors. The resulting cacophony is noisy and confusing, with much conflicting and incompatible information. The simple, clear messages you want to convey can become lost or distorted unless you find ways to reduce the noise level.

Managing Knowledge Building

As Figure 16-2 shows, there should be an extensive, two-way flow of information between the two organizations. One of the primary purposes of

Figure 16-2. Information Highway Between Your Company and Your Strategic Account

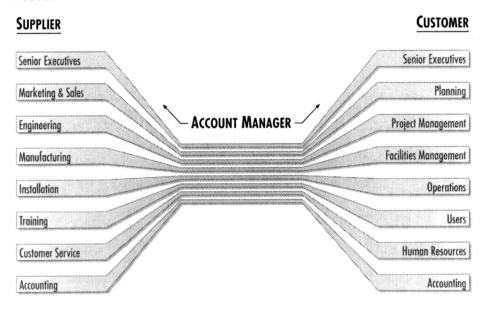

the information flowing from your people to the customer's people is to help build their knowledge of your product areas and the ways in which your products and services solve their problems or enable them to positively impact their business. To accomplish this goal, you should answer the following questions:

- *What are each person's information needs?* You don't provide information to an institution, you provide it to individuals within the institution. So you have to know who in the customer's organization needs the information and what they need. In effect, you have to analyze each person's information needs. What do they want to know more about? What have they asked for? What's relevant to their job function or role? What don't they know? Where are they misinformed or uninformed? What information would enlighten them about your capabilities and their options and solutions? Further, you have to know what constitutes good information for each person. Technical people generally like to see numbers. They want logical arguments presented with facts. Many nontechnical people and busy executives prefer conclusions, highlights, and summaries.
- *What is each person's information style?* How does each person prefer to receive information? Some people want it in written form so they can study it at their leisure. Others prefer to see demonstrations. Some want proofs, technical specifications, and test results. Some prefer to be briefed, and in briefings some people want a formal presentation whereas others prefer an informal, interactive dialogue. Everyone has an information style, and you impact people more when you recognize and adapt to their preferred style.

- *How will each person use the information?* The information you give people—and the form it takes—may depend on how they're going to use it. Will they use it to write or modify their specifications or evaluation criteria? Will they use it to brief their own managers on their options? Will it become part of their plans? Impact their schedule? Help them make decisions on future directions? Once you know how they'll use the information, you can adapt it for their needs. For example, if your contact is going to use your information in a presentation to her senior executives, then you can package it for that purpose and orient your information toward the needs and interests of that senior audience.
- *When does each person prefer to receive the information?* If you give some people the information too soon, they file it away and don't attend to it because they're too preoccupied when they receive it. I've visited with customers 6 months after I sent them something they asked for only to discover that they hadn't even opened the package yet. These types of customers are impulse-actors—they take in information moment by moment and either act on it right away or file it and forget it. Other people want briefings very early, and if you send them information they will read it even though they don't intend to act on it for months. These people are reader-thinkers—they read constantly, absorb the information, and let it gestate in their minds for months before acting. Timing is a complicated and difficult skill to perfect because it relies on intimate knowledge of each customer's working style and the stresses and "information density" of their jobs.

A best practice for managing information flow to customers is to create a map of each key person in the customer's organization, what information they need, and the source of that information. Figure 16-3 offers an example.

To this point, I've focused on providing information as a means of building the customer's knowledge of your products and solutions and their applications to the customer's business. But if you are nothing more than an information source your impact on the customer will be limited. To achieve higher impact, you also must stimulate their thinking by helping them apply the information: challenging their assumptions, encouraging them to explore alternatives, and asking questions that enable them to see the implications of their actions. When you simply provide information, you're in a *tell* mode, and your customers play a more *passive*, listening role, which is less stimulating. When you're in an *ask* mode, they are forced to be *active* respondents and partners in the dialogue, which is more interesting for them and enlightening for you. Neil Rackham, who has done extensive research on selling effectiveness and customer responses to sales messages, formalized this approach in his SPIN selling technique. SPIN is one methodology for asking a sequence of questions designed to stimulate customers' thinking processes and to help them identify their explicit needs and appreciate more fully the implications of not fulfilling those needs.[1]

---

1. Neil Rackham, *SPIN Selling* (New York: McGraw-Hill), 1988.

Figure 16-3. Information Needs Map

Contact	Information Needs	Sources	Comments
Jerry Steiner, VP, ASPAC	■ Traffic analysis past five years ■ Analysis of route plans and discounts for ASPAC shipping ■ Warehousing services available in Tokyo	■ Char Baker ■ Tom J. & Monica S. ■ Dennis Scheer	Jerry wants to see a detailed analysis of their alternatives for shipping from West Coast to Southeast Asia. He doesn't need this information until Jan. 6, when they begin their planning cycle
Melinda MacMillan	Comparison of scheduling software for tracking intermodal shipments	Hugh Nilsen or Barb Weber	Melinda's a hands-on person; need to give her comparative demos
Ron Zapata	Revised accident report for loss on 10/1 near Sisters, Oregon	Jane Petrie	He wasn't happy with our initial report; Jane will revise to include details on safety systems
Sue Sbuelz	■ Wants to see driver hours on traffic reports ■ Could benefit from seeing cost breakdowns on loading/unloading charges	Jay Figueroa	None
Nick Henke	Brochure on new refrigeration systems and safeguards	RLS	Sent on 11/14; need to follow up within three weeks
Ramon Glanz, Cathie Focht, Robert Ma, Pat Goldbach	New video on 2-day guaranteed coast-to-coast deliveries	RLS	They're skeptical about the guarantees; need to follow up video with site visit; take Neil Harris
Andreas Berthold	Proposal on customizing their consignment system	Steve Batz and RLS	Not a firm need yet, but Andreas is interested in learning more about the options. They need to know how to make their system faster and more efficient. Follwo up with Steve; need proposal by next Wednesday
Patrik Kubicka	Our capabilities and performance records for Southern California; capacity for next 18 months	Hsiang Tsen	Patrik is new to the job; needs a full capabilities briefing. Find out from him: ■ Background; experience with shippers ■ Thoughts on new job, directions he plans to take ■ Biases; favorite shippers?

The highest form of knowledge building with customers occurs when you are truly a thought partner with them. As a thought partner, you help them explore their issues and concerns in an objective, unbiased way by asking thought-provoking questions that challenge them to consider their options, explore the implications of their actions, and think more creatively about how they might solve their problems. This approach is clearly at odds with the traditional buyer–seller relationships in which sellers present their wares and the object is to close the deal. In high-trust strategic account relationships, sellers act as consultants to, and advocates for, their customers, and the object is to find the right solutions for the customers. As a thought partner, you're more of a facilitator than a seller.

Managing Noise and Uncertainty

Life would be easy if you could visit the customer, assemble all the key decision makers and influencers, have their undivided attention, and convey your message clearly in a dialogue that helps them identify and implement the right solution. Typically, however, you can't assemble the right people. Some are off site, have conflicting meetings, are on vacation, or are pulled away at the last moment. Those who are present often have many other things on their mind; are distracted by other priorities; have conflicting opinions about what should or can be done; or have been meeting with your competitors, whose views on the subject obviously are contrary to your own. The result is noise and uncertainty.

According to Jeremy Campbell, "noise is anything which corrupts the integrity of a message: static in a radio set, garbling in a printed text, distortion of the picture on a television screen."[2] I think noise also includes conflicting views on how to solve a problem and on the value and application of your products. No matter how well you communicate with your customers, there will always be a certain amount of noise in the system—misinformation, partial truths, emotional biases, propaganda from your competitors, past experiences that affect their judgment today, and conflicting opinions among themselves. A large part of your challenge as an account manager is to reduce this noise and to provide clarity in their understanding so they have the right perceptions of you and your products and solutions.

Noise introduces uncertainty, which creates confusion and delays action—or, worse, causes customers to choose your competitors. In complex strategic account relationships, you have to manage noise across a spectrum of people, departments, business units, and geographic locations. This can be a daunting prospect, because your competitors are working those same hallways, and there may be people in your customer's own organization who think that they can solve the problem or meet the need internally. Noise abounds. To reduce it, keep these principles in mind:

- *Information has a short shelf life.* How much of the information you received last year do you remember now? How much do you remember from last week? Unless information affects you in a dramatic or personal way, you tend to file and forget most of it. Information deteriorates with age. It loses its impact and relevance. The context changes and is reshaped by other in-

---

2. Jeremy Campbell, *Grammatical Man* (New York: Simon and Schuster, 1982), p. 26.

formation and events. Just because you sent them that report last year doesn't mean they remember it, value it, or will act on it. To reduce noise, you must ensure that information is current and is sent relatively close to the moment customers need it.

- *Clarity improves with simple, redundant messages.* Redundant messages are easier to remember because the core information is repeated and reinforced. To prevent customers from reacting adversely to repeated messages, don't say the same thing the same way all the time. Vary the format and medium of the message—but find ways to repeat the information you want customers to remember clearly. We've probably all seen powerful advertising that succeeds because of its strong, simple message—for example: "Where's the beef?" Similarly, some proposals are powerful because they address the customer's key issues and concerns in simple, dramatic ways—over and over. Themes are powerful because they introduce redundancy and thus reduce noise and uncertainty.
- *Interesting messages have more impact.* Information is more memorable and impactful if it's new, surprising, or interesting in some way. If we've heard the message before or it follows a familiar pattern, we tend to tune out. It's like driving down a long, familiar highway. Often you don't remember taking the trip. Many selling messages are this way because they don't convey new information in novel ways. It's a case of the bland being spoken by the boring. Or worse, they're so self-focused and self-promoting that they antagonize customers with their hype and hyperbole. Genuinely interesting messages are, first of all, focused on the customer, not on your company or its products. People are always more interested in their organization and what directly affects them.[3] Also, the message should be about something new, different, or unusual. It should educate those who receive it, show them a new application, talk about how someone else just used the product effectively, or link to something customers will find interesting.[4]
- *Information must appear in context.* To reduce noise, the information must be relevant to customers. Remember that customers receive information within

---

3. This is why direct mailings are considered good if they generate only a 1 percent response rate. Direct mail pieces can't be rewritten and customized for each recipient, so by necessity they focus entirely on the sender's products or services. That's why 99 percent of direct mail is thrown into the trash.

4. Michael Hume and the LoDo Air Band from Denver taught me something about making messages interesting. At the time I was writing this book there was a commercial on television for Rogaine, a men's hair care product. The commercial, featuring Utah Jazz great Karl Malone, is forgettable, and I hadn't thought much about the product until I heard one of LoDo's catchy tunes (sung to the tune of Eric Clapton's *Cocaine)*:

> If you used to have hair, but now there ain't nothing there, Rogaine.
> If you used to look fine, but now you're starting to shine, Rogaine.
> It's all right, it's all right, it's all right, Rogaine.
> If you check out your dome, and it's shining like chrome, Rogaine.
> If the mirror reflects, a bowling ball with a neck, Rogaine.
> It's all right, it's all right, it's all right, Rogaine.
> If you'd like to have fuzz, where it formerly was, Rogaine.
> You can be a new man, if it's on your health plan, Rogaine.
> It's all right, it's all right, it's all right, Rogaine.

Used with permission by Michael Hume.

the context of their daily work and lives. This context includes the complex interplay of knowledge, information, and meaning that derives from what they do in their jobs, including their ongoing fears, joys, problems, challenges, and opportunities—few of which in the normal course of things involve you. So, in a sense, what you communicate to them either is always out of context or is a very small part of their total picture. When you provide new information, a simple question goes through their heads: "So what?" How and why is this information useful? How does it relate to what I'm doing? Why do I need to know it? How can it help me?

You must establish the context for them. You must tell them what it means and why it's important to them. Most salespeople make one or two mistakes. First, they present information about themselves entirely from their own context. I've seen it a thousand times in bids and proposals— here's who *we* are, here's what *we* do, here's what *our* product is capable of, here's why *we're* great, and so on. Or salespeople fail to build a context and assume that the relevance of their products to customers somehow is self-evident. But customers have a different world view and different priorities; they bring an entirely different set of experiences to interpreting the information and generally don't see it precisely as the seller intended.

You should never allow customers to interpret your information on their own. Create the meaning for them by putting it in their business context. By itself, information does not create meaning; interpretation does. When you cite features (information) *and* benefits (relevance), you go part way toward establishing meaning, but to complete the journey you should show how those benefits solve your customer's current business problems in the most efficient and cost-effective way. In short, the information you provide should add value by helping customers make decisions.

Telephone billing statements that analyze your call patterns and show you how to reduce the cost of your bills by timing your calls more effectively are adding value through information. Similarly, Amazon.com (an Internet-based book service) tracks which types of books you purchase and recommends other books you might like. Amazon also provides reviews of many of its books and lists the other books that buyers of any particular book also bought. Learningworks.com, another Internet publisher, offers on-line views of many of its products so buyers can sample the products before buying them. In each case, the sellers are adding value through information that helps buyers determine the relevance of the information to them and thus make more informed buying decisions.

What if part of your message is bad news? What if your product has limitations or it can't be applied or customized the way customers would like? In my experience, it's best to be forthright and not to filter information. Customers may not want to hear something, but sooner or later they'll get the bad news, and if it hasn't come from you, they'll distrust you in the future. So the information you provide should always be accurate and complete.

It may be useful to think of building the customer's knowledge base as *impression management*. In sales, what counts is what customers perceive, and they may misperceive your company and its capabilities. That's an impression you should correct. They may be listening to your competitors and believe that there's little difference between your solutions and theirs. That's another impression you should correct. Information is one of the most important resources you have, and it's the account manager's responsibility to manage its flow to the customer so that the right impressions are created at the right time. When I talk about impression management, I don't mean to imply that you should use smoke and mirrors to fool customers. Quite the contrary, you should convey the right facts from the right people in your company to ensure that customers are well and correctly informed and therefore can make better decisions.

Working With Difficult Customers

Some years ago, I was helping a client prepare a bid for a major engineering project in a foreign country. The client's prospect was the foreign government because the industry was nationalized. Our suspicions became aroused when the government's contracting officials began asking for very detailed technical information. In particular, they asked what approach my client would take, how they would solve numerous technical problems, what materials and equipment they would use, how they would organize the project, how they would price it, and so on. Asking for this type of information in a bid is not unusual, but the amount of detail the government wanted was extraordinary, including preliminary engineering drawings. My client considered them an attractive potential key account, so they bent over backwards responding to the customer's many requests for information. In the end, the government didn't select my client or any of the other bidders, many of whom had spent millions of dollars responding to the bid request. Instead, the foreign government did the project themselves.

After getting all that free consulting, the customer didn't need any of the bidders.

Obviously, there are unscrupulous customers. Sometimes they use your information to teach themselves how to solve the problem. Other times, they feed your technical information to the supplier they actually intend to give the job to so that supplier can become smarter. And, at times, they ask you to bid so they can beat down someone else on price. You usually can't tell whether you're dealing with dishonest customers until they've manipulated you, but in the worse of cases you can refuse to work with them again. It's also fair to ask what they intend to do with the information. It's fair to insist on a nondisclosure agreement. It's fair to talk to them about any instances in

continued

> which you weren't treated appropriately. And, in the most egregious of cases, such as the one I just described, it's fair to document what's taken place and to sue them.
>
> If you've worked with a customer long enough for them to become a strategic account, then presumably these issues either have never arisen or have been resolved. But sometimes unscrupulous people rise to power in customer organizations that have had a high-trust relationship with you, and you need to remain alert and be willing to act if the trust base that you've established starts eroding because of unscrupulous behavior by a customer contact.

You also should be willing to confide in customers, to give them information you don't give to everyone, or to give the information to your key customers first. When you confide in customers, you enlarge your arena and encourage them to confide in you. Consider releasing information to them before releasing it publicly. This strategy actually makes them special, but more importantly it makes them *feel* special.

Finally, avoid using information as a form of barter. Don't set up a tit-for-tat information exchange. If you do that, you establish a transactional relationship, which will lower trust in the long run. Instead, use information as a way to enlarge the arena for both of you and to invite greater disclosure on your customer's part. The more disclosure on both sides, the greater the trust between you.

According to Jeremy Campbell, "Chaos is the easiest, most predictable state, and it lasts indefinitely. Order is improbable and hard to create."[5] If you don't constantly manage information flow to the customer and manage their impressions, what they know and perceive about your company and its capabilities and solutions will become chaotic and disorganized. How many times have you lost some business with strategic account customers because they had the wrong impression about your company or your products, did not have all the facts, or were acting on misleading information they got from some other source? It doesn't have to occur very often before you realize the value of information management.

Developing Your Own Information Base

The account manager should be the repository of information on the customer, not just during account planning but throughout the life of the relationship. It's common sense that the person who manages the relationship

---

5. Jeremy Campbell, *Grammatical Man* (New York: Simon and Schuster, 1982), p. 42.

should be aware of everything that's happening in the account and should be a source of customer information to others in the company. Yet, as strange as it may seem, in some companies I've worked with the account managers suffer benign neglect from technical managers and other professionals who meet with key contacts in the customer organization and pick up vital information but fail to pass it on to the account managers. This kind of neglect would be unthinkable in companies with established account management programs and a strong customer and sales orientation. Here's how it should work:

- *Centralized knowledge base.* The account manager should collect or receive, organize, interpret, and disseminate all information on the strategic account. Clearly, the technical areas that serve the customer should maintain their own information bases, but their information should be replicated in the central knowledge base maintained by the account manager.
- *Intelligence needs.* The account manager should always know what information the company needs from the customer. A best practice for managing this process is to keep an ongoing *intelligence needs list*, which is simply a listing of what intelligence is needed and who can potentially acquire it (see Figure 16-4). If you systematize your intelligence gathering, you stand a better chance of acquiring all the customer information you do need without acquiring irrelevant information.
- *Contact planning.* People in your company who are going to visit the customer should contact the account manager prior to the visit, and the account manager should brief them on current events in the account. They should determine *jointly* what information the person visiting the customer should try to get. In short, each visit should have information goals developed by answering these questions: Where are our knowledge gaps? What don't we know? What can we learn from this contact? What information would he or she have? Effective salespeople typically develop objectives for their meetings with customers. It's useful for them to do the same for technical people and senior executives who are meeting with their counterparts, especially when those people are meeting with deep private sources.
- *Contact reports.* All information coming from the customer organization should be copied to the account manager, no matter who receives it. This should be a standing company policy, applicable to the chief executive officer and everyone else. People throughout the company shouldn't call the account manager every time they talk to a customer contact, but if they learn anything new during a visit or phone call with a customer, they should pass that information to the account manager. Some companies ask that anyone who contacts a customer write a contact report and copy it to the account manager.
- *Internal communication.* Finally, all internal information that pertains to the customer, including changes in delivery schedules, results of field tests, order delays, early project completions, and so on, should be passed on to the account manager. The account manager should be aware of *everything* that impacts the customer's orders or satisfaction.

Figure 16-4. Intelligence Needs Map

Priority	Intelligence Need	Comments
A	■ Criteria for selecting shippers for container loads to Japan ■ Expected size of each shipment ■ Insurance requirements ■ Probable dates for grain shipments next year	Char Baker and Dennis Scheer are responsible for getting this info Due no later than 12/5
A	RFQ for Trans-Canada has been delayed for two months: ■ What's behind the delay? ■ Will the specs change? Need deep private info on what's behind this. Is our position eroding?	Urgent intelligence need! RLS and J. Petrie are on it Notify TYN, FES, and PAS *ASAP*
A	They just acquired Umesato port facilities in Kobe. ■ Impact on Tokyo shipments? ■ Will this be a hub? ■ Alliances with other shippers? Are they looking for partners? ■ Plans for intermodal traffic in Japan?	Get Bill Lewis and Terry Adkins to Kobe *ASAP* to meet with Jerry Steiner, Koji Oshima, and Ken Kadonaga
B	Confirm possible reorganization of their Central Region	H. Nilsen heard the rumor; he will follow up; due on 1/6
B	They used Pacific Consolidated for $2.5 million in shipments from LA to South America last year. Why? Who's making the call? What criteria? How satisfied are they?	Jim Coyle will check it out Due back on 12/17
B	Emma Sayles has taken over their San Diego office. Plans? Changes in direction? Other personnel changes? Plus: what's the internal reading on her?	Mike Ross knows her; will inquire RLS
C	Who's likely to replace Hans van den Berg after he retires next August?	Nick Henke looks to be in line; RLS to confirm with Jerry Steiner and Deb Seymour
C	Personal info on R. Glanz, Joe Sinngh, Carl Tilanus, & Bob Ma	RLS is responsible
C	Their internal intermodal survey results are due on 12/15	RLS to get copy
C	Alberto Garcia's reaction to new FCC rulings?	Steve Batz will ask

---

Information Sensitivity and Reliability

Information sharing is a trust issue, and it's possible to destroy your relationship quickly if you misuse information a customer gives you or if a customer contact believes you're sharing sensitive information with their competitors. So be sure when you're getting information from customers to protect what's sensitive and proprietary. As a general rule, *never* share any information about any customer with any other customer unless that information is already completely in the public domain. People need to know that you are discreet and are as concerned as they are about protecting their competitively sensitive information.

Also, beware of asking for deeper information than a customer contact is comfortable providing. If you ask a normal customer contact for deep private information, for instance, you're likely to generate mistrust—precisely the opposite of the effect you want. You should never ask for deep private information from anyone other than a customer sponsor—someone who has confided to you already and who is biased toward you. If you push too hard for someone to give you sensitive information, his or her guard will go up. It's best to wait for the relationship to develop and for the contact to show a predisposition to trusting you with deeper, more sensitive information.

Finally, you should confirm all information you intend to act on. Unless you have a strongly reliable source, it's best to confirm information from at least one other source before acting on it. I've seen a number of account managers misled by information from one source who turned out to be unreliable for one reason or another.

Using an Information Plan

One of my principal messages in this chapter is that information should be managed, that it is ineffective to rely on serendipity to ensure that you get the right information from the customer and they get the right information from you. If you learn critical pieces of information about the customer by accident, then your account management effort is a wreck.

A best practice in strategic account management is to create an information plan, which becomes part of your account plan. The information plan describes how you will manage information flow to and from the customer and usually details what information various customer contacts need (see Fig. 16-3) and what information you need (see Fig. 16-4). You can use the information plan to brief people who are meeting with the customer and to ensure that the right customer contacts are made so you can get the information you need from them and ensure they receive the right information from you.

An information plan should reflect your account strategies and action plans. For instance, if one of your strategies is to position your company to support your customer's planned expansion into Malaysia, then your information plan should identify all the information you need from them about their expansion plans and all the information they need about your capabilities in Malaysia. No matter what your account strategies are, you will not be able to accomplish them without having excellent information on your customer; competitors; market conditions; and your own products, technologies, and new developments. Similarly, you won't be able to accomplish your strategies without providing your customer with the right information at the right time. So information management is fundamentally important to achieving your goals, and it should be a conscious part of your daily management of the account.

Analyzing and Interpreting Information

I said earlier that information has value to customers only if it's *relevant* and *timely*. Those criteria also apply to information distributed internally. Information does not become knowledge until it has been analyzed and interpreted, put into context, and given meaning, because it impacts your understanding of the customer and leads you to make better, more informed decisions. For these conditions to be true, the information you receive from customers must be relevant to the customer's need for your products, and you must receive the information in time to do something about it.

Sometimes, the relevance and importance of the information are not immediately apparent. For example, one of my clients in the engineering and construction industry learned that a large energy company—one of their strategic accounts—was looking into alternatives for ethylene production. They inquired about the customer's interest and were asked if they could give the customer a 2-hour presentation on their approach to design-to-build ethylene production plants. My client said yes and then assigned several engineers to deliver their standard presentation on that capability. Four days before the presentation, the account manager received a call from one of his friends in the customer's organization, who asked:

"Do you understand what this is about?"
"I think so. They want to see how we approach building ethylene plants."
"Wrong. They want to evaluate you to see whether they should talk to you further."

His friend then informed the account manager that the customer had asked thirteen firms to give 2-hour presentations on their ethylene capability, and the customer's intention was to short list the top three firms and send requests for proposals to them. This was more than a casual request.

A project worth $100 million was at stake. Needless to say, my client completely rethought the company's approach, dedicated a high-level team to the presentation, and worked day and night to ensure that their presentation had high impact.

Here's an even better example of a company using seemingly innocuous information to their advantage. A worldwide consortium of oil companies decided to build the largest offshore oil platform in the world off the coast of Newfoundland, and this information became public knowledge about 1 year before the consortium intended to begin construction. Given the magnitude and importance of this project, one company—which I'll call Apex—assigned an account manager to the consortium. He began gathering information on the consortium and its key people and learned, among other things, that the president of the consortium had graduated from the engineering school of the university in St. John's, Newfoundland. He also learned that the president was a civic-minded person who devoted some time to charities.

All the interested suppliers were invited to St. John's to spend a day meeting with the consortium president, but Apex went far beyond that. They identified their proposed project team 1 year ahead of the project and moved them, including the account manager, to St. John's. Soon, their team members had their kids in school there, were coaching soccer teams, and were joining civic groups. Then, 3 months before the release of the request for proposal, Apex hired the entire graduating class of engineers from the university in St. John's. While other suppliers voiced their commitment to the consortium, Apex lived it and won the award.

Information becomes intelligence when you analyze it and derive value from it in the context of the situation. Intelligence leads to *smart* account management when you act on the information and build a competitive advantage, as Apex did in Newfoundland.

Maintaining and Distributing Information

It's best if you maintain information electronically because it can be distributed more easily to others in your company who need access to it. The past 20 years have seen a revolution in information management. Not too long ago, account records and customer information were maintained in fat manila folders in the account manager's filing cabinet. Very few people had access to the information, and it was difficult to update it or send it to dozens of people at once. Just a few years ago, those records were moved to databases accessible on the company's network—a better solution but not accessible outside of connected workstations. Today, those records can be maintained on intranets or over the Internet. A number of companies are creating secure Internet sites for their customer records, which permits authorized users from around the world to have virtually immediate access to critical customer information, competitor intelligence, and even the account plans on line. It's a remarkable improvement in a very short period.

There are essentially two forms of customer information distribution—*push* and *pull*. In the more common pull form, the information is available on line but authorized users have to know it's there and go get it. The system itself is passive. Pull forms of database management include contact management software such as Act! and Goldmine, which can alert users to scheduled events when the due dates have arrived but do not send other forms of information to users.

In the more evolutionary push form of information management, the system knows the authorized users and periodically sends them new information via e-mail—for instance, when information that could affect their area becomes available. Push forms are like on-line newsletters with subscribers who periodically receive new additions by e-mail. In the past few years, push technologies have evolved quickly, and it's now possible to distribute strategic account information to account team members, executive sponsors, and virtual team members via e-mail. It's possible, too, for these users to select the information they are most interested in and to have the account information sent to them customized according to their preferences. We're rapidly entering an era where account managers can *push* the information out to others in their company in an efficient and highly customized manner. The types of information that should be pushed include:

- Updates on the customer, including key personnel changes
- Account plan changes, including updates to action plans
- Account sales and performance figures
- Order or project updates
- Bid and proposal intelligence and strategies

In addition to push technologies for distributing information, some multinational companies are using global account web sites for interactive conferencing among account team members spread across the globe. Chat rooms are ideal for discussing global customer issues on line with account team members in geographically dispersed locations.

However you manage and distribute customer information, the key is to know who in your company needs the information and how they will use it. Some information is more time critical, so it must be possible for you to distribute information promptly, when necessary, and to alert people that the information is coming.

— 17 —

Managing Customer Delight

Perhaps it's a sign of the times. It's not enough to *satisfy* customers anymore. You must *delight* them, and this is not simply a matter of semantics. Suppliers who can't satisfy the customer won't even be in the game. Satisfaction is the price of admission, but it's not enough anymore. We're now decades into the quality movements that began with Deming and Juran. Dozens of high-quality, global companies are competing in every product and service arena. To win today, you have to go far beyond the meager standard of satisfying customers. Practically everyone can do that.

The new standard is delight. Delighted customers are surprised at the quality and level of service they receive. The service exceeds their expectations and sets a new standard by which they judge all future services of a similar kind. When you *delight* customers, you raise the bar for everyone and make it harder for your competitors to *satisfy* customers in the future unless your competitors meet the new standard. So long as you are the one raising the bar, your customer remains delighted with you and will come back for more.

Managing customer delight is one of an account manager's most visible roles, especially to your customers. It's the role that can transform you in their minds from seller to consultant—from vendor to preferred supplier and from there to partner and ally. Clearly, it requires a great deal of internal coordination and influence, because you have to impact the way your company does business with the customer throughout the entire order cycle. You have to motivate people to care more and do more than they do for normal customers—no matter how high their customer service standard might already be. Strategic accounts deserve and expect that higher level of service.

There are four aspects to managing customer delight. First, you must try to execute work and fulfill orders as well as possible. Achieving zero defects in project execution obviously is difficult, but it's the standard you should try to meet. Nonetheless, mistakes will occur from time to time. Even the most proficient companies will stumble occasionally, so resolving problems and handling complaints are crucial parts of managing customer delight. Resolve problems swiftly and passionately. Show that no problem is too small to be concerned about and that the highest priority for you and your company is resolving any problems they are experiencing.

Second, you should continually measure customer delight and use those metrics both as a communication vehicle and as a means of joint continuous improvement. When you measure delight, you show that you care about how you're doing and how sound the relationship is and that you're listening to your customer. Measuring delight indicates that you are dedicated to helping them achieve greater business impact through the quality of your services and your attention to anything that prevents them from being delighted with your products and services and your relationship.

Third, you have to keep your edge. It's essential to institutionalize your services so you can predictably and reliably serve your customers over time. However, the very practice of institutionalizing your services makes them routine, and routines devolve in time to complacency. As Theodore Levitt notes, "Nothing degrades so easily as the practices and the behavioral routines that are and must be institutionalized. This necessary formalization of routines generally degenerates into faceless activity. It is too easy to take action instead of spending time. It is all too easy to act first and then try to fix the relationship, instead of the other way round. It is all too easy to say, `We'll look into it and call you back.'"[1] Extraordinary service remains extraordinary only if it is constantly renewed, so an essential task of the account manager is to fight complacency and loss of focus on the customer relationships that really matter. There are countless stories of such problems in companies, but a noteworthy group of customer defections occurred to the advertising firm Ogilvy & Mather in the time frame from 1989 to 1991, when they lost major assignments from Shell, Unilever, Seagrams, NutraSweet, and Campbell's Soup. It took a renewal of leadership under Charlotte Beers to reverse the agency's declining fortunes.

Finally, and perhaps most importantly, managing customer delight depends on anticipating changes in the customer's markets, consumers, products, and needs. To capture their attention and delight them with the value you bring, you must *lead the need*. Anticipating the market trends that affect them and being aligned with their internal drivers and directions put you in a commanding position to help them achieve greater business impact, and nothing delights customers more than this.

Executing Work and Resolving Problems

In chapter 15, I argued that the baseline of trust between your company and your customer is built on your ability to meet their requirements and fulfill

---

1. Theodore Levitt, *The Marketing Imagination* (New York: The Free Press, 1986), p. 124.

their needs. The front lines of customer delight are all those interface points where the people in your company execute their part of the project or fulfill their part of the order. Your fortunes rise or fall based on those hundreds of moments of truth every day when customer orders are taken, transmitted, produced, inspected, packaged, shipped, received, installed, invoiced, and serviced. Benson Shapiro et al. argue that "every time the order is handled, the customer is handled.... The order is simply a surrogate for the customer."[2] Their advice is to staple yourself to the order.

Stapling Yourself to the Order

Periodically throughout the year, you should force yourself to see the order from the customer's perspective. How does it look to them? What's pleasing and what's aggravating? What seems conscientious and what seems thoughtless? More to the point, where are they delighted by the service and treatment by receive, where are they merely satisfied by it, and where—heaven forbid—are they unhappy?

When you staple yourself to the order, you follow the process—and the customer's experience of it—from one end of order fulfillment or project execution to the other. Your purpose is to see how the orders are handled and to understand how and why the customer's perceptions of your company are formed. It's not always good news, but at least it gives you a chance to correct any problems.

The key to appreciating the customer's experience of your company is to look at the process objectively. You can do that only if you aren't trying to sell or defend your company's practices at the same time. You must act like a business consultant, calmly examining the facts and seeing the experience with a fresh pair of eyes. Write up your findings, the way a consultant would, and then syndicate your impressions with the people in your company who manage those interfaces with the customer. Syndicate the good news, too, because it helps them to know what they're doing right.

Setting Joint Expectations and Measuring Results

A best practice in managing order fulfillment is to make it a joint responsibility, much as Procter & Gamble (P&G) has done in its alliance with Wal-Mart. Together, they've formed a supplier–buyer team that sets mutual expectations, has a team charter, strives for joint continuous improvement, and measures the results jointly. Before they undertook this initiative, both parties characterized their relationship as adversarial and internally fo-

---

2. Benson P. Shapiro, V. Kasturi Rangan, and John J. Sviokla, "Staple Yourself to an Order," in *Keeping Customers*, ed. John J. Sviokla and Benson P. Shapiro (Boston: Harvard Business School Press, 1993), p. 60.

cused. They worked entirely on the transactional basis of buying and sell-ing. Senior management made a strong commitment to improving the re-lationship and creating a win-win situation. So they formed the P&G/Wal-Mart interface team and created a common vision, mutual goals and working processes, and protocols for extensive data sharing. It's smart for Wal-Mart to invest in this relationship, because they get preferential treat-ment from one of the largest consumer goods manufacturers in the coun-try. Together, they've reduced prices, improved quality, reduced invento-ries in stock, and made themselves mutually responsible for the future improvements that will benefit both companies. It's smart business, and it helps P&G manage its order fulfillment system about as flawlessly as one can do it.[3]

Resolving Problems Through SWAT Teams

General Electric created another best practice with its Work-Outs. Work-Outs are a team problem-solving process, which Jack Welch initially put in place to overcome inertia among middle managers in GE when he was try-ing to accelerate the speed of change and to encourage behavior without boundary. He felt that many GE staffers had excellent ideas, but they were being frustrated by their inability to get their managers to listen and to im-plement suggestions. Work-Outs are focused problem-solving efforts in which teams of people are asked to identify performance problems and spend a day or two in intense, almost physical "workouts" where they ex-amine the problems and their causes, identify alternatives, and then pro-duce a set of recommendations for management. Near the end of the pro-cess, the manager who is responsible sits in the room with the team and hears its recommendations. The manager is asked to respond to each sug-gestion as soon as it is given. To complicate it, the manager is discouraged from making eye contact with his or her superior, so there can't be nonver-bal signals about what to approve and what not to. It forces managers to listen to ideas, to respond quickly, and to be decisive. Work-Outs aren't universally admired, but most people credit the practice with having a sig-nificant impact on GE's successes during the past 2 decades.

Work-Outs initially were practiced only within GE. Once they refined the tool and learned how to use it well, GE began holding joint Work-Outs with customers. In these, representatives of the customer's organization join in the problem-solving process and help identify and suggest means for improving processes and quality. At the end, the GE manager who is re-

---

3. For more information on the P&G/Wal-Mart Interface Team, see Tom A. Muccio,"Organization-to-Organization Trust: A Case Study of Procter & Gamble/Wal-Mart," in *The Trust Imperative*, ed. Roger Dow, Lisa Napolitano, and Mike Pusateri (Chicago: National Account Management Association, 1998), pp. 96-113.

sponsible has to face customers as well as other GE people. As a joint problem-solving process, Work-Outs are hard to beat. They demand that people move quickly and accept the responsibility for making decisions that can impact the business right away. They're not for the faint of heart.

Work-Outs are like the special weapons and tactics (SWAT) teams used by police departments. When you need the extraordinary done quickly or when you're faced with difficult and perilous situations, you don't call in one neighborhood, uniformed cop. You bring in a squad of specially trained and equipped people who can do the job quickly. IBM's legendary customer service teams were like SWAT teams. When customers had a problem with an IBM 360, a platoon of IBMers arrived on the scene within hours and worked concertedly until the problem was fixed. From the 1950s to the 1970s, IBM dominated the large mainframe market and built extraordinary relationships with customers based on their SWAT team approach to problem resolution.

The primary point of these examples is that extraordinary execution necessitates an extraordinary approach. You simply can't do *business as usual* with strategic account customers. The service they receive, throughout every part of your order cycle, must be *unusual.*

The most difficult transition for many companies to make from a traditional sales system to strategic account management is to view account managers as customer managers and to grant them the power and authority to make extraordinary things happen. However, it's critical to the success of strategic account management that this transition occur. Account managers should not have to wait for approval from line managers to get problems resolved. The most damaging words account managers can say to unhappy key customers are, "I have a call into the person who can help you." Those words convey two bad messages: (1) the problem isn't being resolved and (2) the account manager is powerless. The question is, who serves whom? If your account managers represent your most important customers and are responsible for managing those relationships, then shouldn't the line managers in a sense report to the account managers? What's most important to you—managing internal operations or serving your key accounts exceptionally well?

Afterwards, Ray Thomas decided that following an order from the customer's standpoint was the best education he'd ever had. At the time, however, it just seemed like torture. Ray worked for Sykora, a manufacturer of fine furniture in Winston-Salem, North Carolina. For several years, he'd been the strategic account manager for Hudson House, a strategic retailer of quality furniture with 182 showrooms nationwide and a thriving catalog distribution network that extended into Canada and Mexico. Sales to Hudson House had remained steady, but Ray felt the account had much more potential. His company's items weren't getting

continued

prime floor display space in showrooms, and this alone was probably costing them 15 to 20 percent in store volume annually. One store manager told Ray that Sykora items weren't displayed more prominently because Sykora furniture wasn't discounted, and most customers shop for bargains. Yet when Ray compared the marked prices of the store's discounted items with comparable Sykora items, there was little difference. He also got the impression from some buyers that Sykora was difficult to work with.

To get to the bottom of these problems, Ray decided to track an order from start to finish. To his chagrin, he learned that the process was anything but simple. Ordering took an inordinate amount of time when customers called, as Sykora's order clerks searched through catalogs to find items, cross-checked availabilities, and verified shipping costs using the new shipping rate charts. Sometimes, a clerk had to check three or four different catalogs and then put customers on hold while checking to see if discontinued items were available from other sources. Delivery dates could not be guaranteed, and the store was notified 2 weeks later that some items on the order were unavailable for at least 2 months because of a strike in Honduras. The list went on and on.

Rather than bringing his experiences forward without knowing whether they were isolated incidents, Ray worked with his customer contacts to create a satisfaction survey. He sent it to his contacts in more than fifty stores and received forty-three responses. The results were no surprise. They showed a pattern of order fulfillment problems and frustrations. He sent his report to Sykora's executive board and asked for a hearing to address them on obstacles to growing the business, a topic he knew would interest them. After he presented the results, Ray proposed a number of suggestions that he and his Hudson House contacts had originated. Most were adopted immediately and resulted in some quick-win improvements, the most important of which was greater flexibility on pricing, which allowed more competitive discounting. After communicating the results and Sykora's corrective actions to Hudson House, Ray found the store managers more willing to give Sykora prominent floor display space, and their sales increased substantially. Now Ray staples himself to an order at least once a quarter in different showrooms around the country.

Assessing the Relationship and Measuring Delight

The old adage that "management begins with measurement" is absolutely true in managing customer delight. First, you have to know what you mean by it. What exactly is customer delight? How will you know when you see it? Defining customer *satisfaction* is relatively straightforward by comparison. You just have to know their product requirements and their expectations about the fulfillment services (e.g., ordering, shipping, installation, postsale service) that accompany the product. Knowing what they *require* and *expect* gives you a clear sense of what will satisfy their needs. However, if you want to delight them you also must know what actions or results would *exceed* their expectations. Sometimes, they can articulate that fairly easily because they've experienced it before or they've done things for their customers that exceed expectations. But often they can't articulate it because they haven't considered it. In this circumstance, you have the remarkable opportunity to raise the bar with them, to codefine delight.

Having set a very high standard, you should periodically assess the relationship and measure the extent to which you are exceeding their expectations. There are no rules of thumb on how often to measure customer delight. It's an ongoing process, conducted informally every time you meet with a customer. Nonetheless, you're probably negligent if you aren't conducting a formal assessment at least once a year. Here are some guidelines on formal assessments:

1. *Set clear objectives for the assessment.* Know why you're conducting the assessment and set clear parameters for both the process and the outcomes. If your intention is to measure delight, as opposed to satisfaction, then be clear about that purpose and develop an assessment that will measure delight. Syndicate your objectives with your executives and your contacts in the customer organization. Incorporate their thoughts and be sure they support the program.

2. *Ensure that assessments of customer delight are linked to your customer's strategic and tactical targets.* Figure 17-1 shows the linkages that should exist between your measures of customer delight and your company's strategic and tactical processes and the customer's processes. First and foremost, what you measure should be aligned with your customer's mission, operating principles, and strategic plans. For example, Jack Welch of GE has long promoted the concepts of speed, simplicity, and self-confidence. They are the driving principles of GE today, particularly speed of change, speed of implementation, and speed in responsiveness to market

Figure 17-1. Customer Delight Linkages

conditions and customer needs. If GE were your strategic account, one of your measures of customer delight should certainly be your own speed and responsiveness. Further, your measures should reflect the customer's unit performance goals as well as the objectives and standards of their quality assurance systems. If your measures of customer delight are not aligned with the customer's principles and goals, then you will be less likely to impact their business significantly and will not be critical to them as suppliers.

3. *Ensure that your assessments also are linked to your own company's strategic and tactical goals and processes.* What you measure and what you deliver to customers also should reflect your company's mission, operating principles, strategic plans, account plan, and quality systems. Your company's direction and standards for excellence must be consistent with what you are trying to deliver to customers, and because the ISO 9000 criteria include measures of customer satisfaction, your measures of customer delight should reflect your quality goals and program. On the tactical level, your assessment measures should reflect relevant project goals and the criteria from your performance management and compensation systems. For example, if your account managers are being measured and compensated on their ability to consult with customers and help them develop total, high-impact solutions, then your customer delight assessment should include this criterion. Finally, as shown in Figure 17-1, if your company and your customer have developed joint performance goals, then those goals obviously should be measured.

Figure 17-2. Customer Delight Circumplex

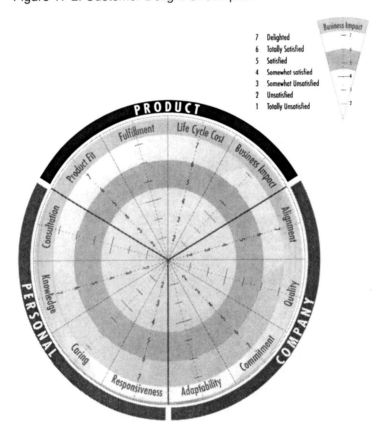

7	Delighted
6	Totally Satisfied
5	Satisfied
4	Somewhat satisfied
3	Somewhat Unsatisfied
2	Unsatisfied
1	Totally Unsatisfied

The litmus test of alignment between your company and your customer is whether your measures of customer delight can be linked directly to the strategic and tactical goals of both organizations. Any measures that do not link both ways indicate a lack of alignment.

4. *In your assessments, measure the extent of the customer's delight in three domains: your products, your company, and yourself.* Within these three domains are logical categories you might wish to explore, and each of the categories would include a number of questions. Figure 17-2 shows one possible scheme for assessing the three domains. In this circumplex, each domain has four subcategories.

The *product* domain measures product fit, fulfillment, life cycle cost, and business impact. The design suggests that customers will be delighted if the product fits (if it does what they need it to do), if your order fulfillment processes exceed their expectations, if they are satisfied with the life cycle cost of the product, and if the product has a positive impact on their business. Figure 17-3 lists the kinds of questions that might be asked under this and the other domains.

Customers will be delighted with your *company* if they feel that your principles and culture are aligned with theirs, if you are focused on quality and contin-

Figure 17-3. The Domains, Categories, and Questions for Measuring Customer Delight

Product

Product fit: How delighted are you with our product? Does it meet all your requirements and specifications? Is it solving your problem as you expected it to? Is it exceeding your expectations for products of this type?

Fulfillment: How delighted are you with our pre-sale and post-sale services? With our order fulfillment process? Delivery? Shipping? Packaging? Installation? Customer service? Training? Maintenance and service?

Life cycle cost: Does the life cycle cost of our product meet your expectations? Do you feel that you're getting excellent value for the total solution cost?

Business impact: How much impact are our products having on your business? Is that impact measurable? Can you trace the impact to your bottom line?

Company

Alignment: How delighted are you with the way our two organizations are working together? Are our cultures compatible? Are you satisfied that we understand and are aligned with your mission and objectives?

Quality: How delighted are you with the quality of our products and our organizational emphasis on quality and continuous improvement? Is our quality program compatible with yours? Are we exceeding your expectations for quality improvement and continuous innovation?

Commitment: How delighted are you with our total company commitment to serving your needs? Do you see that commitment in the actions of everyone in every function of our company? Do you see that commitment from our senior executives?

Adaptability: How delighted are you with our flexibility and adaptability? Do you see our willingness to deliver precisely what you need and require?

Personal

Responsiveness: How delighted are you with our people's attentiveness and responsiveness to your needs and requests? Are you satisfied that we are listening? Do our representatives promptly return calls, answer questions, and provide all the information you need? Are we always there when you need us?

Caring: How satisfied are you that our people care about and are committed to you, your organization, and your success? Do our people consistently demonstrate caring in their treatment of you and your organization?

Knowledge: How delighted are you with our people's knowledge and expertise? Do they consistently demonstrate superior knowledge of your organization and industry, our products and services, and your business needs and metrics?

Consultation: How delighted are you with our people's ability to add value to your solutions? Do they meet or exceed your expectations as consultants to your organization? Are they helping you achieve higher quality solutions?

uous improvement, if everyone in your company demonstrates a strong commitment to the customer, and if your company is adaptable and responsive to their specific needs and requirements.

The final domain reflects their experience with you and other people in your company they work closely with. They'll be delighted if the *people* they work with are responsive to their needs, show genuine caring for them and their organization, are knowledgeable and expert in relevant areas, and provide high solution value through consultative skills.

In actual surveys, these areas and the questions related to them would be customized for the product and would reflect your customer's and your company's strategic and tactical objectives as discussed previously. The circumplex is a useful way to visualize how well you are meeting and exceeding the customer's expectations, because it shows at a glance where you are strongest and weakest. Figure 17-4 is an example of a company with significant strengths in the product and personal domains. Except for order fulfillment, this customer is delighted with the product and with the people they work with most closely. However, they are not delighted with the company, particularly with the company's adaptability and commitment—areas of significant weakness. The company probably appears inflexible, perhaps in its order fulfillment policies and practices, and the customer is not totally satisfied by the company's quality assurance programs. To delight this customer, some major systemic changes need to be made throughout the company.

5. *Involve customers in defining the criteria and writing the questions.* Some companies use blind surveys conducted by consulting firms to measure customer satisfaction. The theory is that a blind survey is more objective and yields more accurate and honest results. I don't favor this approach because you lose several

Figure 17-4. Example of a Customer Delight Circumplex

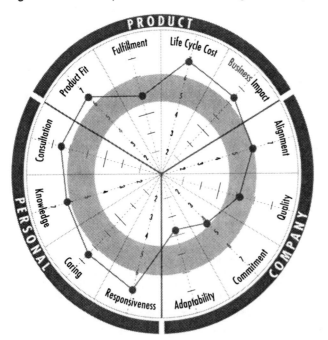

significant advantages. First, conducting the survey yourself shows the customer that you care about whether you are delighting them. When you follow up afterwards, you show that you were listening and are committed to continuous improvement. These actions are critical relationship builders. Second, conducting the survey yourself gives you the chance to involve the customer in the process and increase their sense of ownership.

Consequently, a best practice is to engage your customer in defining the criteria and writing the questions. Ask them, What do you think is important? What should we measure? What do you want to know? One of my clients became so engaged in this process that the client assigned a task force to it and assumed joint ownership of the process and the results. It became a soul-searching event for both of us and resulted in significant changes that improved both the relationship and the customer's business.

6. *Include narrative-response questions in your assessments.* Often, the most useful information from customer delight assessments is not in the numerical results but in customers' responses to questions that require a narrative response, such as "What's the most important improvement you would like to see us make?" or "What single change would have the biggest positive impact on your business?" You can get narrative feedback either in writing or through face-to-face or telephone interviews. If you've been talking to customers and asking these questions all along, the results may not surprise you, but it's useful to compile responses from thirty or more customer contacts and identify the clusters of suggestions. Hearing suggestions in the customer's own words usually has a powerful impact on your own executives and department managers who can effect the changes being recommended.

7. *Communicate the assessment results openly and candidly, and use them as a springboard for action.* Finally, when the results are available, be open and candid in communicating them to your customer. They already know what they think, so it usually isn't a surprise to them, and it signals your willingness to hear the feedback. Once the results have been shared, it's a good practice to call a meeting between your key people and the customer's. Discuss the results and open a dialogue on where to go from here. What areas need the most urgent attention? What would they like to see changed? How can you work together to improve on these results? What are the time frames for action? What commitments are the parties willing to make? Ideally, a joint plan of action should come from the postassessment meeting. You may have most of the action items, but your customer contacts should agree to share their impressions and feedback at various intervals and to help you measure progress. However, because the improvements you make could directly impact their business, they may want to play a stronger, more active role, and they may decide to make some changes in their own systems and practices as well. Clearly, a customer delight assessment can become a catalyst for joint problem solving and performance improvement.

Guarding Against Complacency

Aldous Huxley said that most people have an almost infinite capacity for taking things for granted. We like to think that the customers we've won are ours. We worked hard to get them. We have a right to them. The fact that we have to keep working hard to retain them is frustrating. We want to be able to rest on our laurels and focus on the next big conquests. The people in our company who serve the customer day in and day out also want to see the work become more routine and predictable. This doesn't mean they don't always work hard to serve customers; it simply means they prefer what's familiar and steady. As Eric Hoffer observed in *The Ordeal of Change*, "We can never be really prepared for that which is wholly new. We have to adjust ourselves, and every radical adjustment is a crisis in self-esteem: we undergo a test, we have to prove ourselves. It needs inordinate self-confidence to face drastic change without inner trembling."[4]

People prefer what's known and comfortable, but being responsive to key customers and providing extraordinary service *as the norm* means being embroiled in change. Key customers are always asking for something new, different, special, and unique. They remain key customers because you accede to their demands and treat them specially, but that treatment can strain your systems and create an environment of nearly constant invention and reinvention, a more-or-less permanent white-water condition.

Some people thrive in this environment, but most don't. If you leave your strategic account unattended, your company will tend to become complacent in its treatment of the customer, and the relationship will degrade eventually. To guard against complacency, you need to renew people's sense of the importance of the customer, their urgency in meeting the customer's needs, and their care in handling the customer's requests and demands. I don't mean to sound too Disneyesque about it, but you really need to renew their sense of wonder—that feeling of joy and pride in having won the customer, of serving this *interesting* organization, and of doing it exceptionally well.

Here are some best practices for guarding against complacency:

- *Remain enthusiastic yourself.* As the account manager, you are the primary source of energy and enthusiasm for the customer within your company. If you're not filled with a sense of wonder, why should anyone else be? This best practice sounds like a platitude and ought to be obvious to everyone, but the fact is a number of account managers are uninspiring and don't manifest the energy to mobilize others. Managers of critically important strategic accounts have to be leaders within their own company and leaders in the customer organization as well. They must be visionary, inspirational, energetic drivers. Otherwise, the account will drift.
- *Share the successes and the kudos.* Nothing motivates like success. People want to know about and share in the glory, so a key practice for guarding against complacency is to overcommunicate the successes and the kudos received from customers. Dictionaries define *kudo* as the prestige or acclaim that results from a notable achievement. It encourages people to hear that the company has done well, that the customer is delighted, and that the project ex-

---

4. Eric Hoffer, *The Ordeal of Change* (New York: Buccaneer Books, 1976), p. 3.

ceeded their expectations. Kudos build pride and give people a positive sense of completion. Every time you receive a letter of thanks from a customer, you should announce it, share it, distribute it, and congratulate everyone involved. One of the account managers I know had each such letter copied onto a nice certificate that he awarded to everyone who worked on his customer's projects. When you passed by people's offices, you could see them on the walls. Some people had three or four framed certificates above their desks. Every time that account manager awarded another certificate, he built more cachet for his account—and received special attention whenever he needed it for his customer.

- *Share the results of customer delight assessments and other surveys.* Another part of overcommunicating on the account is sharing the results of customer delight assessments and other feedback from customers. Although the news may not always be good, it helps people feel involved if you make them aware of any issues and then ask for their ideas on resolving those issues.

- *Engage people in continuous improvement programs.* One of the account managers I worked with recently had created a continuous improvement program for her account. She convened regular quality assurance meetings with people from various departments in her company, as well as customer representatives, and they brainstormed ways to enhance the product and ensure continuous quality in the interactions between the two organizations. Involving people in her company who normally would not have been involved in this kind of effort helped them feel more ownership for customer impact and led to substantial increases in quality for the customer.

- *Sponsor customer panels and other forums for connecting people with customers.* Customer panels and other forums that bring customers together with people in your company are superb tools for stimulating interest in the customer and avoiding complacency. Ask customers on the panel to speak about what delights them as well as what they think you could be doing better or where they see opportunities for further synergies between the two organizations. Your audience should include representatives of every department that interfaces with the customer, as well as senior executives in your company. Allowing a question-and-answer period will enable people to interact directly with the customer panelists rather than just being passive listeners.

- *Help people see the bigger picture.* Sometimes the problem is that people don't see the bigger picture and they develop myopia about their role and the customer. For example, account managers for some of my clients have occasional difficulty with their legal departments. The attorneys are trained to see the downside and protect against it, but they are often so zealous in that pursuit that they don't see the harm complex legal documents can do to a key customer relationship. There are times to cover every contingency and to be paranoid and protective about potential problems and breaches—and there are times to relax and let the terms and conditions be played out more casually among friends. Many lawyers would consider this a naïve viewpoint, but they aren't responsible for building the relationships and don't have to deal with the fallout that occurs when trusting customers feel they've been nuked by a 200-page contract. Similarly, operations people want to get their job done right, as they should, and they sometimes are inflexible about how that must be done, regardless of what the customer wants. Giving people the big picture is the best practice I've seen for helping them move away from intransigent positions and stay focused on giving the customer extraordinary treatment.

Two common themes run through all these best practices: overcommunicating and having extraordinary levels of participation in the account from many people in your company. In a nutshell, that's how you keep everyone energized and guard against complacency.

The secret to managing customer delight is having a *high care/high touch* attitude. By and large, the things you must do as a company to delight your key customers—to take them beyond satisfaction—do not occur automatically. They must be stimulated and managed by someone who assumes a leadership role in the account. *High care/high touch* means high frequency of interaction between people in both organizations, extraordinary levels of communication, and enough participation by enough people in your company to build a strong sense of ownership of the account and commitment to the customer.

Anticipating Change

Finally, as I will discuss further in the next chapter, customers are delighted when you anticipate both the changes they are making of their own accord and the changes their markets and customers are compelling them to make. In today's fast-paced marketplace, what you did for customers in the past and what you're doing for them now are less important than how you're evolving to meet their future needs. The pace of change is accelerating, and time to market is becoming not merely a competitive advantage but a necessity. To delight your customers, you must be able to look ahead and anticipate the evolutions and revolutions to come by innovating in areas that are aligned with your customer's expected changes and by accelerating the pace of your company's innovations so that your new products and services are ready before the customer needs them.

An account manager who is merely a traffic manager and networker is not likely to rise to this challenge. Anticipating change requires account managers who are thoroughly immersed in the changes in their and their customer's industries, who are avid readers and consumers of the literature on technological advances, and who are skilled at quality assurance and continuous improvement techniques. Periodically, you should meet with your customers and facilitate brainstorming sessions on current trends and future directions. Ask them to imagine what their products and services will be like in 3 to 5 years. What are their prognostications for their industry and organization? How will their needs change as new technologies become practicable and the competitive environment in their industry evolves?

Effective strategic account managers *lead the need* by developing the answers before their customers think of the questions. They know that to remain static is to stagnate. The only way to delight customers in the long run is to be slightly ahead of them. Customer delight involves measuring the past and managing the present, but its heart and soul are in anticipating the future.

Managing Customer Delight

1. Execute projects well and resolve problems quickly
2. Assess the relationship and measure delight continually
3. Guard against complacency
4. Anticipate change (*lead the need*)

— 18 —

Managing Momentum

Managing a strategic account is like running a marathon with the customer in the lead. You can't sprint the entire distance. It would either kill you or leave you lying breathless on the track while your customer finishes the race. To win, you have to manage your energy—start fast; settle into a quick but steady pace with the customer, running stride for stride; go faster or slower as the customer changes pace; conserve your energy in the long, middle miles; and then sprint with the customer at the end so you finish together.

Accounts work this way, too. When opportunities arise, you have to mobilize your energy and your company's resources to respond. The concerted effort necessary to rally behind the new opportunities demands that people in your company set aside what they've been doing, focus on your customer, and perhaps work long hours to respond. They go into a "high-alert" mode and divert their attention from other tasks and projects so they can meet your needs. You can't keep them in this mode for long without losing their goodwill and running out of favors. To retain their cooperation when you need it most, you have to know when to apply pressure and when to ease off. Your own pace as account manager is likely to remain at a constant high, but others in your company are like firefighters—intense and alert when they're needed and focused elsewhere when they're not.

Dictionaries define *momentum* as the product of a body's mass and velocity. It's the speed or force of motion. Sometimes you need a lot of momentum in the account. You need many of the people in your company supporting you at various times through such activities as marketing campaigns, product introductions, preliminary engineering design efforts, on-site demonstrations, trade shows, and proposal efforts. As account manager, you are the impetus or driving force that ramps up everyone else's energy, gives that energy direction, and guides their efforts toward accomplishment of your goals. Part of the art of account management is knowing when to build that momentum and how to manage it. Without question, this is one of the advanced skills of strategic account managers. It requires leadership, judgment, timing, and political savvy. You must be able to influence laterally and upward, to build favors and call them in at the right moments, to coordinate the diverse activities of many people and departments, and to read the signs in your customer's organization so you know when to act and when to wait. By monitoring your customer's activities and pace, you determine just when to signal your colleagues "Go!"

The key to managing momentum is *anticipation*, which the dictionary defines as "acting in advance so as to prevent." I would modify that definition by saying that you act in advance so as to position yourself for opportunities. When you anticipate what's to come, you plan where and how to apply your resources for maximum effect. You recognize, for instance, that the customer has more-or-less regular cycles of demand for your types of products and services, and you position yourself so that you precede their upswings in demand by increasing your level of activity in the account. I call this *precycling*. You also anticipate the events and activities that impact the customer's needs and the timing of opportunities. You do this by preparing to respond—or *presponding*. Finally, you manage momentum by anticipating the technological or business advances in the customer's industry or other industries that signal market or technology trends, the innovations that will cause your customer's business to evolve. If you can evolve before your customer does, then you have positioned yourself to meet their future needs, and I call this *prevolving*.

Managing momentum is the most artful of an account manager's ongoing account management responsibilities. Those who do it well are masters of timing. Efficient, economical in their use of resources, and clever in bringing together the diverse talents of many people in pursuit of a common cause—they are true customer leaders.

Precycling—Positioning for Your Customer's Demand Cycles

In most industries, demand for suppliers' products fluctuates throughout the year, often in predictable cycles. In retail industries, demand fluctuates with consumer buying patterns and usually is seasonal. In rapidly changing industries, such as computer hardware, supplier demand fluctuates with consumer sales and the supply of hardware on the market, but it's also impacted by new technological developments and product introductions throughout the industry. In heavy industry and construction, demand fluctuates according to larger macroeconomic forces and usually cycles over longer periods. The building construction cycle, for instance, typically runs from 16 to 20 years.

Precycling—The Micro Factors That Impact Demand

The micro factors that may cause your customer's demand for your products to fluctuate annually or in the short term could include:

- Rising or falling demand for your customer's products, which may be cyclic and predictable if they depend on seasonal consumer buying cycles

- Your customer's project cycles (e.g., new housing starts in the spring and summer)
- Your customer's budgeting cycle and fiscal year spending patterns. For example, my strategic account customers have new money available at the beginning of their new fiscal year, so they may delay spending until the start of the new fiscal year. Conversely, if they have excess money in their budget as the end of the fiscal year draws near, they may need to spend money before they lose it. Other times, they spend money at the end of a fiscal year because they've already made the year's profit goals, and spending money in the next fiscal year could jeopardize their chance of reaching their profit goals for that year. In some industries, the demand for your products depends on these kinds of factors, and you can predict the effect these factors will have every year.

     A classic example of budget cycles is the United States government, which is the largest customer on the planet. Major suppliers to the government know when procurement and budget planning occur in each agency and know when spending peaks and plummets. They often structure their own fiscal year to coincide with the government's September–October fiscal year cycle.
- Your customer's other spending priorities, which may delay their purchase of your products (often these other purchases fall in cycles and are predictable)
- Trade show timing. For example, the Computer Distributors Exhibition (Comdex), which is held semiannually, is the largest and most important exhibition of information technology in the world. Most electronics manufacturers unveil new products at these shows. Demand for supplier's products and services often shifts direction and increases or decreases—depending on the product—after Comdex.
- Your customer's new product introductions and marketing campaigns, which stimulate demand for their products and correspondingly increase their demand for your products (in some cases, introductions and campaigns occur at regular intervals or are scheduled far in advance)
- Contract rebids (contracts coming up for renewal indicate moments where demand could increase or decrease sharply depending on whether you win or lose the rebids)
- Your customer's recent purchases of your types of products (e.g., if they've just installed systems, equipment, or hardware that you provide, they won't need the same products or services until their organization has grown or these products become obsolete); often, these types of purchases are regular and recurring

These factors tend to produce near- or short-term effects on your customer's demand for your products.

Precycling—The Macro Factors That Impact Demand

Demand also is subject to longer-term or macroeconomic forces that impact your customer's industry and business. These macro forces include interest rate fluctuations, stock market trends, industrywide technology evolutions, fluctuations in the price of raw materials, tax rate or tariff changes, changes in foreign exchange rates, global geopolitical events, the general health of the economy, and even national and global weather patterns and conditions. The El Niño weather phenomenon, for instance, increases demand for building construction services (to repair damage), which increases demand for lumber and other building supplies. A drop in the price of oil can have an extraordinary impact on the demand for oil field supplies and services. When oil prices plummet, the entire energy industry becomes depressed. Companies such as Texaco and Shell spend less money on exploration and oil field services, which in turn impacts oil field service companies such as Halliburton and Schlumberger, as well as their suppliers and subcontractors down the line.

Your customer's demand for your types of products typically follows short cycles (the micro forces I discussed earlier) and long cycles (the macroeconomic forces discussed here). In combination, these cycles produce a complex demand pattern like that shown in Figure 18-1. This figure represents the seasonal demand cycle for a sporting goods manufacturer with multiple product lines and three major regions in the United States with different consumer sporting interests. Demand climbs through the weeks leading to midsummer and declines through the remainder of the year, except for the Christmas shopping season. Several spikes in the year represent major sporting goods expositions and the retailer buying that oc-

Figure 18-1. Seasonal Cycle Demand

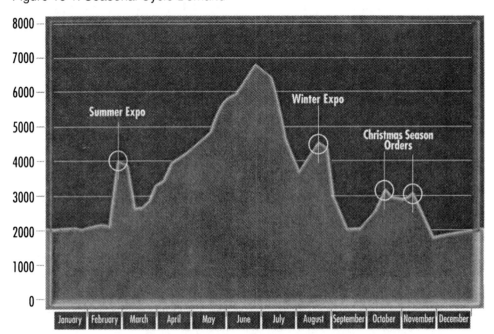

curs during and immediately after those expositions as the retailers build inventories for the coming season. This manufacturer can also plot the demand cycles for each of their major customers, and their account managers can determine how to increase or decrease momentum in their accounts accordingly. In this example, product design and marketing planning for each summer seasonal demand increase must begin 4 months before the summer exposition, which typically is held in late February or early March. Account managers start planning their campaigns for the summer season in early January.

As in Figure 18-1, you should be able to see some predictable points where demand will increase or decline. What I am calling *precycling* is your ability to predict and precede these cycles by taking actions that position you for changes in demand level. For instance, if you are reasonably certain that demand will increase in 2 months, then you should anticipate the up cycle by taking steps now to prepare for it. Your objective should be to have no surprises. Being forced to react to changes in customer demand indicates that you're asleep at the wheel.

Precycling—Recognizing Demand Fluctuations

You should be aware of how the customer's demand for your products normally fluctuates throughout the year and over longer periods, if relevant. To build that awareness, you can create a cycle graph like the one shown in Figure 18-1. The patterns of fluctuation may not be apparent until you see the peaks and valleys displayed over the longer term and the cycles become apparent on the graph. So one way to predict future fluctuations is to notice what has occurred in the past. You should also do the following:

- Remain aware of the larger, macroeconomic forces that impact the customer's business and ask key customer contacts how macroeconomic changes, such as changes in tax or interest rates, might increase or decrease demand for your products.
- Read your customer's industry trade publications as well as your own. The trade publications often signal changes in demand across their industry and suggest how your customer will be impacted.
- Read the sources of public and deep public information on economic and business trends. Sources such as *ValueLine*, *Standard & Poor's*, *Predicasts*, *Forbes*, and *Fortune* usually are helpful, as are your customer's annual reports and published or unpublished plans and predictions.
- Pay special attention to your customer's growth rates and expansion plans. If demand for your products is tied to growth, then their rate of expansion is a good indicator. You often can identify long-term project plans, project completions, plant overhauls, and openings of new offices that may increase demand for your products.

- Look at changes in your relationship with the customer and the changing relationships of your competitors. Obviously, if you are becoming a preferred supplier and a key competitor is losing favor, then demand for your products is likely to increase.
- Identify the critical events on your customer's calendar that could impact demand (e.g., new product introductions, trade shows, fiscal planning and spending).
- Talk to your customer sponsors. The people in the customer's organization who are most supportive of you usually can provide insight about changes in demand. It depends on how well placed they are in their organization and how much they know. However, a typical high-level sponsor can tell you when to be more active in the account and when not to. A sponsor also can read the signs and interpret them for you. For example, recently an important buyer in a customer organization wasn't returning my phone calls. I asked my sponsor about it, and he told me that this person was so overloaded he wasn't returning internal e-mail either. It put my mind at ease, and I knew to back off for a while.

Between the historical demand cycles and your intelligence gathering, you should be able to recognize how demand will rise and fall in the months and perhaps years ahead.

Precycling—Anticipating Demand Fluctuations

Clearly, effective precycling is more than just knowing how and when demand will change; you have to anticipate those changes by taking action. There are numerous ways to position your company for upswings and downswings in demand.

To anticipate upswings in demand, do the following with the customer:

- Time your new product introductions to precede an upswing. Try to generate favorable buzz and excitement about the products just before the demand for them increases.
- Time your marketing and sales campaigns to precede upswings and focus the campaigns so that the messages reach the right key customers at the right time.
- Time on-site demonstrations or site visits to coincide with upswings. Focus those events on aspects of your products or services that meet the customer's rising needs.
- Schedule your senior executive meetings with their customer counterparts to coincide with the increases in demand.
- Develop and deliver your capability presentations before the upswings. Ensure that customers are aware of your capabilities before they need to make decisions about products.

- Step up the frequency and breadth of your own customer contacts. Develop an intelligence needs list and manage the network of contacts between your company and the customer's organization. Ensure that you know who will be making and influencing the buying decisions once demand starts to increase.

To anticipate upswings in demand, do the following internally:

- Communicate your expectations to the departments or units that will need to help you respond. Develop response strategies with them.
- Revise your account plan as necessary by updating your action plans. Then syndicate the changes and gain necessary commitments.
- Begin lining up senior executive support. Enlist your executive sponsor's help in mobilizing other senior executives to reach out to their customer counterparts. Revise your relationship management plan accordingly and set up the calls and site visits, focusing on the people in the customer's buying chain who will make or influence the buying decisions.
- Initiate information-gathering activities focused on the emerging need and distribute information to the appropriate people internally.
- Develop your marketing and sales campaign literature, as well as product demonstrations, software, models, and presentations.

To anticipate downswings in demand, do the following with the customer:

- Begin shifting the focus of your messages from product sales to after-sales support, services, training, maintenance, and upgrades.
- Begin looking for collateral services to provide and for referrals to other units or locations in the customer's organization. During lulls with your primary buying units, devote time to consolidating your position in other units.
- Emphasize quality installation and effective use of the products you recently sold and delivered to the customer; initiate customer delight surveys so that you can communicate results and resolve problems before the next upswing.
- Devote time to relationship building, joint planning, and joint problem solving. Ensure that a number of your contacts are purely social, with no pressure on the customer to buy or on you to sell.
- Work your information management plan (see chapter 16).
- Position your company and products for the next upswing.

Precycling is a matter of timing. It requires great awareness of the micro and macro forces that impact the customer's demand for your products. It necessitates that you look at the customer's organization and industry holistically, to see all the factors that can influence your customer's business and to predict how those factors will cause demand for your products to rise or fall. Finally, it requires you to manage the commitment of your own resources in a timely manner so you lead the need. When it's done well, precycling enables account managers to predict the cyclic changes in demand and to prepare for those changes by increasing or decreasing their company's activity and momentum in the account.

Presponding—Positioning for Shifts in Momentum

Cyclic fluctuations in demand are somewhat predictable because they are based on recurring or scheduled events, but customer demand for your products also can rise or fall suddenly because of unscheduled, nonrecurring events or circumstances, such as an accident at a plant that suddenly reduces their production capacity or a foreign bank failure that depresses one of their foreign markets. Although you obviously can't foresee everything that could impact the customer's demand for your products, if you're alert you often can sense where problems and opportunities might occur and can be prepared to respond, which I call *presponding*. Anticipating sudden shifts in demand might mean developing contingency plans for the most likely events that could occur; however, in some circumstances you can prespond by undertaking initiatives that themselves create the shift in demand. The key is to think ahead of the customer's potential problems or opportunities and have the resources available to respond quickly when these events occur.

Sometimes you hear rumors of impending changes. The customer's tightening its belt. There's a move afoot to reduce expenses. Nothing's been announced to you yet, but you hear the buzz in the hallways. So you prespond by examining expenses and formulating a cost-cutting plan. Perhaps you institute cost-cutting measures before they ask you to. In any case, you're alert and ready. Obviously, the better your relationship with the customer and the deeper your information sources, the less likely you are to be surprised by your customer's shifts in direction. What may appear to other suppliers as a complete surprise will be something you've already anticipated.

Some changes in the customer's business direction result from larger market forces, and presponding means paying attention, noting the business phenomena that are occurring, and anticipating the impacts on your customer. As I write this, for instance, Internet commerce is rapidly changing the face of retail business throughout the country. Amazon.com's remarkable success as an on-line bookseller has transformed the book retail business almost overnight. It prompted retailers Barnes & Noble and Borders to launch on-line sites, and one wonders what will become of Waldenbooks, Book Stop, B. Dalton, and Brentano's if they don't jump on the Internet bandwagon. Amazon's market capitalization is now twice that of Borders and Barnes & Noble combined—two retailers that have dominated the retail book industry in recent years through their network of supersize bookstores. According to John Neuman of A.T. Kearney, the volume of Internet commerce is doubling every 100 days—and that pace is accelerating.[1] Internet commerce is transforming numerous markets and giving global access to small- and medium-sized retailers and manufacturers in many industries. If you're alert, you won't be surprised when your customer announces a major initiative to develop on-line distribution channels, and you will have prepared for it by anticipating what effect that change will have on the products you supply.

Table 18-1 identifies some of the factors that can suddenly increase or decrease your customer's demand for your products. Events such as these are difficult and perhaps impossible to anticipate, especially catastrophic events such as plant closures due to fires, but you should always be pre-

---

1. John Neuman, in a speech given at the National Account Management Association 34th Annual Conference, San Diego, California, May 4, 1998.

Table 18-1. Nonrecurring Events That Can Impact Demand for Your Products

Events That Increase Demand	Events That Decrease Demand
A customer product experiences higher-than-forecast demand from consumers (e.g., the Beanie Baby phenomenon)	A customer product that was expected to do well fails in the marketplace (e.g., Apple's Newton)
A customer plant goes on line sooner than expected	A customer plant experiences a catastrophic problem, such as a fire, and is suddenly shut down
A key customer executive is suddenly replaced, and the new executive charts a different path, which increases their use of your product	A key customer executive is suddenly replaced and the new executive changes course, which decreases their use of your product
Unexpectedly good financial returns lead the customer to increase the budgets that impact the purchase of your product	Unexpectedly bad financial returns lead the customer to freeze budgets, resulting in a sudden loss of funding for your products
Your customer wins a new contract, so the customer suddenly requires more of your product	Your customer loses a key contract, so they no longer need your product; or they lose a major bid in which your product would have played a key role
The price of raw materials suddenly goes down, which enables your customer to increase its production	The price of raw materials suddenly goes up, which forces your customer to scale back on production
Your customer's executives announce a new initiative that will require more of your product	Your customer's executives announce a new initiative that will divert funds and attention away from your product

Table 18-2.   PMEA Program Deliveries to American Telecom

Year	Program	J	F	M	A	M	J	J	A	S	O	N	D
1996		0	2	6	9	11	5	2	0	6	10	5	2
1997	Project	1	2	7	10	12	7	1	1	8	12	6	3
1998	Management	2	4	7	11	13	9	3	2	8	14	8	2
1996		0	0	1	3	4	2	0	0	2	3	2	1
1997	Project	1	0	2	2	3	4	1	0	2	2	2	2
1998	Estimating	1	2	3	2	5	3	1	1	2	4	3	1
1996		2	4	2	2	2	2	0	0	2	4	2	1
1997	Project	2	2	2	2	2	2	1	1	3	3	2	2
1998	Scheduling	2	3	3	4	4	2	0	0	4	4	2	2
1996		2	2	4	6	6	4	2	1	3	4	4	2
1997	Contract	2	3	4	5	7	3	3	2	3	5	3	1
1998	Negotiations	3	4	4	6	8	6	2	2	2	6	4	2
	Totals	18	28	41	62	77	47	16	10	45	71	43	21

pared to respond. Identify the contingencies that reasonably could occur and think through your options. How will you mobilize your resources? Who will you call? How could your company meet the demand? The sudden firing or replacement of a customer decision maker may catch you unaware, but most of the time you can estimate someone's tenure in a position. Even when you can't, you can anticipate change. One of my clients recently underwent a massive reorganization and lost 75 percent of its top executives and many of its middle managers. We couldn't predict exactly who would leave and who would occupy the remaining positions, but we were aware of the impending turmoil and followed the events closely as they unfolded. We knew which executives were likely to be retained in the top positions and who was likely to move up. We presponded to these changes by focusing on the customer's needs after the reorganization and thinking through our strategy with each of the potential key executives who remained. When the changes occurred, we were ready to move quickly and to help the customer continue performing well through the chaos wrought by massive change.

After 5 years as a sales representative for Project Management Education Associates (PMEA), Jody Katzenbach was promoted to manager of the American Telecom account. Every year, PMEA delivers a number of training workshops to American Telecom professionals, including programs in project management, estimating, scheduling, and contract negotiation. To understand how demand in this account varies throughout the year, Jody mapped out the number of deliveries of each program for the past 3 years. The results—shown in Table 18-2 and plotted in Figure 18-2—reveal that American Telecom's demand for programs peaks in the spring and fall months and drops substantially during the late sum-
continued

Figure 18-2. American Telecom Annual Demand Cycle for PMEA Programs

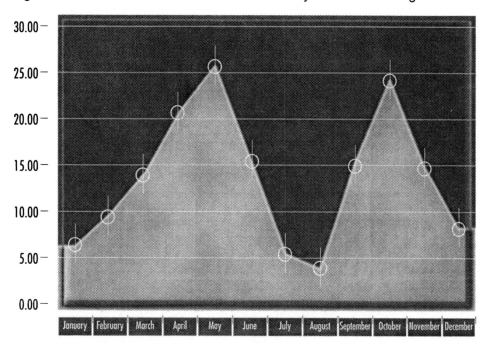

mer, when many of their people take vacation, and midwinter, when people are catching up from the winter holiday season and kicking off the new fiscal year. Jody also noticed that demand for programs has grown each year. PMEA's volume grew from 141 programs in 1996 to 156 programs in 1997 (a growth rate of 11 percent) and to 192 programs in 1998 (a growth rate of 23 percent). These growth rates paralleled American Telecom's growth during these periods. In Jody's industry, demand is tied to the growth in the workforce as new hires and recently promoted employees receive training in project-related job skills.

Using these demand cycle charts, Jody estimated program demand levels for each month in the coming year. American Telecom's annual report estimated that it would grow by 18 percent in the coming year, so she adjusted her estimate accordingly, using the 1998 actual figures as a baseline. Table 18-3 shows the result.

When she shared these estimates with Larry Norton, the director of training for American Telecom, he confirmed that the scope of effort was about right but told her that they were about to receive a mandate from their executive board to upgrade their negotiation skills immediately. Problems with several recent contracts had led their chief executive officer to believe that their entire middle management group should receive advanced negotiations training, and the executive board wanted to accelerate contract negotiation classes for their project managers. Consequently, Norton told her, they wanted twenty more contract negotiation programs in the first quarter of the new year, and eight of those needed to include advanced skills for senior managers. To accommodate this increase in the number of contract negotiation programs, they wanted to schedule twenty fewer project management programs, including all of those scheduled in July, August, and December.

continued

Table 18-3. Estimated Program Volume for American Telecom for 1999 Based on Growth

Program	J	F	M	A	M	J	J	A	S	O	N	D	Total
Project Management	3	5	8	13	15	10	4	2	10	16	9	3	98
Project Estimating	1	2	3	3	7	3	1	1	3	5	3	1	33
Project Scheduling	2	3	4	5	5	2	0	0	5	5	2	2	35
Contract Negotiations	3	5	5	7	9	7	2	2	4	7	5	2	58
Totals	9	15	20	28	36	22	7	5	22	33	19	8	224

Realizing the potential impact on PMEA, Jody immediately contacted Roger MacDonald, her company's operations manager, and was told that the need for that many contract negotiation programs early in the year was a huge problem. PMEA didn't have the resources necessary to deliver that volume. "What can we do about it?" she asked. Roger said he would solve the problem one way or another but that they probably would have to try to move some scheduled programs for other customers and may need to hire and train more instructors. Both of these alternatives were risky, and he wouldn't be able to do it without some top-level support, so Jody called her executive sponsor in PMEA and enlisted his aid. He went to work at the executive level and gained the necessary commitments, but it wasn't easy. He said he'd had to call in a lot of favors to pull it off.

Then Jody received a call from Suzanne Fernandez, one of her sponsors at American Telecom. Suzanne told her that their manager of project scheduling had just announced his retirement, and he was being replaced by Armin Selah, a hotshot scheduling manager who had been recruited from one of American Telecom's competitors. Selah had published a number of articles on the art and science of project scheduling, and he was known as a strong advocate of PrimaTempo software—one of the industry standard software systems for managing complex projects. Her heart sank. PMEA's scheduling program was based on a different software system, and Selah was likely to insist that American Telecom convert to PrimaTempo.

Jody planned to confirm that assumption when Selah came on board. In the meantime, she contacted the head of research and development (R&D) for PMEA and asked about converting their scheduling program to PrimaTempo. She was told that it would require a substantial R&D effort and would divert resources from other scheduled development projects. PMEA also would have to retrain its instructors to ensure that they were competent in PrimaTempo. The head of R&D

continued

was unwilling to make that commitment, so Jody went up through the channels. If her customer made the switch to PrimaTempo, she told them, they would probably need to retrain everyone who had to use the new software, not just the new group of schedulers and project managers, so she expected their demand to increase substantially, at least in the short term. The PrimaTempo company had its own software training program, so PMEA would be competing with the manufacturer. They could win only if they demonstrated a strong commitment to the conversion process and expertise in the PrimaTempo software system.

It was a convincing argument, and her executives decided to invest in the software and the program conversion. Shortly thereafter, she met with Armin Selah and tried to persuade him that it made more sense for American Telecom to use PMEA for all their project-related training needs and assured him that PMEA was as committed to PrimaTempo as he was. She'd developed a business case showing him the benefits, and she introduced him to PMEA's R&D director, who suggested that they begin the conversion project immediately. Selah agreed and said he wanted to complete the conversion no later than the end of the second quarter. She pointed out that this would require additional scheduling courses, and Selah agreed to fund those programs. He felt that what American Telecom gained from using the new software far outweighed the investment they would need to make in the training.

Back in her office, Jody wiped the sweat off her brow and created a revised demand schedule for the coming year. It's shown in Table 18-4. By precycling and presponding to events that would impact the demand for her products, Jody was able to anticipate her key customer's needs and capture the business.

Table 18-4. Estimated Program Volume for American Telecom for 1999 Based on Growth and Changes in Program Need

Program	J	F	M	A	M	J	J	A	S	O	N	D	Total
Project Management	2	3	7	11	13	9	0	0	10	15	8	0	78
Project Estimating	1	2	3	3	7	3	1	1	3	5	3	1	33
Project Scheduling	1	6	8	9	9	6	0	0	5	5	2	2	53
Advanced Contract Negotiations	2	3	3										8
Contract Negotiations	6	9	10	7	9	7	2	2	4	7	5	2	70
Totals	12	23	31	30	38	25	3	3	22	32	18	5	242

So one key to presponding is to think ahead and develop contingency plans for the most likely changes that could occur. You don't necessarily need formal, written contingency plans, but they may be helpful with your most strategically important customers and the worst or best possible contingencies, especially where you'd need a massive response from your company.

Presponding also means acting quickly once the event occurs. Whether the customer experiences a problem or an unexpected opportunity, you should be poised and available to help. Your ability to respond quickly depends, in part, on the availability of key people in your company, so you should alert them when circumstances arise indicating that a problem is imminent. You may need to convene a rapid-response task force to help deal with the customer's problem or need. If a sudden, large opportunity surfaces, you may need to assemble a 16-hour-a-day proposal team to formulate a quick response to them. You may need to rally your estimators to produce a quick-and-dirty estimate or call on your finance specialists to work their connections in the financial community to help the customer with emergency project financing. Finally, you may need to mobilize your senior executives and persuade them to exert their influence and devote their time to making things happen quickly.

Occasionally, you can stimulate shifts in the customer's demand by compelling them to see a new way, to shift their paradigms about how they do things. Xerox's Document Centre product—which faxes, copies, prints, scans, and e-mails documents—is a paradigm-shifting product, a method of redesigning office work and uniting people from remote offices. It has the capacity to increase demand from customers because it offers a new way of thinking about intraoffice and interoffice communication. Technological advances and new products are the most obvious ways of stimulating demand, but you also can do it by offering paradigm-shifting solutions to the customer's problems. Thinking creatively about meeting the customer's needs and being proactive in solving their current and emerging problems are perhaps the best ways to prespond.

Conversely, if you don't learn about the customer's needs and problems until they release a request for quotation, you're already too late. They and your brighter competitors have already been thinking about the solution—and perhaps working on it together.

Prevolving—Positioning for Market Trends and Innovation

In technology-driven industries, you also can manage momentum by anticipating how your customer's technology will evolve and developing your supporting products and services just ahead of the customer's technology evolutions. However, staying ahead of the technology curve is becoming increasingly difficult as the twenty-first century draws near. The pace of technological change is accelerating almost more rapidly than we can keep up with it. This century has seen extraordinary innovations in technology, with revolutionary advances in medicine, electronics, computing, telecommunication, aviation, and miniaturization—and physicist Michio Kaku argues that we are on the threshold of yet another revolution. "Human knowledge is doubling every ten years. In the past decade, more scientific knowledge has been created than in all of human history. Computer power is doubling every eighteen months. The Internet is doubling every year. The number of DNA sequences we can analyze is doubling every two years. Almost daily, the headlines herald new advances in computers, telecommunications, biotechnology, and space exploration. In the wake of this technological upheaval, entire industries and lifestyles are being overturned, only to give rise to entirely new ones."[2]

Clearly, account managers alone cannot impact the rate at which their company's technology advances, but they are a vital link between the customer's emerging technology needs and their company's research and engineering efforts. Account managers are close to the customer and can indicate how they envision the customer's technology and product or service needs evolving. Ten years ago, for instance, a graphic artist's primary tools were a knife, a waxer, and a light board—tools that seem quaint today. Carefully pieced-together masters were photographed, and the negatives were used to create an impression on an offset plate that was attached to a cylinder in the printing press. This process was time consuming and expensive, so professional color printing could be done economically only in large print runs. Today, art is created on a computer and transmitted to the press, which forms an electronic image on the cylinder. Gone are the expensive negatives and the offset plates. The process is simpler, faster, and cheaper, so short runs now are feasible. Suppliers who supported printers, publishers, advertising agencies, design agencies, and art supply retailers should have noticed that personal computers and software such as Adobe Illustrator and PageMaker were revolutionizing the field. However, the change occurred so quickly that many printers and suppliers were ill prepared and either declined or went out of business.

Today's marketplace does not permit security. To stay alive, you must keep pushing the frontiers, not only in technology but also in solutions, project methodologies, and customer service. Here are some ideas:

- Stay ahead of your customer's development curve. Keep your ear to the ground and know where they are developing their technologies. In 1997, MCI claimed that by the year 2000, more than half of their revenue would come from products they hadn't developed yet. If you were one of their sup-

2. Michio Kaku, *Visions: How Science Will Revolutionize the 21st Century* (New York: Anchor Books, 1998), p. 4.

pliers, you'd want to know what they envisioned and what technologies they were investing in.

- Be an avid reader of your customer's industry journals. Know how their industry is evolving and what advances are likely to occur.
- Pay attention to related fields or general technological developments, such as the Internet, that could impact your customer's business.
- Look for substitutes for your customer's products or your products. What emerging technologies or materials could be used in place of what you or your customer provides?
- Do some creative thinking about your products and your customer's products. Ask these kinds of questions: What could make the product obsolete? How will customers use the product differently in the future? What could make it better, faster, cheaper, more convenient, less time consuming, more modular, more serviceable, or more direct? What could be outsourced or vertically integrated? What cost pressures will your customer experience in the future, and how will they respond to those pressures?
- Read the books and articles by futurists such as Faith Popcorn, John Naisbitt, and Alvin Toffler.[3] What do they envision? If their predictions come true, what will be the impact on your products and your customer?

Prevolving is the most challenging of the three skills I've discussed in this chapter. It requires considerable foresight as well as your company's facility in evolving its technologies faster than the customer's needs evolve. Clearly, it's one of the best ways to position your company for the future, but most companies do not demonstrate that level of foresight. Only a handful of companies consistently evolve faster than their customer's needs evolve. Today, those companies are the best-in-class performers in their industries: Microsoft, IBM, Intel, Dell Computer, General Electric, Sony, Hewlett-Packard, Canon, BASF, Siemens, Matsushita, Enron, Shell, and Motorola, to name a few. The most common characteristic among these top performers is that they are forward thinking and invest heavily in research and development. They prevolve.

Account managers manage momentum in their accounts by looking ahead, by anticipating how demand for their company's products will change through the year, and by calling on their internal resources to support their account efforts at the right time. In effect, managing momentum is good energy management, and it's one of an account manager's most advanced skills.

---

3. See Faith Popcorn and Lys Marigold, *Clicking: 17 Trends that Drive Your Business—and Your Life* (New York: Harperbusiness, 1998); Faith Popcorn, *The Popcorn Report* (New York: Harperbusiness, 1992); John Naisbitt, Patricia Aburdene, and Pat Aburdene, *Megatrends 2000* (New York: Avon, 1997); Alvin Toffler, *The Third Wave* (New York: Mass Market Paperbacks, 1991).

— 19 —

Managing Opportunities

Account managers generally know of many opportunities in their accounts while they are developing their account strategies and putting action plans in place. Typically, some account strategies include action plans focused on winning specific opportunities. However, it's not possible to anticipate every opportunity. Depending on your types of products and customers, numerous opportunities may develop while you are working the account day by day. In some industries, account managers pursue these opportunities on their own as part of their selling activities. In other industries, such as aerospace, defense, engineering and construction, telecommunications, and industrial goods, account managers can't respond to these opportunities without the support of many other people.

In aerospace, for example, pursuing an opportunity may require a supplier to create preliminary engineering designs; to locate and form teaming agreements with component or subsystem manufacturers; to research alternative materials or processes; and to develop preliminary solutions in areas such as systems integration, modularization, configuration management, software design, and ergonomics. In the engineering and construction industry, pursuits may require site investigations, soil analyses, preliminary engineering drawings, feasibility studies, and teaming with subcontractors. Account managers can't possibly do all this work, but they are responsible for managing opportunity pursuits and coordinating the efforts of many people in their company to ensure that they are positioned to win.

The account manager's role typically includes assessing new opportunities and gathering enough information about them to make logical pursuit decisions. Sound decisions are based on the value of the opportunity and an analysis of the customer's key issues and decision-making processes. If the company decides to pursue the opportunity, the account manager must develop an opportunity pursuit strategy, which includes the company's key selling messages, and then manage the pursuit by coordinating the activities of all key people, including senior executives. In some industries, such as aerospace, managing a single, large opportunity pursuit can occupy much of an account manager's time, but the reward can be major contracts worth hundreds of millions of dollars to the company. Conversely, if the pursuits are not managed well, the value of the lost opportunities can climb into the hundreds of millions of dollars as well.

The first rule in managing opportunities is to learn about them well in advance. If you don't learn of opportunities until the customer has released a request for proposal (RFP), then you're already too late. You've missed the chance to influence the requirements, develop and presell a distinctive solution, and create a favored position for your products or your project team. Furthermore, if your customer hasn't given you early warning about the opportunity, then your relationship with that customer probably is not good. You certainly aren't in the favored position. If your competitors have known about the opportunity longer than you have, then they probably have been working with the customer in the interim, and your chances of winning the work are considerably reduced. It's imperative to learn about new opportunities early so you can launch what amounts to a preemptive strike. The rule of thumb is

If you don't learn about an opportunity before the customer releases an RFP, then you've probably already lost it.

Assessing Opportunities

As soon as an opportunity arises you should assess it, and the best assessments are systematic and thorough. One of the best practices I've seen is to create an opportunity diagnostic checklist, like the one shown in Table 19-1, and use it to help the people in your company ask the right questions. The answers to these questions will help you determine how well positioned you are and whether pursuing the opportunity is worthwhile.

Table 19-1 is representative of the questions you might ask. However, the checklist you use should be tailored to your industry, types of products, and customers. With experience, you can create a relevant and rigorous set of diagnostics that applies to every opportunity that surfaces. The purpose of this tool is to ensure that you are looking at opportunities objectively and exhaustively, that you're asking enough of the right questions, and that you are well positioned for any opportunities you choose to pursue.

The questions themselves help you gather the right information about the opportunity and help discipline the people in your company who are prone to chase every opportunity no matter how undesirable some of them might be. These questions also help you determine, at least preliminarily, what your solution strategy might be. The answers to these questions should be insightful. They should tell you whether your company can offer a differentiated solution and whether the opportunity is valuable enough for you to analyze further.

Table 19-1. Opportunity Diagnostic Checklists

Customer Assessment				
Question	**Yes**	**No**	**?**	**Comments/Action Items**
1. Do we have a strong relationship with this customer?				
2. Are we the preferred supplier?				
3. Have we worked with this buying unit of the customer's organization before?				
4. Do we have a good track record with this buying unit? Do they trust us?				
5. Do we know all the decision makers and influencers in this buying unit?				
6. Do we know how the buying decision will be made and who will make it?				
7. Are the people in this buying unit willing to discuss their needs and the underlying issues openly and candidly?				
8. Do we understand what problems or opportunities are motivating the customer to act now?				
9. Are the customer's business and project needs clear?				
10. Do we understand the customer's business objectives and strategies?				
11. Do we know how this project will contribute toward achievement of their business objectives and strategies?				
12. Do we understand the customer's culture?				
13. Do we know how the customer' culture affects their decision processes and priorities?				
14. Do we understand the best possible outcome for the customer in this situation? Do we know what their ideal solution is?				
15. Do our products, services, and approaches fit the customer's ideal solution? Would our solution be the best possible outcome for the customer?				
16. Do we know how they will measure the success of this project or purchase? What metrics they will use?				
17. Do we understand the needs, motivations, interests, concerns, and priorities of each of the people who will be involved in the buying decision?				
18. Is the customer determined to compete this opportunity?				
19. Would they consider sole-sourcing the bid to the right supplier?				
20. Is this a highly visible project or purchase in the customer's organization?				
21. Will their top executives be involved in the selection process?				
22. Do we know the selection or evaluation criteria?				
23. Do those criteria favor us?				
24. Have we influenced the selection criteria?				
25. Does the customer now have an installed base of our products?				

Continued

Table 19-1.   Continued

	Project Assessment				
	Question	**Yes**	**No**	**?**	**Comments/Action Items**
1.	Is the project real? Has it been funded? Approved by the customer's executives? Do we have evidence that the project is real?				
2.	Do we know where the money to fund this project will come from?				
3.	Has the customer thoroughly scoped the job and communicated the requirements to us?				
4.	Do we understand the scope of work?				
5.	Do we understand the impact this project will have on the customer's business? Is that impact significant?				
6.	Do we have a clearly defined approach or solution?				
7.	Does our solution meet the customer's needs and address the issues?				
8.	Do the customer's requirements favor our products or services?				
9.	Do the customer's requirements mandate any products or services that are unique to our competitors?				
10.	Are the customer's requirements sound? Do they reflect generally accepted technical principles and sound business judgment?				
11.	Would any alternative approaches be better for the customer?				
12.	Is the customer open to discussing alternatives?				
13.	Do we know the timetable or schedule?				
14.	Is the schedule realistic?				

	Capabilities and Differentiators Assessment				
	Question	**Yes**	**No**	**?**	**Comments/Action Items**
1.	Can we provide all the services the customer expects?				
2.	Do we have the right experience?				
3.	Do we have the right products?				
4.	Do we have the right technology?				
5.	Do we have the right people?				
6.	Is the project location favorable to us?				
7.	Would we need subcontractors, teaming partners, or other companies to perform this project well?				
8.	Have we made preliminary arrangements with teaming partners or suppliers?				
9.	Does our proposed solution meet all the customer's needs?				
10.	Can we address all the customer's key issues and requirements?				
11.	Will the customer perceive our solution to be uniquely advantageous for them?				
12.	Do we have clear and powerful differentiators in our products or solution? Will the customer clearly perceive that we have a uniquely different and better solution than our competitors?				

Question	Yes	No	?	Comments/Action Items
13. Are we well positioned with this buying unit? Have we presold our company, products, and potential solutions to them?				
14. Have we demonstrated an appropriate level of commitment to the customer?				
15. Do we have the right senior-level presence in this buying unit? Have we established good senior-level, peer-to-peer relationships?				
16. Have we introduced all our key people to the customer, especially our proposed project manager or team leader?				
17. Is the customer comfortable with our key people? Have we built personal trust between our key people and theirs?				
18. Do we have any debilitating weaknesses?				
19. If we have weaknesses, do we know how to overcome them?				
20. Have we already taken appropriate actions toward overcoming those weaknesses?				
21. Have we successfully completed similar work for this buying unit? Or for other buying units in the customer's organization?				
22. Is our solution or approach superior in any way?				
23. Are the people we would need for this project available?				
24. Are we confident in our ability to perform on time, within budget, and according to specifications?				
25. If not, do we know what's necessary to raise our confidence level?				
26. Have we taken actions toward that end?				
26. Have we introduced our key people to the customer?				
27. Is the customer comfortable with our project team?				
27. Is the customer confident in our capabilities?				
28. If not, do we know what's necessary to raise their confidence level?				
29. Have we taken action toward that end?				
30. Have we fully examined every alternative approach to solving the customer's problem?				
31. Does our solution or approach have any disadvantages?				
32. Is pursuing this opportunity consistent with our account strategy? Does it meet our needs?				

Continued

Table 19-1.   Continued

Competitor Assessment				
Question	Yes	No	?	Comments/Action Items
1. Do we know who will be competing with us for this business?				
2. Do any of the competitors have a history of successful work for this customer? For this buying unit?				
3. Do any of the competitors have close relationships with the customer's decision makers or influencers?				
4. Do we understand each of our competitors' key strengths and weaknesses relative to the customer's issues and requirements?				
5. Do we know how the customer perceives each of our competitors?				
6. Is there an incumbent supplier?				
7. If so, is that incumbent favored?				
8. Do we know what each competitor is likely to offer?				
9. Will any of our competitors' offers be better or more advantageous to the customer than ours?				
10. Do we know how each competitor perceives our strengths and weaknesses?				
11. Do we know each competitor's likely win strategy?				
12. Is this business critical for any of our competitors?				
13. Will the customer favor any of our competitors?				
14. Do the customer's requirements appear to have been influenced by any of our competitors?				
15. Are any of our competitors better positioned than we are in the account?				
16. Have we lost previous bids to any of our competitors on this opportunity?				
17. If so, do we know why they won and we lost?				
18. Conversely, have we beaten these competitors on previous bids?				
19. If so, do we understand clearly why we won?				
20. Did we perform well on those previous contracts?				
Cost/Risk/Benefit Assessment				
Question	Yes	No	?	Comments/Action Items
Do we know how much the customer budgeted for this project or purchase? Do we know their ballpark estimate?				
Is their cost estimate reasonable?				
Do we know what terms the customer will expect?				
Can we accept those terms?				
Are any of the probable contract conditions unacceptable to us?				
If so, can we work around those problems?				
Do we have or can we obtain the appropriate performance bonds?				
Do we have an estimate of the total project cost to us?				
Do we have a good idea of our competitors' prices?				

Question	Yes	No	?	Comments/Action Items
Do we know the cost of pursuing this opportunity?				
Have we estimated the profit potential from this opportunity?				
Is the profit potential significantly higher than the pursuit cost?				
Have we examined all possible pricing strategies?				
Are the technical, financial, contractual, and legal requirements consistent with our policies and practices?				
Do we understand the technical risks?				
Do we understand the financial risks?				
Do we understand the contractual risks?				
Can we manage or mitigate all the risks?				
Do we understand the risks, dependencies, or obligations inherent in winning the job?				
Do the benefits of the job outweigh the managed risks?				
Are we well positioned to win on price?				
Will winning the work improve our position for future business with this buying unit?				
Is this a must-win situation for us?				

Making the Pursuit Decision

I once asked one of my clients how selective they were in pursuing opportunities. He said, "We chase everything that moves. If it doesn't move, we kick it to see if it'll move, and then we chase it!" Humor aside, selectivity is one of the hallmarks of effective account management. You shouldn't chase every opportunity. Some won't be right for your company—nor your company for every opportunity. Perhaps some of your key customer's needs should be met by lower-priced, commodity suppliers or by niche suppliers who have special expertise. You should ensure that the opportunities you pursue are ones that are aligned with your vision for the account; are compatible with your strategies; provide suitable returns; and are the best fit between the customer's needs and your products, people, and solutions.

The account manager is responsible for bringing the right information to the table so the company can decide whether to pursue an opportunity. In most companies, the pursuit decision is made by sales management or by a joint sales and operations committee. Pursuits of large opportunities can cost millions of dollars and involve dozens of people, so the decisions must be made judiciously and in light of all the other opportunities the company is pursuing.[1]

---

1. Many years ago I worked with General Dynamics' Electric Boat Division on their bid for the design of the SSN21, the U.S. Navy's new nuclear attack submarine. Electric Boat began working on the opportunity years before the Navy released its formal RFP. The account manager formed a pursuit team and, with the cooperation of numerous technical departments, initiated preliminary design and technology feasibility studies. For at least 2 years before the Navy evaluated the bids and selected a contractor, Electric Boat committed tens of thousands of man-hours to the pursuit and completed an extraordinary amount of technical work on the design. Pursuits of this magnitude require nothing less than the full support and involvement of the chief executive officer, who becomes, by default if not by choice, the executive sponsor of the effort.

The decision to pursue an opportunity should be made objectively based on an analysis of the opportunity value, your competitive position, the biases and preferences of the customer's decision makers, and other factors that form your selection criteria. Each of these elements is important, so I will discuss them at length.

Determining Opportunity Value

Most of my clients will admit that, at one time or another, they spent more money chasing an opportunity than the opportunity was worth. It's best to view opportunity pursuits as investment decisions, so to make a sound pursuit decision you have to calculate the return on your investment. The key question is this: *What is the opportunity worth to us?* What is its value? Opportunity value is a measure of the return your company is likely to receive if it pursues the opportunity. To calculate opportunity value, you have to estimate the potential profit from the job and then multiply that figure by the probability of the contract being awarded and the probability that you will receive the contract. To clarify, here are some key terms and the process for calculating opportunity value.

Definitions

Go percentage	The probability of a contract actually being awarded to your company or any other supplier
Get percentage	The probability of a contract being awarded to your company
Opportunity value	The product of the potential profit from the contract and the Go and Get percentages
Pursuit budget	The recommended amount of money you should invest in this opportunity if you decide to pursue it

Process

Step 1: Determine the Go Percentage

This figure represents the probability that the contract actually will occur, that the customer will fund it and award it to a supplier like your company. If there are multiple prime bidders and your company is acting as a subcontractor, the Go percentage is the probability that the contract will be awarded to a prime contractor.

The Go parameters are as follows:

100 Percent Probability

- The job has been funded and the funds released. There are no financial holds, dependencies, or pending approvals.
- The customer has a strong and compelling need for the product or service; time is of the essence.
- No alternatives are being considered.

80 Percent Probability

- The customer expects to receive a strong return on its investment for this job.
- The job has been budgeted and funded, but the contract go-ahead depends on the customer getting the right price for the job.
- The customer has indicated a strong intention to go to contract.
- The customer has a strong need for the product or service, but delays and substitute products would be acceptable, although they are not being considered at this time.
- The customer is not seriously considering alternatives to this job.

60 Percent Probability

- The job has been budgeted but has not been funded. Key people are still looking for funding, but it is not certain.
- The return on investment for the customer is acceptable.
- The person driving this opportunity is likely to prevail but does not yet have total management support for the project.
- The customer has several alternatives to this project.

40 Percent Probability

- The return on investment for the customer is marginal.
- The job has not been funded. Key people are looking for funding, and they may not get it. Funds are tight, and this project is not yet a top priority.
- Some serious obstacles would have to be overcome before this job could go ahead. For example, the job may depend on regulatory changes, hazardous waste cleanup, or receiving local support for the project.
- The person driving this opportunity may not prevail.
- Alternatives to the project are being seriously considered.

20 Percent Probability

- The return on investment for the customer is questionable.
- The job has not been funded or budgeted.
- Funds are very tight, and this is a low-priority project.

- The obstacles that would have to be overcome before this job could go ahead are formidable and are unlikely to be overcome in the near term.
- No one in the customer's organization is driving this project. A significant increase in interest is necessary before this job could become a reality.
- The customer has many compelling alternatives.

10 Percent Probability

- The job is in the feasibility study stage.
- The job is not scheduled to be awarded for 3 or more years.

Step 2: Determine the Get Percentage

This figure represents the probability that your company will get the contract. Although it is difficult to determine a precise Get percentage, you can establish a rough-order-of-magnitude figure by using the following guidelines:

- First, determine the unadjusted Get percentage. For every supplier this figure is 100 divided by the number of serious contenders. So if there are four serious bidders, then each bidder's unadjusted Get percentage is 25 percent. I am using the word *serious* to acknowledge that, in most competitive situations, some bidders aren't serious contenders because they're too small, too inexperienced, or unqualified in some way. Their Get percentage is near zero, so they can be eliminated from further consideration most of the time.
- Adjust the Get percentage based on incumbency. History shows that incumbents who are performing well and who remain competitively priced win about 95 percent of rebids. Interestingly, even if incumbents are performing poorly, if they remain competitively priced they will win rebids about 50 percent of the time. Presumably the evil the customer knows is preferable to the evil they don't know, and in rebid situations, poorly performing incumbents usually bend over backward to correct their errors, and some customers use rebids to force incumbent suppliers to clean up their act. In any case, if there is an incumbent supplier, that company is likely to have a higher Get percentage. If your company is not the incumbent, your Get percentage should be lowered.
- Adjust your Get percentage based on customer preference. Obviously, if you're in a partnership or strategic alliance with a customer, your Get percentage will be very high, perhaps 100 percent. If you're in a preferred supplier position, your Get percentage may be in the 60 to 80 percent range, depending on other factors, such as the strength of your competition. If you're not the preferred supplier but are well positioned for this opportunity because of your people, technology, products, or relationships with the customer's decision makers, then your Get percentage is also likely to be high.
- Adjust your Get percentage based on your competitors' positions. If a key competitor is well positioned for the opportunity, then your Get percentage will be lower.

Clearly, calculating your Get percentage is far more art than science. Nonetheless, in practice, and with experience, it's possible to estimate Get percentages fairly accurately. If you know enough about your customer, your competitors, and the opportunity, then you should have a fairly clear sense of your probability of winning the work. If you don't know enough to calculate a Get percentage, then you have many bigger problems to deal with.

Step 3: Calculate the Opportunity Value

First, you need to estimate the potential profit from this opportunity. I can't offer firm guidelines here because this calculation depends on your industry and the typical margins your company can earn from its products and services. However, based on the size of the opportunity and the typical margins for such work, you should be able to identify the potential profit from the job. Opportunity value is this figure multiplied by the Go and Get percentages. For example, if the potential profit from the job is $1.5 million, the Go percentage is 100, and your Get percentage is 50, then the opportunity value would be $750,000. As you consider whether to pursue this opportunity or other opportunities, this is the figure you should bear in mind. It's how much money you stand to make on this opportunity at this time. Obviously, as the Go and Get percentages change, the opportunity value changes.

Step 4: Estimate Your Pursuit Budget

If you choose to pursue this opportunity, how much should you spend pursuing it? It doesn't make sense to spend more money chasing the work than it is worth to you if you get it, so your pursuit budget should be based on the opportunity value. At this point, another concept becomes important—your investment ratio. How much of the opportunity value are you willing to invest to get the job? A 1:1 investment ratio would mean that you're willing to invest as much as you expect to earn. In my experience, this situation occurs rarely and only when the potential for future work with the customer is great. An investment ratio of 1:2 would mean you're willing to invest half of what you expect to earn, and so on. Common ratios in industry range from 1:5 to 1:10.

To continue my earlier example, if your opportunity value is $750,000 and your investment ratio is 1:5, then your pursuit budget should be no more than $750,000 × 0.2$ or $150,000. This is the amount of money you should spend developing the opportunity and preparing your bid. In this example, the Get percentage was 50 percent. If your Get percentage had been higher, then this opportunity would have been worth a larger pursuit budget.

Calculating opportunity value is an important step because it helps ensure that any further time you spend analyzing the opportunity is warranted and it helps you determine how much you should invest in the pursuit. Clearly, the investment ratio is the key to determining pursuit budget, and this ratio depends on many factors, which I will discuss later when I talk about applying selection criteria.

Bret Martin's firm, Market Research Associates (MRA), was considering a bid on the second phase of a large study for Bret's strategic account, Quick Foods Corporation (QFC), one of the nation's largest grocery chains. QFC was considering going global with its Foodique store concept, which had proven successful in selected U.S. markets. Foodique stores featured lavish delis, seafood counters, sushi bars, European-style bakeries, fresh flowers, in-store herb gardens, coffee bars, cookbooks and magazines, specialty cookware and applicances, and classes in gourmet cooking and flower arranging on a membership basis.

QFC's target markets were locations whose demographics featured highly educated, middle- to high-income families with luxury lifestyles. Furthermore, the locations had a high number of "foodies"—people who love to cook and eat. *Gourmet* magazine subscriptions were high in these markets, as were catalog sales through Williams-Sonoma and other cookware specialty retailers.

During phase one of its feasibility study, QFC determined that similar markets existed in Europe, Canada, Mexico, Japan, Australia-New Zealand, and other developed countries. The goal of phase two was to determine what specific changes would be required for Foodique to take off in each market. Phases three and four would determine the selection of test markets and the design of prototype stores in those markets.

MRA had a long-standing relationship with QFC and a successful track record, so Bret was surprised when they lost the phase one study to a small, relatively unknown firm named Archer, Landau & Curtis. The word on the street was that Archer Landau was eager to grow market share and was doing it by trimming their margins to the bone and making lots of promises. Bret's sponsor in QFC told him that Archer Landau had kept their promises so far, but it was clearly stretching them almost beyond their capacity. QFC executives were concerned about their ability to deliver reliable studies on all the target markets in phase two, particularly in Europe and Asia, where Archer Landau has limited presence. Also, rumor had it that Susan Landau, one of their partners, had left the partnership and was forming her own firm. It's not clear what impact her departure would have on their performance, but Bret's sponsor said QFC was concerned.

His sponsor also told him that one of QFC's four corporate officers had a change of heart and was recommending that QFC postpone phase two for at least a year while they expanded in the U.S. market. This recommendation was being taken seriously, although the other three officers, including the chief executive officer, still seemed committed to overseas expansion.

As he was assessing the opportunity, Bret learned that two other firms were now interested in the phase two study, including Globe Market Research, MRA's largest rival, which had a similar relationship with QFC. Brent felt that among the

continued

four contenders for phase two, Archer Landau (the incumbent), MRA, and Globe were the three firms with the strongest competitive positions. Bret's key issue analysis (KIA) confirmed his intuition. As shown in Figure 19-1, of a possible 690 points, Archer Landau scored 502, MRA scored 536, and Globe scored 541. Bret knew his firm would have to make a hard push to win. The question was, could they afford to do it? Was the investment they'd have to make worth the potential return?

Bret estimated that the Go probability was about 80 percent; the one reluctant QFC officer could force a postponement, but it was unlikely. He estimated that MRA's Get percentage was no better than 40 at this point. The potential profit from phase two, as well as phases three and four, was $600,000, and he assumed that if they won phase two and performed well they would be given the last two phases. It was a reasonable assumption, and Bret's sponsor confirmed it. Based on these assumptions, Bret calculated the opportunity value to be $192,000 ($600,000 × 0.8 × 0.4). He took this figure to the bid review committee for consideration with other opportunities MRA was facing.

Although the QFC study opportunity was by no means a shoo-in, the committee did approve pursuing it, largely because QFC was an important client and because Bret made a compelling case. The committee also approved an investment ratio of 1:2, which gave Bret a pursuit budget of $96,000. A strategy was already forming in his head as he thanked the committee members and left the room.

Analyzing the Customer's Key Issues

If the opportunity value is high enough to warrant further analysis, the next step is to analyze the customer's key issues and determine your competitive posture, vis-à-vis, your competitors. The primary question you're trying to answer is, *Can we win this?* It's good discipline at this point to force yourself and others in your company to take a hard look at what the customer needs and expects and how your solution compares with your competitors' solutions. The tool I recommend is called, appropriately, a key issues analysis (KIA), the first part of which is shown in Figure 19-1 (the second part will appear later in the chapter). This figure offers an example based on the Quick Foods Corporation case study. As shown in this example, here's how to do a KIA:

1. In the left column, list the customer's key issues, requirements, or concerns based on your conversations with their decision makers and influencers. What are they looking for? What are they primarily concerned about? What do they want in a solution, and how will they evaluate potential suppliers? If the customer eventually releases an RFP, these key issues typically would be published as their list of evaluation or selection criteria.

2. In the next column, assign each key issue a weight based on the customer's priorities and concerns. The weights typically go from 10 to 1, reflecting the de-

Figure 19-1. Key Issues Analysis, Part I

Key Issues What are the customer's main concerns?	Weights What are the customer's priorities?	Metrics How will the customer measure supplier capability?	Competitors (Please Identify)			Us
			A Archer, Landau & Curtis	B Globe Market Research	C Faast & Associates	Current Score
Worldwide market research experience	10	Global customer base Established foreign offices/affilitates	5 50	9 90	8 80	9 90
Availability of qualified resources to conduct studies around the world	10	Staff size Successful global projects of similar scope	5 50	9 90	7 70	9 90
Understanding of FIP project (continuity from Phase One)	10	Successful similar projects Personnel expertise Correct response to criteria/questions	10 100	7 70	3 30	5 50
Ability of deliver reliable data	9	Proven methodologies Statistical validity from previous projects	9 81	9 81	6 54	9 81
Cost	9	Not to exceed $6 million for Phase Two Price within competitive range	10 90	6 54	8 72	7 63
Track record with QFC	8	Successful previous projects with QFC Referrals from QFC project managers/alumni Reputation in QFC network	8 64	8 64	0 0	8 64
Ability to deliver on schedule	7	Study completed within six months of start Schedule track record on similar global projects	7 49	8 56	5 35	8 56
Key personnel	6	Expertise of key personnel (years, projects, education) Guaranteed availability/ assignment of key people	3 18	6 36	5 30	7 42
	Total Weighted Scores (best possible: 690)		502	541	371	536

creasing weight of the issues. As shown in Figure 19-1, some key issues may be weighted equally, and the weights may not fall below 5 or 6 (issues with lower weights wouldn't be strong factors anyway). The weights must be based on the customer's perceptions, not yours, and it's best to ask them how they would weight these issues.

3. In the "Metrics" column, identify how the customer will measure a supplier's ability to satisfy the requirements. What metrics will they use? How will they measure success? The metrics column is particularly important because it establishes a performance benchmark and tells everyone in your company who works on the opportunity what the customer expects.

4. Next, identify your primary competitors and give them a 1 to 10 score (with 10 as the highest) for each issue. The scores should reflect the *customer's perceptions* of each competitor's ability to address each issue. In Figure 19-1, for example, the customer will perceive that competitor B has significant worldwide market research experience. Competitor A will be perceived to have much less experience in this area. How can you know what the customer perceives? The best way is to ask them, particularly your sponsors. But you also can glean much of this information from your conversations with other customer representatives, from the comments they make about work your competitors have done for them, and from general industry perceptions of your competitors, which your customers are likely to have heard. After assigning scores for each competitor and each issue, multiply the scores by the issue weights and then add the weighted scores in each competitor's column. The result will show relative competitor strength.

5. Finally, in the column labeled "Us," score your company on each issue using the same 1 to 10 scale. Your scores should be based on your current standing in the eyes of the customer. What do they think of your company and its products and solutions now? What are their *current* perceptions of your company and your ability to address their key issues? Again, base your scores on the *customer's perceptions*, not yours. What you think doesn't matter. Multiply your current scores by the issue weights and then calculate your total weighted score.

As I noted earlier, this kind of analysis is more art than science. It relies on uncertain numbers, but nonetheless it gives you a ballpark estimate of your competitive position relative to your primary competitors. Further, it forces the people in your company to look at the opportunity from the customer's perspective—to focus on their key issues, to see how they would weigh the issues, and to assess your competitors and your own company as the customer is likely to. In practice, the KIA is an eye-opening exercise, and the results often are surprising. It's best for the account manager to lead members of the pursuit team through this exercise and for the team to come to consensus about your company's strengths and weaknesses in pursuing this opportunity. Later, I'll show how you can use this tool to develop your opportunity strategy.

In the example illustrated in Figure 19-1, we are in a close race with competitors A and B. KIA scores within 10 to 15 percent of each other are essentially equal. Competitor C is a distant fourth and probably is not a serious contender. According to this analysis, our current unadjusted Get percentage would be about 33 percent. At this point, there is little to distinguish us from competitors A and B. When we return to this example later, I'll show how we can improve the odds considerably.

Analyzing the Customer's Decision Makers

Next, it's crucial to identify who in the customer's organization will make and influence the buying decision for this opportunity. Your account plan should have already identified and profiled many of the customer's key people, but a different set of people may be involved in making the buying decision for a particular opportunity. In my experience, the decision-making group in the customer's organization usually varies from opportunity to opportunity as different operators and advisors become involved. To make a sensible pursuit decision, you need to know how the buying decision will be made for the specific opportunity you're analyzing. If you've learned about the opportunity well before the decision will be made, then you can still try to improve your relationships with the decision makers and influencers; learn more about their biases and preferences; and perhaps influence their specifications, scope of work, and selection criteria. The key questions to answer are these:

- Who will make the final decision on this purchase or project? Why was this person chosen? What is his or her normal role in the customer organization?
- How well do you know the decision maker? Have you worked with him or her previously? What is your relationship?
- Who will influence this decision? Who are the end users or operators, advisors, gatekeepers, and external advisors? Where are these people located? How much influence will they have?
- What role will the gatekeepers play in the decision? What procedural requirements must we meet?
- How will the decision be made? What procedures or decision protocols will they follow? Is there a formal purchasing process in place? If so, how will it help or hinder us in our ability to ethically influence the outcome?
- Who in our company knows the people in the decision-making group for the customer? What are our relationships with them?
- What are the biases of the decision makers and influencers? What are their interests, preferences, and experience with our products or competing products?
- Are any of the customer's people biased toward us or against us? Do any of them favor our competitors?
- What criteria will they use to evaluate products, solutions, and suppliers? Do we fully understand their key issues and concerns?
- Have product or solution specifications been written yet? If not, can we influence them? Would they be open to seeing proof-of-concept or product demonstrations?
- How much access do we have to the customer's decision makers and influencers? Can we work closely with them before the decision? How much contact would they consider to be ethically appropriate?
- With whom do we need to build stronger relationships? How can we do that?

Figure 19-2 illustrates a key person analysis for an opportunity. Mapping your relationships with the opportunity's decision-making group is helpful because it shows how well positioned you are with the customer's key people and it suggests some of your strategies if you decide to pursue the opportunity.

Figure 19-2. Key Person Analysis

Role*	Name & Title	Key Issues concerns, requirements, needs, wants	Biases	Characteristics background and history	Contacts in our company
Decision Maker Has ultimate authority to make the buying decision	Michael Dorsey; Senior VP for Business Development	• System must support 19% sales growth target for upcoming fiscal year • Improve productivity of sales operation • Provide sales group greater competitive edge	Neutral; hard to read; is not biased toward us but has no apparent biases toward our competitors	Texas A&M engineer; Wharton MBA; in sales for 18 years; recently promoted to Sr. VP; very capable at organization; considered an excellent manager; has the CEO's ear; is a big picture person but scrutinizes details before making a decision; will insist on demonstrable benefits	G. Radcliffe M. Fred Mann K. Rogers Dion Salt K.C. (Sonny) Bright
Advisor Advises and supports the decision maker; provides guidance, information, and insight	Marc Arnold; VP for Manufacturing and Distribution	• Change orders—need to be minimized through better forecasts • Fewer returns • Enhance web-based distribution channels	Positive; thinks our approach will help his team	VP for 12 years; loyal company person; active in manufacturing association (past president); known as a strong motivator	G. Radcliffe R. Mars Lu Li
	Joanna Silva, Director, Customer Service	• 24-hour help hotline for online customers • Need to decrease customer complaint response time by half • No down time!	Negative; she had a prior bad experience with us	Hired from UPC; strong customer service background; Duke grad; basketball player in college	G. Radcliffe
	Susan Hunt, Director of Sales	• System cost • Implementation schedule and training—wants entire group up to speed in 90 days! • Functionality and management reporting options	Positive; feels the need for a good solution quickly	5 years in the job; aggressive, no-nonsense mgr; Dorsey's her mentor; champion chess player; tennis; golf; very competitive	G. Radcliffe K. Rogers H. Hurmitz T. Popper R.J. McBride
Operator Will operate, manage, or use the product or service	Gregorio Lopez, Mgr, Sales, Eastern Region	• Companywide acceptance—we need to syndicate the benefits widely • Resources—do we have the people needed to install and ramp up this system in the time frame?	Positive; brought us in and is pushing our proposal; is a sponsor	USC grad; young for position; was with NW Bell; strong track record; good friend of G. Radcliffe; likes Cajun food	G. Radcliffe R. Moss K. Rogers J. Samora C. G. Sanchez
	Rhonda Chin, Mgr, Sales, Western Region	• Speed and simplicity of the system • Minimum burden on field sales reps • Obvious benefits to the reps of using the system • Total installed cost	Neutral; is hard to contact but seems un-biased	A detailer and a reader; considered an expert in the industry; tends to be skeptical of new technology; will be a hard sell	G. Radcliffe T. Popper
Gatekeeper Screens the offer; ensures that bidders comply with all rules; manages the buying process	Boyd Donaldson, MIS Director	• Compatibility with their existing systems • Does our system meet the specs? • Learning curve for system support—it can't be too difficult to maintain and modify as needed	Neutral; goes strictly by the book	Formerly with IBM; has been here 6 years	Lu Li E. Martinez J. Maxey
	Jane Schwedland, Mgr, Procurement	• Must agree to their contract terms • Must provide a performance bond • Must follow their purchasing procedures • Price must be competitive	Negative; is unwilling to revise the contract terms	Former teacher; spouse is County DA; chairs local United Way; tough negotiator	G. Radcliffe R. Hilseberk
External Acts as an external advisor to the decision maker; may be a lawyer, accountant, banker, or consultant	Khalid Toroparvala, Consultant, Global Futures Group	System should be state of the art and enable upgrades as technology advances	Unknown	Occasional columnist for Byte magazine; industry expert on parallel processing and distributed networks	J. Maxey
	Sharlene Washington, Prime Financial Group	Wants minimum of three bids	Neutral	Unknown	None

* Have you identified the person or people filling each role for this opportunity?

Applying Selection Criteria

Whether or not to pursue an opportunity is a business decision, and it should be based on an analysis of the facts and on criteria that indicate how attractive or unattractive the opportunity is. Basing these decisions on your gut is risky and, unless your instincts are unusually accurate, can destroy your credibility with your team and, ultimately, with the customer. The best practice I've seen is to apply a set of positive and negative indicators to the pursuit decision. The positives signal a "go"; the negatives signal "caution" or "stop." Some of the negatives are treated as show stoppers—

if they are present, then you "no bid" the opportunity regardless of any other factors. Here are some examples of positive and negative indicators.

Go Indicators

- The project is aligned with your account vision and strategies and is consistent with your organizational purpose and goals.
- You have a long-term, favored relationship with the customer; you are the preferred supplier, a partner, or an ally.
- You are well positioned for this opportunity and have a Get percentage of at least 66 percent.
- The Go percentage is high (80 percent or higher); this appears to be a real project.
- The project is attractive; it can have a high, positive impact on your company.
- The financial factors are positive—high profit potential with minimal financial risk.
- The contract terms are favorable to your company.
- The national, political, economic, and business conditions are favorable.
- Follow-on projects or multibusiness unit opportunities are likely.
- This is a target industry, location, customer, or service area in your strategic plan.
- You have unique competitive advantages in this situation; you can offer the right solution to the customer and provide unique value.
- You are resource rich in the area and can offer the right people at the right time.

Obviously, not all these positive indicators need to be true for you to give the opportunity the green light, but if a number of these indicators are true, then the opportunity probably is a go.

Stop Indicators

- The project is not aligned with your account vision or strategies and will not contribute to the achievement of your company's strategic plan.
- Strong competitors are incumbent or are otherwise better positioned with the customer; the customer may be asking you to bid just to keep your competitors honest or to drive down the price.
- A competitor is strongly favored by people in the customer's decision-making group and has strong relationships with key customer representatives.
- A competitor is willing to buy into the project and is likely to drive the competitive price range too low.
- Risk is too high compared to the potential return, or the project is otherwise financially dubious.
- Contract terms or national, political, economic, or business conditions are highly unfavorable.

- The customer wants you to make an unacceptable equity commitment in the project.
- Project funding is tenuous or weak, or the customer is financially unsound.
- You are competitively disadvantaged—you lack the right resources, technology, people, or experience to give the customer compelling reasons to choose your company or your products.
- You don't know the people in the buying unit well, didn't learn about the opportunity early, haven't done adequate positioning, or don't understand the scope of work.
- The cost to pursue this opportunity is higher than the potential return. It isn't worth the investment you'd have to make to win the work.

In many pursuit decisions, there is a mix of positive and negative indicators. If there are no clear show stoppers, then you need to weigh the positives and negatives in balance. Companies are typically less selective during market downturns when their plates are empty, and they have the luxury of turning away opportunities when their plates are full. But it's good discipline to follow this process whenever you are faced with a pursuit decision. If you decide to chase a dog, you should at least know that you're doing so.

The account manager's role in opportunity assessment is to guide the process and ensure that the right questions are being asked, the right facts are being considered, and the right people are involved in the pursuit decision. You won't be a dispassionate observer in the process, but it's important to maximize people's involvement in the process and to syndicate the decision with them. You probably will need their support as you develop and implement opportunity strategy.

Developing Opportunity Strategy

Once you've decided to pursue an opportunity, the question becomes: *What will it take to win?* Opportunity strategies are like your account strategies except that they focus on the objectives and actions necessary at the tactical level to capture an opportunity. Like account strategies, opportunity strategies are intended to highlight your strengths and mitigate your weaknesses. However, they also must specify what you must do to neutralize your competitors' strengths and emphasize their weaknesses. The goal of an opportunity strategy is to position you with the customer's decision makers and influencers and to increase their sense of your differentiation and unique value. In short, the goal is to maximize your competitive advantage.

In ideal circumstances, an opportunity strategy is so successful that the customer chooses not to compete the contract but simply awards it to you as the sole source. If possible, you want to presell your company and your products and solution so that you avoid open competition with your rivals. Let's be clear about that last point:

Your goal is to preempt competition.

Of course, you must do this ethically and legally, but it doesn't make sense to compete for work if you don't have to. So a primary goal of any opportunity strategy is to presell your solution and create bias in your favor. If you make a compelling case, customers may be persuaded to award you a sole-source contract or to authorize the work as an extension of a current contract. However, even if you can't get a sole-source contract, your goal should be to bias the competition in your favor by convincing customers ahead of time that yours is the best solution for them. Typical preemptive-strike strategies are to:

- Write an unsolicited proposal while they are still exploring their problems and haven't formalized the need. Help them define the need and solution simultaneously.
- Write a sole-source proposal once you know of the need and before they've solicited proposals or engaged in discussions with other suppliers.
- Try to negotiate a contract before writing a formal proposal.
- Propose doing the work as an extension of a current contract.
- If they are intent on issuing an RFP, propose a solution and set of specifications; try to influence the requirements so the specs favor your approach.

Whether or not you can preempt competition, good opportunity strategies have the following characteristics:

- They answer two fundamental questions: *Why us?* and *Why not our competitors?*
- They address every one of the customer's key issues.
- They highlight your strengths and mitigate your weaknesses.
- They neutralize your competitors' strengths and ghost their weaknesses. The term *ghost* means that you *raise the specter* of your competitors' weaknesses without attacking them by name.
- They focus on your differentiators—the areas where you offer unique advantages to the customer or provide value in ways your competitors can't.
- They establish your *credibility* and *acceptability*, and they build the customer's *preference* for you.

What it Takes to Win

Credibility, which you earn by having

✓ The right products
✓ The right technologies
✓ The right solution
✓ The right team
✓ The right experience

continued

Acceptability, which is based on having

✓ A conducive political environment
✓ Negotiable terms and conditions
✓ A competitive price

Preference, a product of confidence and trust, which comes from

✓ A compelling story
✓ Supportive customer relationships

Because opportunity strategy should be focused on the customer's key issues, an effective tool to use in developing strategy is the KIA. Earlier in this chapter, I discussed part I of the KIA (Figure 19-1). Figure 19-3 shows part II using the same example. This part of the tool is meant to help you develop your opportunity strategy. The question is, what can you do to improve the "Us Current" score that you calculated earlier. What strategic actions can you take at this point? How can you highlight your strengths, mitigate your weaknesses, neutralize your competitors' strengths, and ghost their weaknesses? Finally, how can you differentiate your company and products from your competitors? Here's how to complete this part of the KIA:

1. Determine what you must do to win. Where and how can you realistically improve your scores? In the "Strategic Actions" column, identify what else you can do between now and the buying decision to meet the customer's needs, address their issues, and improve their perception of your capabilities. Going issue by issue forces you to focus on what's important to your customer.

2. In the four columns under "Strategy," check off what each strategic action accomplishes—whether it highlights a strength, mitigates a weakness, neutralizes a competitor strength, or ghosts a competitor weakness. All four elements of strategy should be addressed by at least some of your strategic actions.

3. In the "Us Potential" column, score yourself as you think the customer will perceive your company after you have accomplished your strategic actions. Rating yourself is difficult, but if you have good relationships with some customer representatives you can ask for their help. How do they think you'll be perceived after you've implemented your strategy? When you're finished, multiply the scores by the weights for each key issue and then total your weighted scores. The result is your best possible outcome.

4. If your total weighted score is not appreciably higher than your competitors' weighted scores, then you should revisit your strategic actions. What else can

Figure 19-3. Key Issues Analysis, Part II

Strategic Actions — What do we need to do to maximize our potential score?	Us				Potential Score	Differentiators — What features make us significantly different, positive or negative, from our competitors?
	Strategy (✔)					
	Highlight Our Strength	Mitigate Our Weakness	Neutralize Their Strength	Ghost Their Weakness		
Emphasize past work with QFC and its major competitors internationally	✔		✔	✔	10 / 100	We know you and your competitors More related int'l experience than Globe
Show existing relationships with qualified firms in all countries and get commitments from all of them	✔		✔	✔	10 / 100	Existing relationships in all countries Agreements in place
Do our homework: (1) learn what we can about Phase One results (2) do one country as a sample		✔	✔		8 / 80	Lower learning curve than B or C Sample study saves time & money
Theme of "Experience + Resources + Track record = Reliability" Emphasize A&C's lack of E&R	✔		✔	✔ ✔	10 / 90	Experience & resources
Selected country sample saves $$ Show value added on past studies (we're worth it; they're not)	✔		✔ ✔	✔	9 / 81	Value added (must quantify)
List successful QFC-MRA projects Review our recommendations on Superstore project where Globe failed	✔			✔ ✔	9 / 72	Understanding of QFC's needs and issues, even where we're not involved
Emphasize our resources and past performance Develop sample project plan	✔ ✔		✔	✔ ✔	9 / 63	Sample project plan saves time money
Emphasize zero turnover Propose a team they already know and show their availability	✔ ✔			✔ ✔	10 / 60	Assurance of the right people being on the project for the duration Known performers who know QFC
Highest Potential Score					646	

you do? Clearly, your competitors will be taking their own strategic actions, so you need to consider what you think they'll be doing.[2]

5. Finally, in the "Differentiators" column, identify every way in which the customer will perceive your company and products to be differentiated from your competitors. This column should list your unique advantages, the added value only your company and products can offer.

Opportunity strategy consists of the actions you will take to maximize your competitive position. Along with the strategic actions, you should

---

2. In the most sophisticated opportunity pursuits I've participated in, we put together teams to simulate our key competitors, and they worked as hard at developing a winning strategy as we did. We had to struggle, often through the night, to counter their strategic actions and to develop strategies that would turn the tide in our favor. When the stakes are high, you have to be diligent and determined to find every competitive strength and weakness, and you have to anticipate your competitors' strategies and find the ways and means to defeat them.

identify those who are responsible for the actions and when you expect them to start and to be finished. Responsibilities and deadlines complete the strategy. As I noted earlier, account managers usually aren't responsible for taking all these actions, but they must drive the strategy and manage it to ensure that the actions are taken on time. Further, if you need the cooperation and support of other professionals or managers in your company, you must syndicate your opportunity strategy with them and gain their buy-in. In most cases, they should participate in developing the strategy.

After you implement your strategy, assess the results and modify your strategy as necessary if the results show that you need to do more. Pursuing an opportunity is a dynamic process and is shaped by what you learn from the customer as well as by your competitors' activities. Some common strategic actions include:

- Developing an information plan and gathering information on the customer's needs, project goals, and issues and concerns
- Building relationships with everyone in the customer organization who will make or influence the buying decision; understanding their perceptions of you and managing those perceptions
- Initiating executive-level contacts; selling at the top
- Exploring the customer's budget parameters and trying to understand their estimate of the project cost
- Doing preliminary designs or otherwise showing how your technologies can be applied to the problem
- Doing capabilities presentations, product demonstrations, and proof-of-concept studies
- Establishing preliminary agreements with key subcontractors or team members
- Finding local partners in foreign countries or establishing agreements with key agents
- Establishing your project team and introducing your proposed project manager to key customer representatives; building those relationships
- Creating an executive summary brochure focused on the customer and the project. Your competitors will send their generic brochures that are self-focused and highlight their products and capabilities; yours should focus on the customer's problem and how your company and products meet their needs
- Developing your differentiators and ensuring that the customer is aware of them
- Looking for opportunities to consult on the project; for example, writing the technical specifications and program requirements or identifying ways to reduce technical, contractual, or financial risk for the customer
- Understanding the decision-making process and trying to condition the deal by influencing the RFP if they insist on issuing one
- Initiating a public relations campaign; getting the right articles published and placing the right display ads in the right publications

The fundamental purpose of these strategic actions is to presell your company, products, and solutions. You want to build preference early in the customer's decision-making process so they either give you the work without competing for it or are biased in your favor if the competition goes forward.

Bret knew that he'd need a lot of support to implement his strategy, so he formed a pursuit team of six people including himself and Jack Strater, his executive sponsor. The team reviewed the first part of the KIA and agreed with his findings. Then they locked themselves into a room for 4 hours and hammered out an opportunity strategy by working through the second part of his KIA (shown in Fig. 19-3). Several important concepts emerged:

1. MRA was well positioned globally, with local offices or affiliates in all the target countries. MRA had more international experience and presence than Global and far more than Archer Landau. They could ghost Global here because Global did not have affiliates or offices on Australia or New Zealand.

2. MRA should emphasize its global experience and depth of resources. Global could match them on resource depth, but if MRA heavily emphasized this factor it probably could knock out Archer Landau, about whom the customer was already having resource concerns.

3. One glaring weakness was on issue 3—understanding of the Foodique International Project. Archer Landau would be far ahead of MRA on this issue, and Global could be ahead if they have good sources of deep private information inside QFC, which was likely. So Bret and the pursuit team made a bold decision: they would invest some of their pursuit budget to do a pilot study in one of the target countries. In their proposal, they could show preliminary results, establish their understanding of the project, and excite QFC by demonstrating the feasibility of their idea. To accomplish this, they would need a lot of inside information from Bret's sponsor inside QFC, and he felt that he could get the information if he could show how the pilot study would benefit QFC whether or not they selected MRA for the phase two study.

4. Finally, knowing how hard it is to unseat an incumbent, they decided to attack Archer Landau on the issue of key personnel. Susan Landau's departure gave them the opportunity to ghost the incumbent by stressing how MRA's key people would be dedicated to the project for its duration, so QFC would be guaranteed to get a team of people they know and trust. They'd also emphasize MRA's longevity and stability as a firm.

The commitment to do a pilot study turned out to be the winning maneuver. After MRA had been awarded the contract, Bret met with his sponsor and learned that the evaluations had put MRA and Global into a virtual tie for first place, but QFC's chief executive officer was impressed that MRA had committed to a preliminary study. The results, which MRA reported in its proposal, were indeed stimulating, and they convinced QFC to select MRA for the next phase.

Crafting Your Themes

In chapter 16, I discussed the importance of managing information and said that the clearest messages to customers were relevant and timely. They also should be customer focused and should show how the features of your products benefit them. For at least 40 years, salespeople have been told to link the features of their offer to the benefits the customer receives. That old saw has not lost its edge. Even in this age of consultative selling, it's important to remember the basics. Customers don't buy your products; they buy what your products do for them. Account managers surely are aware of this old adage, but the people in your company who support opportunity pursuits and write your proposals may not be.

Today, the best practice is not only to link features and benefits but to go well beyond that. Your selling messages or themes should link the features of your offer back to your customer's goals and issues. The goals are what the customer is trying to achieve. Their issues signify their requirements and concerns—what they demand from a solution. The features of your offer are the specifics of what you propose to do or provide, and they also should be linked to benefits the customer receives from them. In turn, the benefits should be backed up by proofs—evidence that you've provided these benefits in the past and can do so again now. The most compelling messages focus on the customer's problem and *prove* that you can solve it, and the best-practice tool for creating compelling messages is the IFBP (issues, features, benefits, proofs) matrix, which is described in Figure 19-4 and illustrated in Figure 19-5. To create an IFBP matrix, do the following:

1. Identify the customer's overall project or purchase goal. What are they trying to achieve with this purchase?

2. List the customer's key issues in priority order. If you've done the KIA, then just list the key issues identified there.

Figure 19-4. The IFBP Formula

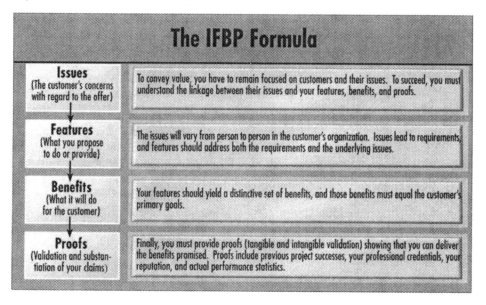

Figure 19-5. IFBP Matrix

Goal: Devex wants to establish rapid, worldwide presence in polyethelene manufacturing and achieve a 10% market share within 3 years.			
Issues	**Features**	**Benefits**	**Proofs**
1) Cost	Worldwide purchasing leverage	Assurance of our ability to procure lowest-priced materials and labor	$23 billion projected purchasing commitments
2) Ability to meet schedule	Fast-track scheduling and modular construction	Early start-up = lower project cost + early operational revenue	Sample fast-track schedule compared to traditional schedule
3) Relevant experience	Specific projects (name and describe) completed or in progress Experience with specific technologies	Assurance of ability to deliver technical excellence on time, within budget	27 similar projects ($2.9 billion in contract value, for 15 clients) Descriptive write-ups with photos Site visits/tours Client testimonials
4) Key personnel qualifications	Seasoned management team with proven skills and 240 years of combined relevant project experience	Assurance that the work will be done right the first time No learning curve means lower project cost and less risk	Client introductions and relationship-building contacts Resumes (with or without photos) in qualifications submittal and proposal Client recommendations
5) Location	Offices or affiliates in 39 countries Office located 15 kilometers from project site	On-site project management Reduced travel/logistical expense In-country presence ensures understanding of project requirements and local issues Ability to maximize foreign country content when appropriate	93 local projects completed or in progress Descriptive write-ups with photos $1.4 billion in subcontracts/partnerships with local firms Site visits/tours Client introductions and relationship-building contacts

3. Identify the features of your offer that respond to or address the requirements of each key issue. For space purposes, I had to compress the example shown in Figure 19-5, but in actual IFBPs there may be four or five features for each key issue. It's important to identify every aspect of your offer that responds to the customer's key issues.

4. Then identify the benefits of each feature. Why is this feature useful to your customer? What value does it provide? How does it address their key issue in some meaningful way? You can imagine some ornery customer standing before you, and every time you state one of the features of your offer the customer says, "So what? What does that do for me?" The benefits of your features answer that question. Of course, the benefits have to be valuable to your customer. Your product may give them some fabulous technical capability, but if they don't need that capability, then it's no benefit—it's just added cost. So you should always view benefits from the customer's perspective. If they agree that it's a value-added benefit, it is; if they don't agree, it isn't.

5. Finally, identify proof that you can deliver the benefits. Proofs can be tangible or intangible and can include previous project results, product quality test results, performance statistics, previous customer testimonials, your professional credentials, and industry rankings. There can be multiple proofs for each benefit. Note that the proofs substantiate your benefits, not your features. A common mistake is to provide proof that you have the features. That's not compelling. What's compelling is tangible proof that you can deliver on your promises, that the benefits you promote are ones the customer will receive.

In practice, IFBPs can be many pages long and can be quite detailed. You can create them in advance by identifying the typical issues your customers have for each of your products. Then you can customize them for each opportunity. They're a remarkable tool for account managers because they help the technical people in your company—who usually don't think this way—to see the importance of linking product features and capabilities to the customer's goals and issues. Further, you can use them to create powerful themes and messages. Just take any issue, feature, benefit, and proof and build it into a sentence or paragraph:

> To ensure that you receive the lowest installed cost, we offer a modular plant design that will accelerate your construction schedule by at least 2 months, reducing your construction cost by an estimated $450,000. We've achieved similar results on fifteen previous projects. The most recent was Edco's Lafayette Pulp Processing Plant....

Messages such as this one become the messages of your presales efforts and the themes in your proposals. You ensure that everyone in your company who contacts the customer knows them, you build them into your letters and presentations, and you ensure that your proposal is filled with them. On one of our major pursuits, we had twenty such themes. Three dozen writers were working on the proposal, all of them technical specialists who knew their fields but were not experts in sales or proposal writing. So we printed all twenty themes on brightly colored bumper stickers and sorted them so the writers received the set of themes they were supposed to write into their sections of the proposal. When I checked later, I found that most of them had taped the bumper stickers to the walls above the desks. There the themes were—eye catching in lime green, canary yellow, and competition orange—so luminous they were impossible to ignore. The writers wove them into their sections and produced the finest winning proposal they'd ever created.

Managing the Pursuit

In managing opportunities, the account manager acts like a theatre director, ensuring that people know their parts, that they're at the right places on time, that they don't stumble over one another, and that the whole thing looks flawless and perfect to the audience—the customer. The tools I've discussed in this chapter are some best-practice methods for putting on a great show.

The intensity level increases when you're pursuing an opportunity, particularly if it's a large one and your fortune in the account depends on success. However, even in less critical pursuits, the pressure is on because a definable piece of business is at stake. Here is where you must increase the momentum—finding the resources to respond, mobilizing supporters, intensifying the information flow between organizations, developing and implementing strategy, managing the customer's perceptions, and coordinating the account team's efforts so that you maximize your potential to win. In chapter 18, I talked about the need to manage momentum, and that need is nowhere more evident than during an opportunity pursuit.

Summary of Part IV

Implementing your account plan and managing the account day by day is like rafting on a white-water river. You alternate between periods of turbulence and calm, not quite knowing what lies ahead but preparing for any eventuality. There's a lot to attend to. You have to syndicate your account plan and build internal support for it. You need to find an executive sponsor and perhaps overcome the resistance of internal departments and people who have other priorities and may not feel the urgency you do for giving your customer special treatment. Ironically, building internal support often is more difficult than selling your products to your customer.

Implementing your plan also means managing the relationships between the key people in your company and their counterparts in your customer's organization. You have to build trust at three levels. Needs-satisfaction trust is the most basic and must be established before you can deepen the relationship. Personal trust exists between individuals in the two organizations, and you must ensure not only that you have personal trust with customers but that other key people in your company build that level of trust as well. The third level of trust, institutional, must be managed over time, and as you build it you transform your company's relationship with the customer from vendor to preferred supplier and then to partner and perhaps strategic ally.

Implementing the plan means building a zippered network between the people at various levels in both organizations. Networks can occur naturally, but building the network you want and need is not likely to happen by serendipity; you must manage it by forging the right connections between people and by arranging the right contacts and interaction at all levels. Once that network is established, you manage the flow of information between the two organizations. You build the customer's knowledge base by providing relevant and timely information. You build your company's knowledge base by acquiring the right information from customers and other sources and then maintaining and distributing that information to the right people internally.

All your efforts should be focused on delighting the customer. You do that by executing projects well and resolving problems quickly. Periodically, you should measure customer delight and use the results both for continuous improvement and relationship building. Your focus on delighting customers illustrates your commitment to them and builds their trust.

The most effective account managers also manage momentum by looking ahead, knowing when the customer's demand for your products will rise or fall, and anticipating those changes by taking action before the customer expects it. You *precycle* by anticipating the cyclic changes in demand, and you *prespond* by moving quickly when nonrecurring events impact the customer's needs. The most advanced companies also *prevolve* by anticipating their customer's evolutions in technology or service need. They have solutions ready just before the customer needs them, so their solutions help the customer advance, which improves the speed and responsiveness to market conditions of both organizations.

When opportunities arise, you must assess them and, if you decide to pursue them, develop and implement opportunity strategies that maximize your potential to win. Managing opportunities is usually an account manager's most visible and time-consuming activity, and it may require the involvement and support of many other people as the preselling effort is launched and a proposal submitted. Managing opportunities, especially in large pursuits, requires all of an account manager's leadership skills.

— 20 —

The Future of
Strategic Account Management

As I write this, we are nearing the twenty-first century. Strategic and global account management programs are proliferating rapidly, and the evidence suggests that they will continue to do so. According to the Strategic Account Management Association, there are now more than 150,000 strategic account managers in the United States.[1] That number will grow as more companies recognize the wisdom of treating their key customers as strategic assets and the necessity of managing those assets strategically.

Strategic account management programs tend to grow with companies by evolution, not revolution. A company's first embrace of the concept usually is tentative and halfhearted. It can represent a significant departure from the way the company has been structured and operated. Those changes don't come easily, especially when they require a paradigm shift in the way senior executives think about their roles and in the way functional managers carry out their responsibilities. It can mean giving account managers more power, authority, autonomy, and visibility than salespeople traditionally enjoy. When it's fully implemented, it can transform the company from an internally driven organization to a market-driven, customer-focused organization, where the true power in the relationship resides not with the company or the customer but with the network of people who form the bridge between them. But that transformation often is painful, and some companies never have the heart or the will to complete it.

As we near the twenty-first century, some notable companies have made the transformation—Hewlett-Packard, 3M, IBM, Xerox, Konica, Weyerhaeuser, Marriott, Pepperidge Farm, Praxair, Siemens, AT&T, and Citicorp, to name a few. For them, the future is now, and much of what I say in this chapter may not be surprising to the global and strategic account managers in those companies. In different ways and to different degrees,

---

1. *National Account Management Association Journal* 33 (1997).

they are on the cutting edge of strategic account management. For many other companies, whose names I won't mention, my prognostications may seem farfetched. Nonetheless, as I've worked with both the novices and the masters at strategic account management, I've seen progress toward the practices and developments discussed in the following. This is what we can expect from the most advanced strategic account management organizations in the coming years:

1. *Strategic account managers will increasingly be viewed as businesspeople, not salespeople.* Some organizations today, such as General Foods, use product line managers as leaders of significant pieces of their business, and product line managers are expected to be well-rounded business managers. Many have profit and loss (P&L) responsibility. As strategic account management evolves, account managers will come to be viewed as business managers whose purview is a strategic or global account, and they also may have P&L responsibility.

Furthermore, as strategic account managers move beyond the traditional sales role, the qualifications for the position will change. Leadership, financial analysis, and general management skills will become more important, and strategic account managers in the future may not necessarily have sales backgrounds—they may come from operations areas and project management. They will be viewed as the customer's representative within the company and will move higher in the company's hierarchy. Already, vice presidents in some companies act as strategic account team leaders. This trend is likely to continue. In the future, some vice presidents will be focused entirely on managing particular key customer relationships. As companies become more externally focused, they are likely to view strategic account customers as key assets, and strategic plans will increasingly focus on customer asset management. These trends reflect the growing sense of the importance of strategic accounts and the reality that supplier relationships are becoming increasingly important to customers. Partnering is likely to grow and, with it, the need for strategic management of business relationships by people who themselves are business leaders, not salespeople.

2. *Supply chain management will drive the virtual integration of suppliers and compel a degree of cooperation unheard of today.* One of the latest trends is supply chain management—the integration of suppliers up and down the supply chain from raw materials providers to end users. Companies are recognizing that many of the costs in the system can be eliminated when suppliers up and down the vertical chain cooperate, and many customers are forcing suppliers in the chain to cooperate in cutting costs, discovering manufacturing and inventory efficiencies, and integrating administrative functions. Some suppliers are recognizing the value of supply chain management to their customers and are taking the lead in their own supply chains. In the future, strategic account managers will likely be at the forefront of this trend, working closely with their own suppliers to improve supply chain performance and helping customers manage other supply chains in their systems. This movement will be part of a broader trend of *outreach* by account managers as they look beyond their own companies to find ways to help customers improve their performance.

3. *Strategic account managers will become leaders of joint cost reduction and performance improvement initiatives.* Many customers are nearing the point of diminishing returns on their quality assurance and continuous improvement initiatives. The process mapping, benchmarking, and best-practice initiatives in these organizations have run their course. They've helped customers improve, but further gains from such initiatives are likely to be incremental, not transformational. In the next 20 years, gains in organizational performance are more likely to come from the *interface* between organizations, so suppliers and customers will work even more closely on joint initiatives to reduce costs and improve efficiency. As managers of the relationship, strategic account managers are likely to be central to this process, and many will lead it. It will be another form of outreach.

4. *Account teams are likely to evolve into total customer service teams.* As the task of managing strategic and global accounts becomes more critical as well as more complex, companies will create larger, formal account teams whose charter is to integrate all the functions in the company in service of the customer. Today, most account teams support the account manager, but team members retain their own functional responsibilities. In the future, the value of having dedicated supporters of key customers will become more evident, and companies are likely to dedicate integrated, cross-functional teams to that purpose. As I noted earlier, in some companies this already is a reality, but many other suppliers remain well behind the power curve in this area.

5. *With increasing globalization, strategic account management will become global account management.* By necessity, global account managers will be located at the highest levels of their organizations, and they will lead cross-functional, cross-national teams who support global customers. It will become increasingly important for these global account managers to be citizens of the world, speaking four or five languages and being cross-cultural in their temperament and outlook. In a very real sense, they will become ambassadors of their corporations and will need to have high-level connections and be politically savvy in many parts of the world.

6. *With supply chain integration will come more outsourcing of critical functions.* Customers will increasingly narrow their definition of their core competencies and areas where they add value in the total value chain, and they will outsource areas where suppliers have more design and development expertise. Automobile designs, for instance, will increasingly rely on design engineering expertise from suppliers who specialize in particular components or manufacturing functions. It won't make sense for General Motors to design dashboards, for instance, if suppliers have more expertise in human interface designs than the auto manufacturer does. The specialization of functions will drive this decentralizing of manufacturing, and the trend is likely to spread to marketing, inventory management, and perhaps sales. Strategic account managers will have numerous opportunities to position their companies for outsourced services.

7. *Strategic account management will be accomplished through virtual communities on the Internet.* We're already feeling the impact of the Internet. Some companies maintain strategic account plans on secure web sites and communicate them to account team members and supporters via the Internet. The people in those compa-

nies who support strategic account teams often are located around the globe, making communication and coordination difficult. With the Internet, these companies have been able to put account plans and strategies on secure web sites, so team members anywhere in the world can access the information they need and provide updates and information to the account manager and their colleagues. By creating chat rooms on their web sites, companies can enable real-time account discussions among members of virtual account teams, including members who are connected from their offices, homes, or hotel rooms around the world. Creating strategic or global virtual account teams through the Internet is on the cutting edge now, but in a few years it will be commonplace.

Competition in the future, especially among technology companies, is likely to be waged less through technical superiority and more through effective communication with customers. Today, experienced people move between companies with impunity, and many second-tier rivals within industries are being consolidated or eliminated. All rivals who remain are technically proficient. It's becoming increasingly difficult for customers to distinguish bidders along technical lines. So the companies that prevail in the future will do so based on their ability to *communicate* business solutions and added value. Because they are information rich and relationship focused, strategic account managers will be prime movers in getting the right messages developed and communicating them to customers.

8. *Joint supplier–customer web sites will strengthen the information pipeline between the two organizations and integrate functionality.* As the value of Internet communities grows and more people become accustomed to accessing the Internet daily, suppliers will create joint web sites with customers for sharing information and ideas and for problem solving and coordinating across the functions in both organizations. Joint web sites are ideal for sharing procedures and processes, guidelines, project plans, schedules, progress reports, order information and processing, inventory updates and product availability, continuous improvement suggestions, customer service and maintenance guides, troubleshooting suggestions, and customer delight surveys and results. In the future, some strategic account managers will have to be web masters. It's easy to imagine how a joint web site would improve communication and strengthen the relationship between the two organizations. Consequently, I think savvy strategic account managers will create these web sites for and with their customers.

9. *The technology for managing strategic accounts will improve and will allow strategic account management principles and methods to be extended to more customers.* As companies and account managers become more adept at managing strategic accounts, the capacity to extend strategic account management methods and tools to less critical customers will grow. Software for account planning, action planning, and information management will facilitate those processes and give account managers both the time and ability to manage more accounts. Likewise, as the technology for artificial intelligence develops, companies will find ways to automate customer service tasks, to create expert systems that diagnose and solve problems rapidly, and to give every customer preferential treatment. At some point, many of the concepts discussed in this book will become commonplace for all customer accounts, not just the critically important ones.

10. *Customers will continue to streamline their procurement processes and work with a smaller number of select suppliers.* I began this book by pointing out that customers are reducing the number of suppliers they work with, in one case from an average of five bidders per contract to 1.7. This trend no doubt will continue because, in their ongoing quest to cut costs, customers will have to trim their procurement process budgets. They'll increasingly see the value of working closely with a few prequalified suppliers and in building partnerships and alliances with the suppliers they most trust. In *The Connected Corporation*, Jordan Lewis makes an eloquent case for the value of close working relationships between suppliers and buyers.[2] Paradoxically, the average company spends more of its annual budget on products, supplies, and services from external suppliers than it does on internal functions, yet it devotes the vast majority of its management time and attention to the internal functions. As the irony of that fact dawns on more and more companies, they will devote increasing attention to their relationships with suppliers, and the role of the strategic account manager will become more critical to the success of both the buying and selling organizations.

As I said at the beginning of this chapter, in some companies today strategic account management is so advanced that much of what I've described here may already be in place. However, many companies are still struggling with the basics. They've implemented some aspects of strategic account management and are learning every day how to do it better, but they have a long way to go. The clock is ticking. Competition in the twenty-first century is likely to be even more fierce than it is today. If you don't have strong partnerships with key customers, you may not have a business, no matter how capable you are at managing your organization. Managing your customer assets wisely will be a key differentiator between the great performers and the merely good ones, and the latter may not survive.

---

2. Jordan Lewis, *The Connected Corporation* (New York: The Free Press, 1995), pp. 1–3.

Appendix: Sample Strategic Account Plan

The sample strategic account plan shown in this appendix was adopted from an account plan for a U.S. strategic less-than-truckload (LTL) truck line. Wellington Distributors (the customer) and PERU Lines (the seller) are not their real names. All names, locations, account facts, and figures have been modified for this sample.

This sample plan is an excellent example of a strategic account plan that follows many of the principles in this book. It was prepared in November 1998, the year before the scope of the plan. PERU Lines follows a calendar year, so this plan is in effect from January 1 to December 31 of each year.

The account manager's name appears on the front page, along with the names of the executive sponsor and the assigned members of the account team. These people helped create the account plan and are jointly responsible for achieving the objectives set forth in the plan.

Throughout this sample plan, I have included annotations where I felt that further explanation would clarify what the account planners were doing or illuminate their use of some of the frameworks described in this book.

Wellington Distributors, Inc.

Strategic Account Plan for 1999

Date: November 14, 1998
Account Manager: Paul H. Hickman
Executive Sponsor: Richard Klein
Account Team: Jenelle Zink
                      Rich Sisneros
                      Carl Wyckoff
                      Debbie Brauhauer

Summary[1]

Wellington Distributors is one of PERU Line's most important customers. They are growing an average of 9.4 percent per year. During the 1998 calendar year, revenues from Wellington will account for 7.3 percent of our annual revenue, and our share of their business will be 11.31 percent. However, both figures are likely to decline in 1999. The majority of our loads come from two of their regions—West and Midwest—where we have excellent relationships with key decision makers. We do relatively little work in their other five regions. Wellington is decentralizing its buying process, so we are likely to experience even greater revenue and market share declines unless we work aggressively to build strong relationships at lower levels and throughout the other five regions. We are in a fiercely competitive market and must leverage our technology and intermodal capabilities in order to meet both Wellington's needs and our objectives.

---

1. The plan begins with a summary that provides highlights for executive readers. The importance of the account is clear—it represents 7.3 percent of PERU's annual volume. Also, the account is likely to decline in the coming year because of one key change the customer is making. This summary gives readers a quick overview before they go further.

Strategic Directions[2]

These are our strategic thrusts as a corporation—the directions PERU has chosen in order to achieve its overall corporate goals. I haven't listed all our corporate strategies here—only the ones that pertain to the Wellington account:

1. Change our image from being a western truck line to a strategic LTL and intermodal carrier.

2. Leverage our state-of-the-art, computerized route and resource management system and create electronic links with major customers that improve our service to them while erecting strong entry and exit barriers that block our competition.

3. Grow our intermodal capabilities and maximize our ability to provide quick and efficient intermodal transport; develop stronger relationships with major providers in other modes.

4. Manage costs through such innovative measures as bonus sharing with drivers and sharing of cost savings with administrative and maintenance personnel.

Account Vision[3]

Our vision is to be one of Wellington's three core shippers. We want them to view us as a professional, full-service, systemwide partner that can meet or exceed all their needs for trailer, refrigerated, and container hauling. Further, we see an integration of our computerized systems with theirs, an integration that adds value to their business while linking them more closely with our logistics and traffic management capabilities.

1999 Account Objectives[4]

Based on our SWOT (strengths, weaknesses, opportunities, and threats) analysis (attached) and our overall strategic direction, here are PERU's 1999 objectives in serving Wellington Distributors:

1. By the end of 1999, we will meet the projected load and revenue volume in each region as shown in this plan. While achieving these goals, we will position

---

2. Next, the author identifies the corporate strategic directions that impact this account. These directions or "thrusts" come from PERU's strategic plan. By listing the strategic directions that impact the Wellington account, the author establishes the links between the overall corporate goals and strategies and his management of this strategic account. As you read the plan further, you'll see that Hickman's action steps reflect the strategic directions identified here.

3. The account vision paints the picture of what the account team wants this account to be. This is the team's long-range aspiration—the broadest statement of what they envision the account can become. Everything else in this plan should support the vision and show how progress will be made to attain it.

4. Next are the account objectives. These are specific, short-range goals, aimed almost entirely at what the team wants to accomplish during the coming year, but they also should point the way toward the long-range vision. I should point out here that Hickman and his team arrived at these objectives only

ourselves through relationship building and proactive customer service to grow revenue throughout Wellington by at least 8 percent above 1999 levels in the year 2000.

2. We will consolidate our position in the East, Canada, Central America, and Caribbean regions in trailer loads and penetrate those regions in the refrigerated and container shipments. Specifically, by the end of 1999, we will achieve 15 percent growth in the East and Canada regions and 50 percent growth in the Central America and Caribbean regions.[5]

3. We will work aggressively to build strong relationships with these key people: Emery Nakai, Harvey Frost, Marjean Cortney, Maynard Lutts, Carla Dawes, Karl Deterding, José Désocio, Ruth Spitzer, and René de Clerc. Evidence of success will be a minimum number of quality contacts in 1999 (see contact plan), achievement of revenue objectives, and favorable bias shown toward PERU as revealed by their selection of PERU in more than 50 percent of cases of head-to-head competition.[6]

4. We will use innovative cost-saving measures and employee and driver incentives to achieve at least a 4 percent rate reduction for Wellington by the start of the fourth quarter of 1999 in order to stimulate account growth in the year 2000.

5. We will market our intermodal capabilities more aggressively to increase intermodal service to Wellington by at least 8 percent in 1999 and 14 percent in 2000.

6. We will complete our new total customer service (TCS) web site on March 31, 1999, and transition all Wellington shipping departments and facilities managers to our new system by June 1, 1999. We will measure the process improvements and administrative cost savings from June to October and use the results in a Wellington-wide promotional campaign in the last quarter of 1999.[7]

---

after conducting a lengthy analysis of the customer and assessing PERU's position in the account, as well as the positions of their competitors. In developing an account plan, you must profile the customer, analyze your competitors, and analyze your own position before you develop account objectives and action plans. However, most readers of the plan won't be as interested in the detail of the analysis as they will the plan of action, so account managers like Paul Hickman often include the customer profile and analyses as an attachment to the account strategies, as shown here.

5. Each of these objectives should be SMART—specific, measurable, attainable, relevant, and timely. It's challenging to make every objective SMART, but doing so creates a more manageable plan. Each objective should indicate how you know when it will be attained. In other words, the means of measuring success should be part of the objective. For more detail, see chapter 13.

6. It sometimes is difficult to make objectives measurable, particularly in the softer areas, such as customer bias. They had to ask themselves, "How will we know when the customers are favorably biased toward us?" The answer is that they'll win a greater percentage of head-to-head competitions with their rivals. When customers are biased toward you, they decide in your favor when all other factors are relatively equal—and often when they aren't equal.

7. Some objectives may indicate not only what you intend to achieve but also how you intend to achieve it. The action list will elaborate on the steps you need to take. Note the precise dates in this objective. The more concrete and specific you make it, the more actionable and measurable the objective is. It's easy to become lazy when writing objectives, but with discipline you can create objectives that truly enable you to *manage* the account.

7. We will defend our position against InterContinental Corp.'s (IC) attack on our existing contracts such that we lose no business on balance to IC through 1999. We will accomplish this, beginning immediately, by tripling our frequency of contact with key customers (see contact plan), matching their rates and time-to-destination guarantees, and instituting top-to-top executive contacts where most threatened.

My action plans for achieving these objectives start on the next page. These plans will be updated continuously throughout the year. They are available at Wellington.sap, which is located on PERU's intranet at Sales/pub/hickman.

Action Plans[8]

Objective 1. By the end of 1999, we will meet the projected load and revenue volume in each region as shown in this plan. While achieving these goals, we will position ourselves through relationship building and proactive customer service to grow revenue throughout Wellington by at least 8 percent above 1999 levels in the year 2000.[9]

Actions[10]	Who	Start	End	Done
Implement route/load availability concept through our MIS system that proactively identifies routes/rates for Wellington. Promote to key Wellington decision makers through our executive team *[Done: New program has caught on quickly; Wellington is adopting program throughout their system. Kudos to the programming team.]*	DNB PHH	8/98	5/99	✓

---

8. The action plans are the living, dynamic part of the plan. Hickman's reside on PERU's intranet, so he can update them and maintain them in an electronic form that everyone else in the company can access. Whether action plans are maintained in written form or electronically, they should be updated frequently. You may add new action steps as previous ones are completed or as events in the account occur or circumstances change. Action plans that are not current are worthless, so maintaining them is the living, breathing part of an account manager's job.

9. Each action plan should begin with a restatement of the objective. This is what the action plan is trying to accomplish.

10. Next comes an action list or table that identifies the key actions you need to take, who is responsible for completing each step, when you expect the step to begin and end, and a check box indicating whether the step has been completed. Clearly, there are many different ways to structure action plans; you should use whatever works for you. Note that, in this format, when steps are completed the results are written in italics type after the action step. Identifying the person responsible for the step helps establish accountability and commitment. Obviously, no one's name should appear here unless that person has participated in the planning process and/or agreed to accept responsibility for the action.

Actions	Who	Start	End	Done
Target areas where key competitors are vulnerable; identify and secure "must-win" contracts that enable us to penetrate the Central America and Caribbean regions and consolidate our gains in the Canada and East regions	PHH Acct team	11/98	12/99	
Identify other key people in PERU who should serve on an expanded account team, get management approval, and bring new team members on board *[Done: Expanded team in place and functioning.]*	PHH JTZ	1/99	3/99	✓
Initiate broader executive-level contacts with Wellington's regional directors; identify their issues and concerns and modify our approach and strategy as needed	JTZ CBW RRY SWT	1/99	6/99	
Create and deliver Wellington program and social event at the ATA conference; arrange top-to-top contacts and do a full-court press at the senior level[11]	PHH JTZ RES	3/99	6/99	
Move aggressively in the East region, particularly in containers and refrigerated shipments; quadruple the frequency of contacts with key East region VIPs	PHH BNA RES	3/99	9/99	
Achieve the other objectives identified below	PHH	1/99	12/99	

Objective 2. We will consolidate our position in the East, Canada, Central America, and Caribbean regions in trailer loads and penetrate those regions in the refrigerated and container shipments. Specifically, by the end of 1999, we will achieve 15 percent growth in the East and Canada regions and 50 percent growth in the Central America and Caribbean regions.

Actions	Who	Start	End	Done
Institute a defensive campaign against IC's attacks on us in the Midwest and an offensive campaign against them on their refrigerated and container shipment contracts in the East region[12]	PHH JTZ	1/99	12/99	

---

11. Many of the action steps listed are at the "macro" level. To accomplish this task, for instance, the person responsible may need to do a number of subtasks, and the whole process could take months. In account plans, action steps should not be done at the level of a daily schedule, but they should identify the larger tasks that need to be done for you to meet the overall account objective.

12. Some tasks will be defensive, designed to thwart a competitor's attack or defend against an external threat, such as a faltering economy. Others will be more proactive and will be based on new initiatives you are taking to position yourself with the customer or improve and promote your products or services.

Actions	Who	Start	End	Done
Create an image/marketing campaign through-out the East region to overcome impressions left from hijacking incident in 1997 and accidents in 1998 that impacted East region's cargoes	MLP	2/99	4/99	
Locate and employ an East Coast agent who can represent PERU to regional manufacturers and to Wellington's Eastern Regional office *[Done: Hired Pete Turner on 2/13/99; early re-sults are disappointing but Pete's interface with manufacturers has increased to 18 hours/week; three contracts larger than $100K are pending.]*	PHH	2/99	2/99	✓
Increase frequency of contact with key people (down to local warehouse managers) in these four regional offices Goal = 6× with region staffs and 3× with warehouse managers be-ginning 3/99[13]	PHH	3/99	9/99	
Pursue more LTL loads from the Midwest to the four regions; leverage existing relationships in Midwest to establish capability inside Welling-ton *[To date, LTL loads have increased 12.4 percent, exceeding our earlier expectations.]*	PHH	3/99	5/99	✓
Leverage existing refrigerated and container shipments, particularly where interregional in-termodal routing is possible	PHH	3/99	9/99	
Have executives attend 1999 Atlanta Transport Fair and ATA Regional Conference in Orlando to establish high-level presence in the region[14]	WTP	4/99	8/99	
Produce and distribute to Wellington and East-ern shippers a PERU intermodal and refriger-ated container video; revise web site to contain elements of the video	RES	4/99	8/99	
Sponsor a booth at NY Distributors Mart and schedule high-level meetings with Wellington decision makers and influencers	PHH SCV	5/99	5/99	

Objective 3. We will work aggressively to build strong relationships with these key people: Emery Nakai, Harvey Frost, Marjean Cortney, Maynard Lutts, Carla Dawes, Karl Deterding, José Désocio, Ruth Spitzer, and René de Clerc. Evidence of success will be a minimum number of quality contacts in 1999 (see contact plan), achievement of revenue objectives, and favorable bias shown toward PERU as revealed by their se-lection of PERU in more than 50 percent of cases of head-to-head competition.[15]

---

13. The "6×" and "3×" notation refers to the frequency of contact per year. A 6× level means bimonthly contact; 4× is quarterly; 12× is monthly. It's a shorthand method for establishing frequency-of-contact goals. You should know how often you need to be in touch with key customer contacts and then man-age the zippering of your relationships through a contact plan. See chapters 13 and 15 for more details.

14. Action steps should include not only what the account manager must do but also what everyone else in the company has agreed to do to achieve the objectives. In this case, Hickman is citing responsi-bilities from PERU's executive and marketing teams.

15. Note that this objective cites specific people with the customer's organization. When specific people are key to your success, then you should develop an objective that relates directly to building stronger relationships with them.

Actions[16]	Who	Start	End	Done
See contact plan	PHH	1/99	12/99	

Objective 4. We will use innovative cost-saving measures and employee and driver incentives to achieve at least a 4 percent rate reduction for Wellington by the start of the fourth quarter of 1999 in order to stimulate account growth in the year 2000.[17]

Actions	Who	Start	End	Done
Communicate rate reduction commitment to Bob Munson and other senior Wellington executives *[It was a very successful meeting; Munson is encouraging a 5.5 percent reduction but promised more business if we can achieve it; Fred Warner has sent the challenge on to the company.]*[18]	FPW	11/98	11/98	✓
Communicate rate reduction goal to all appropriate VIPs throughout Wellington regions; solicit Wellington participation in cost-reduction/savings programs *[The program was well received; competitors have learned of it, as we expected; the West, Midwest, and Canada regions have held joint meetings with us on cost reductions; program appears successful but too early to see impact.]*	PHH FPW RLK	11/98	2/99	✓
Institute incentive-based cost-saving program for all nondriver employees *[Done: this program was already in progress; to date it has yielded 3.34 percent cost savings; ongoing.]*	TNM	1/99	12/99	✓
Create incentive-based program for drivers; set goal of 8 percent cost reduction through 1999	TNM RLK	1/99	12/99	
Realize cost reductions through ongoing administrative and operational improvements (part of TQM program)[19]	RLK	1/99	12/99	
Institute rate reductions and communication campaign for Wellington to begin 10/1/99	RLK PHH ZAS	9/99	10/99	

16. In this case, every action step needed is contained within the contact plan.

17. This objective is really geared toward improving PERU's position for the year following the scope of the account plan. However, it is a vital objective because it positions PERU for the longer term, and the actions necessary to build that position must be accomplished during the year being managed.

18. Fred Warner is PERU's chief executive. The action result in this case was a high-level executive meeting. A more detailed report on the meeting also exists, but people reading the action plan can grasp very quickly what the outcome of that meeting was.

19. If there are ongoing internal programs that impact the account, they should be cited in the account plan. In this case, PERU's TQM program should result in improvements that help achieve the account objective. The question to ask, for each objective, is "What will it take to achieve this?" If the answer includes some existing internal programs, then they should be cited so the people responsible for those programs understand that success in the account depends in part on the outcomes of their programs.

Objective 5. We will market our intermodal capabilities more aggressively and increase intermodal service to Wellington by at least 8 percent in 1999 and 14 percent in 2000.

Actions	Who	Start	End	Done
Create joint marketing/communication campaign with our rail, air, and sea transport partners *[Done: the campaign was very successful—but mainly outside Wellington. Marketing is renewing the program in June.]*	MLP PHH	12/98	3/99	✓
Create new intermodal web site with links to our intermodal partners and intermodal planning tools for customers and prospects *[Done: the web site has generated an average of 34 leads/week, 15 from Wellington in 2 months.]*	MLP MEM	12/98	4/99	✓
Target Wellington's primary intermodal distributors from East region and initiate high-level sales calls with their key executives worldwide and domestically	PHH CBW WTP RLK	2/99	8/99	
Increase frequency of contact with Wellington's intermodal shippers (see contact plan)	PHH	1/99	12/99	
Submit at least six preemptive proposals for Wellington intermodal services in 1999	PHH	1/99	12/99	
Leverage existing intermodal contracts by offering rate incentives to extend the contracts to 12/99 *[Done: three contracts were extended on 5/12/99; four others are in discussion.]*	PHH LES	1/99	3/99	✓
Substantially increase our presence at the 1999 Intermodal Transport Association conference in San Diego; use conference to gain buzz and generate at least 100 leads	PHH MLP	4/99	7/99	

Objective 6. We will complete our new TCS web site on March 31, 1999, and transition all Wellington shipping departments and facilities managers to our new system by June 1, 1999. We will measure the process improvements and administrative cost savings from June to October and use the results in a Wellington-wide promotional campaign in the last quarter of 1999.

---

20. Here, a key program has been delayed for reasons that aren't cited but are probably well known within PERU. So the living action plan shows the delay and cites the new start and end dates. When events such as this occur, it's important to assess the impact on achieving your overall account objectives and identifying any new actions necessary to close the gap. When things go wrong, you need to determine how the situation has changed and what effect it could have on revenue and profit or on the customer. The white water of account management, which I referred to in the introduction to part IV, means responding to these kinds of delays and other potentially catastrophic events. You usually can't change your goal, so the challenge is to figure out how to respond and make up the gap.

Actions	Who	Start	End	Done
Complete TCS system and bring on line *[This program is delayed by 2 months and should now be completed on 6/12/99.]* [20]	MLP MEM	3/98	~~4/99~~ 6/99	
Create transition plan and implementation guides for customers *[Delayed.]*	MEM GTH	~~3/99~~ 5/99	~~5/99~~ 7/99	
Create customer communication program and implement through sales and account representatives	RRT	~~4/99~~ 6/99	~~5/99~~ 7/99	
Conduct road show meetings with Wellington shipping departments and gain commitments to implement	PHH	~~6/99~~ 7/99	~~6/99~~ 8/99	
Implement, train users, resolve problems, and institute program more broadly through customer networks	MEM	7/99	12/99	

Objective 7. We will defend our position against IC's attack on our existing contracts such that we lose no business on balance to IC through 1999. We will accomplish this, beginning immediately, by tripling our frequency of contact with key customers (see contact plan), matching their rates and time-to-des-tination guarantees, and instituting top-to-top executive contacts where most threatened.[21]

Actions	Who	Start	End	Done
Move aggressively to meet with IC's targeted contracts and contacts and counter their initiative *[Done: PHH/RLK road trip in November–December 1998 was largely successful, but we lost $70K in Dover shipments; RLK to meet again with Maynard Lutts on 6/9/99.]*	PHH JTZ RLK	ASAP	12/99	✓
Triple frequency of contact with IC-targeted accounts throughout all levels of Wellington *[Done: see contact plan.]*	PHH JTZ	ASAP	N/A	✓
Where loads are threatened, approve spot rate reductions to match IC's offer and time-to-destination guarantees *[Done: We've had to reduce rates in five instances but have kept the contracts; Terry Pesek knows what IC is doing and isn't buying it, but can't justify higher rates, so we've had to match them.]*	PHH CBW	ASAP	12/99	✓
Initiate senior executive contacts in Midwest and East regions	PHH RLK	1/99	12/99	
Respond aggressively to each of IC's actions as they occur	PHH	Ongoing		

21. This entire objective is based on a prominent competitor threat, which was identified in PERU's self-SWOT analysis. The action steps show that an aggressive response was warranted. Still, they lost some business, but Hickman may have stemmed the tide. Note that some rate reductions were necessary because a low-balling competitor was trying to steal customer share.

Contact Plan[22]

PERU	Wellington Contact	Title	Frequency	Next Contact
PHH	Robert Munson	President and CEO	Semiannually	7/99[23]
	Bobby Ray Hogan	VP, Transportation	Monthly	Ongoing
	Carl Devlin	Manager, Surface Shipping	Monthly	Ongoing
	Harvey Frost	Purchasing Director	Bimonthly	6/99
	Elaine Stauffer	Manager, Strategic Planning	Semiannually	5/99
	Susan Boyle	Midwest Region Manager	Bimonthly	6/99
	Orval Frye	Midwest Transportation Manager	Weekly	Ongoing
	Terry Pesek	Midwest Shipping Manager	Weekly	Ongoing
	Marjean Cortney	Midwest Warehouses Manager	Biweekly	Ongoing
	John Bousquet	West Region Manager	Monthly	Ongoing
	Tom Myszkowski	West Transportation Manager	Weekly	Ongoing
	Emery Nakai	West Shipping Manager	Weekly	Ongoing
	Kathryn Clites	West Warehouses Manager	Biweekly	Ongoing
	Ginette Adams	East Region Manager	Bimonthly	5/99
	Maynard Lutts	East Transportation Manager	Biweekly	5/99
	Carla Dawes	East Shipping Manager	Biweekly	5/99
	Karl Deterding	East Warehouses Manager	Biweekly	5/99
	José Désocio	Director, Central America	Monthly	Ongoing
	Ruth Spitzer	Director, Caribbean	Monthly	Ongoing
	Frank Wilson	Director, Western Canada	Biweekly	Ongoing
	René de Clerc	Director, Eastern Canada	Monthly	Ongoing
RLK	Robert Munson	President and CEO	Semiannually	5/99
	Bobby Ray Hogan	VP, Transportation	Semiannually	5/99
	Susan Boyle	Midwest Region Manager	Semiannually	6/99
	John Bousquet	West Region Manager	Semiannually	6/99
	Ginette Adams	East Region Manager	Semiannually	6/99
	José Désocio	Director, Central America	Annually	4/00
	Ruth Spitzer	Director, Caribbean	Annually	9/99
	Frank Wilson	Director, Western Canada	Annually	6/99
	René de Clerc	Director, Eastern Canada	Annually	6/99

---

22. In chapter 15, I discuss how account managers should create zippered relationships between all relevant levels of their organization and the customer's organization. The contact plan is a method for managing the zippering of the two organizations. Hickman has used it to show which key people in PERU should contact various key people in Wellington, how frequent their contacts should be, and when the next contact should occur. This is very much a living part of the account plan, updated frequently as contacts occur. It should list not only your planned contacts with the key customers you already know but also your planned contacts with key people you don't know or who don't have a good relationship with you now. A contact plan that lists only your existing contacts is next to worthless because it doesn't indicate how you are building for the future or extending your customer network to all key parts of the customer's organization and the key people therein. So ensure that your contact plans indicate how you are going to build relationships with the key people you know about (because you've done your homework) but who don't know you.

23. The date of next contact should be updated every time a contact occurs. The people making the contact should tell the account manager what they learned, what they told the customer, and what's happening next. In many companies, this communication takes the form of a contact report. However, contact management software is quickly supplanting the old written contact reports.

PERU	Wellington Contact	Title	Frequency	Next Contact
CBW	Robert Munson	President and CEO	Semiannually	9/99
	Bobby Ray Hogan	VP, Transportation	Annually	8/99
	Ginette Adams	East Region Manager	Occasionally	9/99
	José Désocio	Director, Central America	Occasionally	8/99
	Ruth Spitzer	Director, Caribbean	Occasionally	6/99
	Frank Wilson	Director, Western Canada	Occasionally	?
	René de Clerc	Director, Eastern Canada	Occasionally	8/99
JTZ	Bobby Ray Hogan	VP, Transportation	Quarterly	6/99
	Susan Boyle	Midwest Region Manager	Quarterly	5/99
	John Bousquet	West Region Manager	Quarterly	6/99
	Ginette Adams	East Region Manager	Semiannually	5/99
RES	Ginette Adams[24]	East Region Manager	Bimonthly	5/99
	Maynard Lutts	East Transportation Manager	Bimonthly	7/99
	Carla Dawes	East Shipping Manager	Monthly	5/99
	Karl Deterding	East Warehouses Manager	Monthly	5/99
GTY	Elaine Stauffer	Manager, Strategic Planning	Quarterly	6/99
LOP	Bobby Ray Hogan	VP, Transportation	Quarterly	5/99
	Carl Devlin	Manager, Surface Shipping	Quarterly	5/99
	Ross Jenkins	Manager, Intermodal Planning	Bimonthly	6/99
	Rob Dennis	Intermodal Coordinator, West	Quarterly	6/99
	Bruce Smith	Intermodal Coordinator, East	Quarterly	6/99
	Maureen Davies	Intermodal Coordinator, Midwest	Quarterly	6/99
	David Beltzer	Intermodal Coordinator, Canada	Quarterly	6/99
	Ruth Spitzer	Director, Caribbean	Semiannually	5/99
	José Désocio	Director, Central America	Semiannually	6/99
DNB	Elaine Stauffer	Manager, Strategic Planning	Occasionally	7/99
	Harvey Frost	Director of Purchasing	Bimonthly	6/99
	Kellen Marks	MIS Director	Quarterly	5/99
TAD	Larry Little	Quality Director	Quarterly	6/99

Note: All contacts—whether by letter, telephone, or meeting—require a brief contact report. Please submit these reports to Paul Hickman, Wellington Account Manager, and to others in PERU who have a need to know.

---

24. Some customers, such as Ginette Adams, appear more than once in the contact plan because more than one PERU representative is scheduled to meet with her throughout the year. Multiple contacts by different people should be coordinated to ensure that customers do not feel overwhelmed and that they receive a coordinated set of messages from everyone they meet with. In chapter 16, I discuss managing information flow to and from the customer. The account manager's role is to coordinate the information flow throughout the account and to ensure that everyone internally who talks to the customer is also communicating with everyone else who has relationships with the same customer representatives. It sounds complicated—and it is—but it's essential in managing the account.

Profiles and Analysis[25]

Customer Profile

Wellington Distributors operates a warehousing and distribution network for North America and the Caribbean and is one of the world's largest privately owned corporations. Projected revenues for 1999 are about $8.58 billion. They are organized by regions and are located as follows:

Group	Location	Primary Contacts	
Corporate Headquarters	Chicago	Robert Munson, President	312-555-1001
		Bobby Ray Hogan, VP Transportation	312-555-2221
		David Montague, Facilities Director[26]	312-555-0987
		Carl Devlin, Surface Shipping	312-555-7995
		Harvey Frost, Purchasing Director	312-555-3765
Midwest Regional Office	St. Louis	Susan Boyle, Region Manager	314-555-0880
		Orval Frye, Transportation Manager	314-555-3581
		Terry Pesek, Shipping Manager	314-555-3562
		Marjean Cortney, Warehouse Manager	314-555-3893
West Regional Office	Seattle	John Bousquet, Region Manager	206-555-0732
		Tom Myszkowski, Transportation Manager	206-555-1493
		Emery Nakai, Shipping Manager	206-555-2211
		Kathryn Clites, Warehouse Manager	206-555-3043

---

25. The customer profile and competitor and position analyses must be done before developing account objectives and action plans, but you may want to put them at the end of the account plan. The people who are interested in this information can read it, but those who aren't interested don't have to wade through pages of analysis before they reach your objectives and action plans, which are the most important parts of the account plan. Some account managers omit the profiles and analyses altogether. Their account plans consist of little more than summary, vision, objectives, and action plans. The details of their analysis, including the customer profile, are available on request. I think this is an acceptable practice, particularly in companies where the customer and competitors are well known.

26. David Montague's name does not appear on the contact plan because he does not participate in shipping buying decisions, nor can he influence those decisions.

Group	Location	Primary Contacts	
East Regional Office	Atlanta	Ginette Adams, Region Manager	404-555-4567
		Maynard Lutts, Transportation Manager	404-555-4589
		Carla Dawes, Shipping Manager	404-555-4599
		Karl Deterding, Warehouse Manager	404-555-4772
Mexico and Central America	El Paso	José Désocio, Director	915-555-4713
Caribbean	Miami	Ruth Spitzer, Director	305-555-2334
Western Canada	Detroit	Frank Wilson, Director	313-555-8523
Eastern Canada	Buffalo	René de Clerc, Director	315-555-5557

Background[27]

Our relationship with Wellington began in 1986, when George Hurtig (our former President) met with John Bousquet (who was the shipping manager for Wellington's West region at that time) and sold two shipments from Denver to Seattle. We continued to grow the account into a $3.4 million contract by 1994 when George retired. Since then I've developed a good relationship with Orval Frye, the Manager of Transportation for Wellington's Midwest region. Between these two key contacts, we have been able to build the business with Wellington to 1998's level of more than $23 million. Although we've been in a strong growth mode in the West and Midwest regions, we have struggled to consolidate our position in Wellington's other regions.

This year our customer share of Wellington's shipping will be 11.31 percent.[28] However, most of this business stems from two relationships, and Wellington is now pushing the authority for shipping down to lower levels as their business grows. In particular, the shipping manager for the West region is a new person, Emery Nakai, and John is saying that he needs to give Emery the authority to make all shipping decisions. Although it is unlikely that Nakai will move all the loads away from PERU, it isn't clear whether he will maintain us at our current level. Consequently, we are now in a defensive mode in this account.

We have had several very large contracts to move auto parts from midwestern manufacturers throughout North America, and these contracts are up

27. Some background information on the customer and your company's business relationship with them may be helpful. Once this brief history is written, it probably won't need to be updated, so it can become "boiler plate" in succeeding revisions of the plan.

28. This part of the profile is very helpful to readers because it summarizes the current state of the relationship and identifies the primary factors that are or can impact your position in the account.

for bid. One of our major competitors, IC, is better positioned for these bids and is likely to get them in early 1999—largely as a result of Dennis Araujo's relationship with the auto parts manufacturers. As of November 14, 1998, I estimate that revenue from Wellington in 1999 will fall to about $19.8 million, which constitutes a 13.9 percent revenue decline, and will reduce our market share to about 9.74 percent. To arrest this decline, we must work aggressively in 1999 to position ourselves more broadly through Wellington's regional offices, especially in light of their move toward decentralization of procurement.

Corporate Philosophy, Vision, and Strategy

Wellington's mission is to provide the most convenient means for manufacturers to get their goods to the right markets at the right times. Their concept is the "hub and spoke," where their warehouses form distribution hubs at strategic points along the transportation network and the spokes are their links to local and regional markets and retailers. By design, Wellington does not handle petroleum products, chemicals, nuclear materials, or hazardous waste. But their warehouses are filled with every other kind of goods—cars, trucks, tires, engines, auto parts, foods and beverages, dry goods, canned goods, electronics, consumer products, frozen foods, and so on. Before Wellington became as large as it is, many manufacturers maintained their own warehouses and shipping fleets. Wellington's vision is to capture much of that in-house shipping service and to enable manufacturers to outsource distribution.

Wellington has its own fleet of trucks and does about 30 percent of its own shipping. However, there are factions among Wellington's management who believe that they should divest the fleet and totally outsource shipping. This has been a growing political battle in their corporation, and it's not yet clear how top management will decide on this issue. In any case, it's unlikely that their fleet will grow—outsourced shipping is less expensive to them than maintaining their own fleet, drivers, maintenance crews, and facilities. If they do divest Fleet Services, PERU will face one of two opportunities. First, we may be able to take over some of the shipments currently being handled by Fleet Services. Second, Wellington may be willing to sell Fleet Services to a carrier such as PERU, and if we are interested in pursuing this possibility, we might be able to acquire Fleet Services with an agreement to retain their current load schedule for a period of years.[29]

---

29. In chapter 10, I noted how important it is to discuss the implications of the information in your customer profile. Here is a good example. The account manager has learned that Wellington may divest its Fleet Services group. The implications are that PERU may face one of two opportunities. When you move beyond purely descriptive information about customers and discuss the implications of the information you've gathered, the account plan becomes a more diagnostic tool, and it helps your management appreciate not only the significance of changes in the customer's situation but the actions you can take now to position your company for the opportunities that may emerge (as shown in this example) or for the threats that are looming.

Market Trends and Impacts[30]

Wellington's market reflects the distribution trends of the past 20 years, which are essentially a move toward speed, simplicity, and just-in-time management of inventories. Their customers expect to maintain the minimum of stocks on hand and to be able to fill inventory requirements very quickly. To meet this need, Wellington maintains a highly sophisticated computer network that tracks goods moving through its distribution system. Wellington is one of the few truck lines to own its own distributed network system, which it uses to track inventory, shipping schedules, orders, capacity, and financial transactions on an instantaneous basis. As a result of their emphasis on speed and responsiveness, they expect carriers such as PERU to be able to respond very quickly to demand for shipping loads, and they expect zero-defect, on-time delivery. So we, like our major competitors, are being forced to offer guaranteed time-to-destination services.

Another market trend is the movement toward containerized shipping. Because of increased foreign trade brought about by the North American Free Trade Agreement (NAFTA) and the General Agreement on Tariffs and Trade (GATT), there is a growing need for intermodal shipping—truck to rail to ship and all variations of intermodal distribution. The need for refrigerated containers is growing especially rapidly. Industry experts estimate that shipping prices for containers (especially refrigerated) will continue to grow through 2000 and will decline thereafter as more carriers acquire container capability and the increase in supply forces rates lower. Clearly, this trend presents an opportunity for us to increase our intermodal shipping with Wellington because it is aligned with our corporate vision and strategy.

Capabilities and Limitations[31]

This section addresses Wellington's ability to meet its own shipping needs. Their capabilities and limitations are as follows:

Capabilities

- One division of Wellington, Fleet Operations, is dedicated to providing truck transport to and from its regional hubs and manufacturers and retailers.

---

30. This section of the customer profile examines how broader market trends are impacting the customer's business and causing them to make decisions that could affect your company.

31. A section on capabilities and limitations can be used in lieu of a customer SWOT analysis (see chapter 10). The point of either approach is to assess where the customer is strong and weak. Their weaknesses often are sources of opportunity for you if you have the right solutions for them. You also may be able to work with them to mitigate or overcome their weaknesses through innovative solutions to their problems.

- About 10 percent of Fleet Ops' trailers are container flatbeds; the rest of their fleet consists of semitractor trailers.
- Sophisticated computer control of the distribution network and the size of their shipping needs enables them to demand just-in-time shipping and inventory management, which requires carriers to be more responsive in terms of scheduling than most carriers are used to.
- Wellington's intermodal ports and truck/rail facilities are among the best in the world.
- Wellington's warehouses are equipped with computer-controlled routing and stacking systems that enable them to move goods efficiently from shipping docks to storage racks and back to docks as orders are fulfilled.

Limitations

- None of Fleet Ops' container flatbeds has refrigeration hookups, so they cannot transport refrigerated containers.
- Wellington has stated publicly that they will not grow Fleet Ops. In fact, there are rumors that Fleet Ops may be divested.
- Wellington has limited warehouses in non-U.S. locations. Their Central America and Caribbean operations are particularly limited. Operations in Canada are restricted somewhat because they have no regional offices located in Canada—a situation they are studying and will probably remedy in the years ahead.

Decision Makers and Influencers

The following table lists the key decision makers and influencers in Wellington who can impact carrier selection decisions.[32] Their roles in the process and their current relationships with our people are indicated.

Name	Title	Role	Relationship
Robert Munson	President and CEO	Advisor	None
Bobby Ray Hogan	VP, Transportation	Decision maker	Positive
David Montague	Director, Facilities	Advisor	Neutral
Carl Devlin	Manager, Surface Shipping	Decision maker	Positive
Elaine Stauffer	Manager, Strategic Planning	Advisor	None
Harvey Frost	Director of Purchasing	Gatekeeper	Blocker
Donald Meyer	Contracts Manager	Gatekeeper	Neutral

---

32. This section identifies the key people who may be involved in buying decisions for the customer. When you write the account plan, you generally don't know who will be responsible for making particular buying decisions, but you can know how the customer's organization is typically wired (see chapter 15). In other words, you can know who typically wields influence in buying decisions, and you should identify those people here. Note that this analysis also identifies each key person's current relationship with PERU. Understanding the current state of each relationship helps you build contact and relationship plans that are systematic and comprehensive.

Name	Title	Role	Relationship
Theresa Espinoza	Senior Accountant	Gatekeeper	Neutral
Bradford Boyle	Manager, Midwest Region	Decision maker	Neutral
Orval Frye	Manager, Transportation, Midwest	Operator	Sponsor
Terry Pesek	Manager, Shipping, Midwest	Operator	Positive
Marjean Cortney	Manager, Warehouses, Midwest	Operator	Neutral
John Bousquet	Manager, West Region	Decision maker	Sponsor
Tom Myszkowski	Manager, Transportation, West	Operator	Positive
Emery Nakai	Manager, Shipping, West	Operator	None
Kathryn Clites	Manager, Warehouses, West	Operator	Positive
Ginette Adams	Manager, East Region	Decision maker	None
Maynard Lutts	Manager, Transportation, East	Operator	Blocker
Carla Dawes	Manager, Shipping, East	Operator	Neutral
Karl Deterding	Manager, Warehouses, East	Operator	None
José Désocio	Director, Mexico/Central America	Decision maker	Neutral
Ruth Spitzer	Director, Caribbean	Decision maker	Neutral
Frank Wilson	Director, Western Canada	Decision maker	Positive
René de Clerc	Director, Eastern Canada	Decision maker	Neutral

As this table shows, PERU has its best contacts in the Midwest and West regions. Our relations in the East region and in corporate purchasing are negative or neutral. The implications are that we will not grow much further in this account unless we can overcome these relationship negatives. It will be particularly difficult to secure corporatewide contracts with a blocker (Frost) playing a key role.

Decision-Making Analysis[33]

Most shipping decisions are made by regional managers; however, Wellington is currently pushing those decisions down to the transportation and shipping manager levels as part of an ongoing empowerment initiative. Some regional managers (such as John Bousquet) are actively avoiding shipping decisions, and we can expect this trend to continue. Some warehouse managers also have considerable say in selecting a truck line. At this point, most shipping decisions are still based on long-term relationships with regional managers, but within the next 4 years we expect decision making to be decentralized and pushed to much lower levels— perhaps even to the warehouse level! The exception will be the large, multiregional or multinational contracts, which are still being made by Bobby

---

33. A good customer profile also discusses how buying decisions typically are made. Note the implications at the end. Although this message is repeated from earlier parts of the plan, it bears repeating because of its criticality. Hickman, the account manager, will need considerable support for the increased level of relationship building he is proposing. Therefore, he needs to emphasize the need for more aggressive relationship building at lower levels in Wellington.

Ray Hogan (Vice President, Transportation) and Carl Devlin (Manager, Surface Shipping) at corporate. A strong player at corporate, although not a direct decision maker, is the purchasing department, which has managed to lobby for and get a "stamp of approval" voice in corporatewide shipping contracts whenever the shipping contracts exceed $100,000.

Obviously, there are profound implications for PERU. We must work aggressively to build relationships with this new, lower level of decision makers or we will not achieve our account objectives. Consequently, we need to develop and work a contact plan that reaches farther down in Wellington than we've previously gone on a systematic basis.

Surface Shipping Load Trends: 1994–2000 (Projected)[34]

The following table shows how much each Wellington regional office has spent on shipping from 1994 to 1998. Also shown are Wellington's projections for surface shipping costs in 1999 and 2000. All figures are in thousands ($U.S.).

Office	Type	1994	1995	1996	1997	1998	1999	2000
West U.S.	Trailers	14,797	17,577	17,794	22,748	28,963	29,391	33,868
	Refrigerated	6,299	7,406	6,888	8,053	7,791	8,583	9,112
	Containers	23,634	29,888	31,009	43,007	36,537	42,790	45,272
Midwest	Trailers	16,837	17,829	18,196	20,352	21,497	23,427	25,080
	Refrigerated	22,053	23,850	22,653	24,818	24,622	29,299	30,606
	Containers	19,466	22,531	23,750	25,946	27,184	33,531	39,751
East U.S.	Trailers	7,274	8,414	8,800	9,216	10,721	11,199	11,892
	Refrigerated	4,016	7,118	10,487	13,542	19,878	22,309	28,712
	Containers	29,353	28,247	33,424	33,090	36,527	38,966	40,303
East Canada	Trailers	1,090	1,483	1,382	1,631	1,893	2,168	2,319
	Refrigerated	1,592	1,700	1,986	2,244	2,640	3,033	3,269
	Containers	3,658	5,187	5,495	6,109	6,596	7,999	8,833
West Canada	Trailers	2,559	2,790	3,476	3,340	3,667	4,212	4,389
	Refrigerated	1,035	1,796	2,016	2,227	2,657	3,102	4,347
	Containers	128	94	1,188	1,693	2,398	3,068	3,091
Central America	Trailers	3,440	5,829	6,019	6,438	7,481	8,261	8,830
	Refrigerated	0	0	57	308	761	861	1,217
	Containers	0	0	0	1,800	2,278	2,975	3,864
Caribbean	Trailers	805	1,144	1,519	1,770	1,857	2,038	2,194
	Refrigerated	140	383	755	793	1,117	1,495	1,652
	Containers	3,175	10,426	14,732	15,324	16,265	17,806	20,703

Source: Wellington Distributors, Inc., Strategic Planning Office.

---

34. This section describes the projected need for PERU's types of services. It helps everyone in PERU understand the projected level of demand—and therefore the changing level of opportunity with this customer.

Position Assessment—PERU Lines

PERU is moderately well positioned with Wellington's West and Midwest regions. We have struggled to consolidate our position in their East and Canada regions and have barely penetrated their Central America and Caribbean regions. As Wellington decentralizes its buying authority for shipping, we have the opportunity for strong gains in all regions, but we must act aggressively to take advantage of these opportunities.

Current Relationship and Business Activities

The following table shows the history of our business with Wellington since 1994, and it includes projections for 1999 based on my best estimate of loads we will receive from Wellington this coming year.[35]

Office	Type	1994	1995	1996	1997	1998	1999
West U.S.	Trailers	496	1,558	2,641	3,118	5,018	4,471
	Refrigerated	0	0	0	0	0	0
	Containers	216	512	3,560	3,149	3,339	3,231
Midwest	Trailers	327	1,311	2,841	3,446	5,875	5,313
	Refrigerated	0	0	188	382	311	309
	Containers	370	633	3,209	3,640	3,872	4,039
East U.S.	Trailers	0	0	30	296	444	401
	Refrigerated	0	0	0	0	0	0
	Containers	0	0	176	420	402	0
East Canada	Trailers	0	0	211	972	168	802
	Refrigerated	0	0	0	0	0	0
	Containers	0	0	107	534	446	431
West Canada	Trailers	0	0	201	328	693	902
	Refrigerated	0	0	0	0	0	0
	Containers	0	0	235	448	294	377
Cental America	Trailers	0	0	0	0	772	501
	Refrigerated	0	0	0	0	0	0
	Containers	0	0	0	0	0	0
Caribbean	Trailers	0	0	0	0	188	140
	Refrigerated	0	0	0	0	0	0
	Containers	0	0	0	0	0	0
	Totals	1,409	4,014	13,399	16,733	21,822	20,917
	Percent Change		248%	234%	24.8%	30.4%	−4.1%

Source: Paul Hickman.

---

35. This section details the account manager's sales projections for the coming year.

As this table shows, we had exponential growth in this account as a whole through 1994, but we have not consolidated our position in regions other than the West and Midwest, where we have been in a growth mode for 6 years. However, we are being put into a defensive position by Wellington's decentralization initiative. In Canada and the East U.S. regions, we remain in a consolidation mode. We haven't successfully penetrated the border regions (Central America and Caribbean). Because Wellington is pushing decision-making authority to lower levels, we will continue to lose market share unless we build better relationships with buyers at lower levels throughout Wellington's organization, and this must be the focus of our strategic initiatives in this account. In summary, this is our current phase in the relationship life cycle with each of Wellington's regions[36]:

Wellington Region	Life Cycle Phase
West	Growth–Defense
Midwest	Growth–Defense
East	Consolidation
Canada	Consolidation
Central America	Penetration
Caribbean	Penetration

Our Capabilities and Resources

Our current capacity would enable us to increase our service to Wellington by about 23 percent if all available trucks and trailers were located where they could serve Wellington's needs and our load volume with other customers remains steady. Realistically, we could increase service to Wellington by about 9.5 percent in 1999 and about 16 percent in 2000—given our current capital spending projections and commitments to other customers. In terms of equipment, we have all the types of trucks and trailers Wellington needs except for such specialized cargo carriers such as grain tanks and lumber trailers, but we have decided to focus on mainstream cargo needs and not provide specialty cargo services to Wellington.

Because growth with Wellington is constrained by our own capacity limitations, we must be careful about the routes and types of loads we pursue. To best make use of our resources, we should try to book round trips or time-definite transits through Wellington's system.

---

36. Hickman is using the relationship life cycle framework to assess PERU's position in each of Wellington's six regions. This is a helpful way of characterizing their relationships and business prospects with each of the buying units.

Wellington's Perceptions of Us

PERU is perceived as a full-service truck line with modern equipment and professional drivers. Our rates are in line with our major competitors' rates but are 3 to 6 percent higher than most local and regional carriers, so we are perceived as a slightly more high-priced carrier and cannot compete favorably when the service is perceived as a commodity. However, we have an excellent safety record (43 percent above our industry norm) and a good record for on-time delivery. Last year, 94.3 percent of our shipments for Wellington arrived on time or before scheduled delivery.

However, we still have image problems stemming from the 1997 hijacking incident in Memphis and two costly accidents in the winter of 1998—all of which involved Wellington cargoes. Our insurance rates still average 15.2 percent higher than our competitors because of these incidents. Unfortunately, some of Wellington's people—particularly those in the East region—still consider us careless and untrustworthy because of these events.[37]

On balance, we are quite well thought of in the West and Midwest regions. We are less well known elsewhere in Wellington's system. The overall impression is that we are professionals whose overall service to Wellington has been excellent over a period of years.

PERU Strategic (SWOT) Analysis[38]

Considering Wellington's characteristics and our competitive position with them, here are our strengths and weaknesses, along with opportunities we face in the near term and threats to our business with Wellington:

Strengths

1. We are an intermodal carrier capable of interfacing with rail, ship, and air transport, and this is a strong and growing need at Wellington.

2. We have invested heavily in refrigerated containers and have a lot of capacity there, which is also a growing need within Wellington that cannot be met by Fleet Services.

---

37. Being forthright about your problems is important. These issues will show up again in Hickman's SWOT analysis and could become the basis for an account objective. Whenever you have performance problems or accidents that impact your business with a major account or skew their impression of you, you should address those problems in the account plan and set objectives for overcoming them.

38. The self-SWOT is the culmination of all the other analyses the account team has done, including the competitor analyses that follow. Essentially, the SWOT is an organized summary of the implications of their analysis. There should be a direct connection between the SWOT and the account objectives. As discussed in chapter 13, the highest-priority items in the SWOT analysis should form the basis for the account objectives, and that is the case in this sample account plan.

3. We have a computerized route and resource management system that, although not as sophisticated as Wellington's system, is considerably more advanced than most of our competitors, particularly the regional and local lines. Therefore, we are perceived to have the same high-tech vision Wellington does.

4. We have modern equipment and professional drivers; we are perceived as being at least as professional as any other carrier.

5. We are among the industry leaders in safety and on-time delivery, although our records do not yet compare to the majors.

6. We have excellent relationships with key decision makers in the Midwest and West regions. We also have a strong, positive relationship with Bobby Ray Hogan (Vice President, Transportation) and Carl Devlin (Manager, Surface Shipping)—the two key corporate people who make broad shipping decisions.

Weaknesses

1. We are headquartered in Denver and have no strong East Coast presence. We are perceived to be a western U.S. truck line rather than a national line.

2. We have no relationship with Emery Nakai, the new shipping manager for the West region, and decisions will be pushed down to his level.

3. We do not have strong, positive relationships with decision makers in Wellington's East region or in the Canada, Central America, or Caribbean regions.

4. By and large, we do not have strong relationships with Wellington's warehouse managers (except in the West). As they extend decision-making authority to local warehouse managers, we face an even bigger challenge.

5. Because of our own capacity limitations, we cannot grow the Wellington account beyond 9.5 percent in 1999 and 16 percent through 2000.

6. We are higher in price than some carriers, particularly the small, mom-and-pop operations.

Opportunities

1. If Wellington chooses to divest Fleet Services, we may have the opportunity to pick up some of their current loads or to acquire Fleet Services and lock in their current load levels as part of the acquisition.

2. Wellington's need for intermodal shipping is growing faster than any other aspect of their transport needs. Further, they have a growing need for refrigerated containerized shipping, which we can provide.

3. Wellington is high-tech focused, and we might have an opportunity to link our computerized routing and resource system with theirs. Beyond resource management and route planning, we also could establish computer links for invoicing and other financial transactions, as well as e-mail, equipment updates, and handling of problems and/or emergencies. We could be the first carrier of our kind to establish such a link with a major customer.

4. Their decentralization of decision making could be an opportunity if we can establish positive relationships with the new level of decision makers.

5. Wellington continues to grow at an impressive rate. Their need for surface transport will continue to grow, so the opportunity for increased service to them is significant.

Threats

1. Their decentralization of decision making could be a threat if it means that the cost of maintaining all those new relationships is higher than our margins can tolerate. It isn't yet clear whether lower-level decision making will result in greater commodity pricing for trucking services—but that is a possibility.

2. We continue to pay higher-than-average insurance rates because of the Memphis hijacking incident and two catastrophic accidents. Another hijacking or substantial loss from other causes could seriously jeopardize our image and increase our rates.

3. Consolidated is seriously threatening our Midwest business by targeting Wellington's customers and by lowballing their rates. It seems clear that they are trying to gain market share through break-even pricing and to capture more business by bringing pressure to bear on Wellington through Wellington's customers. The biggest immediate threat to us is losing the Denny Corporation shipping contract, which is now up for renewal.

4. There is a remote risk that Wellington will reverse its decision to divest Fleet Services. It's possible, but unlikely, that Fleet Services actually might grow.

5. Two of Wellington's key people are blocking PERU—Harvey Frost, Director of Purchasing, and Maynard Lutts, East Region Manager of Transportation. They will remain a threat as long as we have negative relationships with them.

Assessment of Competitors[39]

PERU faces intense, professional competition in every part of Wellington's scope of operations. Three of the majors are well established in Wellington, and IC is moving aggressively to try to take customer share away from us. In addition, we face competition from Wellington's Fleet Services group and from hundreds of smaller LTL carriers.

Current Relationship and Business Activities

PERU has thousands of competitors in each region of the continent, from the mom-and-pop haulers who lease or own their own truck to the major carriers such as Consolidated Freightlines and Northern Amalgamated Freightways. As of March 1998, there were more than 440,000 trucking

---

39. This assessment of the competition is very useful for readers who aren't familiar with your key competitors in the account. Parts of this picture may not change frequently and could therefore become a "boiler plate" part of each annually revised account plan.

companies in the U.S., nearly 70 percent of which operate six or fewer trucks. Our most serious competitors in the U.S. regions are Pacific Freight, Great Western, and Cascade Trucking (West region); Northern Amalgamated, Consolidated, Englund, and Road Runner (Midwest); and Southern Freightways, Watson Brothers, Coastlines, and Interstate Lines (East). The Big Four operate thoughout the U.S. and impact us in every region. We are particularly vulnerable to Highway Express and IC, which combined account for nearly 40 percent of Wellington's customer share domestically.

Competitive Strategies

In each region, we have identified the top five or six competitors and analyzed their competitive strategies. I won't list all that information here, but if anyone is interested, I can show you our competitor files. Suffice it to say that our competitors' strategies fall into these predictable categories:

- *Lowest cost per load.* The principal strategy used by the small regional companies is low cost. They generally can haul freight for 10 to 15 percent less than we can, but many of them are unreliable and unresponsive, and as a group they offer many fewer services. Wellington uses them for short-haul LTL shipments on a limited basis.
- *Regional availability.* "We're there when you need us," is one common strategy for regionally based haulers. Having fleet resources close to the customer and available for spot loads is a key strategy for many truckers.
- *Specialized hauling.* A number of our competitors haul special loads, such as livestock, lumber, autos/trucks, etc. Some also specialize in high-risk hauling (cigarettes, electronics, computer chips).
- *Intermodal links.* Some competitors specialize in intermodal transport and have strong connections with the railroads, airports, and shipping docks.
- *Relationships.* Everyone in this business relies on personal relationships. Where hauling is treated as a commodity, most truckers depend on friendships with buyers, and our competitors are no exception. Our strongest competitors are as active as we are at managing long-term relationships with their customers.

Our principal competitors have been flushing low-yield freight out of their systems and concentrating on making profit margin rather than increasing tonnage. Like us, they have taken steps to reduce costs and have abandoned their hub-and-spoke systems, which were costly to maintain, lengthened transit times, and increased cargo damage.[40] Their vastly improved performance matches our own gains in productivity and cost reduc-

---

40. It's especially important to analyze the competitors' strategies. The situation is never static. They will be adapting as their market and customer conditions change, so you need to remain aware of their competitive strategies and the changes they're making to try to prevail in the marketplace.

tion. Many of the major haulers have invested in web sites that are appealing to the new generation of shippers, and they have equipped their trucks with global positioning system (GPS) systems and radio frequency (RF) systems that enable customers to log onto the Internet and track their own shipments. These innovations have given the majors a distinct competitive advantage, particularly where customers are willing to pay more for expanded services.

Competition from package delivery services, such as UPS, is causing all LTL truckers, including PERU, to provide faster transit times and to guarantee shipment arrivals. But the bar is being raised quickly. Some of our competitors are now offering guaranteed coast-to-coast deliveries in 3 days, which is 2 days faster than we currently can do it. They are using sleeper teams and intermodal partners, such as air transport services, to accomplish these guaranteed rapid transits. A growing segment of customers is demanding faster, guaranteed service, and it seems likely that we will have to match our rivals to remain competitive.[41]

Wellington is so large and so attractive as a customer that we face all these competitor strategies in virtually every region. The effectiveness of each strategy depends on the individual buyer inside Wellington, but the strongest factor we contend with is the customer's perception that a number of truck lines can do the job, so decisions are made based on lowest price and existing relationships between the buyers and the haulers. However, factors such as responsiveness, reliability, safety, and guaranteed time-definite delivery do have significant impact, particularly with the top decision makers.[42]

Wellington's Perceptions of Our Competitors

Our major competitors (Highway Express, IC, Northern Amalgamated, Watson Brothers, Consolidated, Great Western, etc.) are perceived as full-service, intermodal, professional carriers. PERU and the other majors do about 70 percent of Wellington's hauling; the rest is done by Fleet Services and the smaller carriers. Like PERU, most of the majors are willing to do long-distance hauling with driver teams so loads are delivered as quickly as possible. By and large, the smaller carriers are single-driver operations and are unable to move cargo as quickly. Most of the majors also have driver training and safety programs comparable to ours, and their maintenance programs are comparable as well. The smaller carriers are viewed as the mom-and-pop shops that most of them are, and they aren't significant

---

41. You may need to match some steps your competitors have taken so you can remain competitive.

42. Identifying what customers are looking for is crucial, because these themes become the messages you communicate in your meetings, letters, telephone calls, and proposals. Their needs and wants also should drive your company's technical innovations, so this type of information must be passed on to your marketing, engineering, research, and strategic planning departments.

competitors. Most don't have the resource depth that we do or the ability to reliably schedule loads far in advance.

Our Major Competitors[43]

Here are profiles of our three largest competitors in the Wellington account: Highway Express, IC, and Consolidated Freightlines.

Highway Express

Highway Express has the lion's share of business with Wellington, particularly in the East and Midwest regions. They are the nation's largest LTL truckline. Among their strengths[44] are time-definite scheduled delivery; guaranteed on-time delivery; integrated, multicarrier tracking and shipping information; domestic and international services; and a number of programs for customer convenience, such as quick-and-easy rate information over the Internet. Their strategy is to offer rapid, comprehensive LTL services nationwide and to develop close relationships with customers. They are very large and are formidable in competitions where the size of their fleet and network gives them an economy-of-scale advantage. Their express service guarantees have driven them to 9.4 percent growth in the past 2 years.

   Two key people manage their Wellington relationship[45]—Glen Hamilton, a 28-year veteran, is their account manager, and Bob Sullenberger, an executive vice president, is their executive sponsor. Sullenberger knows Bob Munson well and plays golf with him several times a year. The bottom line is that this is a solid team with strong penetration of the account. Consequently, they enjoy tremendous support from within Wellington, especially in corporate headquarters and the East and Midwest regions. However, the decentralization of transport decision making within Wellington will impact this competitor's relationships, too.

InterContinential

IC is an amalgam of five large regional truck lines that have been absorbed into Continental Corp. over the past 35 years. Three of its subsidiaries—Berkhardt, Southern States, and Miera—serve Wellington regions. IC's

---

43. It wouldn't be feasible to profile every competitor you face. There may be too many of them, and the value of those profiles probably would be marginal. Nonetheless, it's helpful to profile your key competitors. You should thoroughly understand the competitors you face every day. They have a significant impact on your business prospects and ability to capture opportunities.

44. The account manager is using the four pillars framework to analyze the competition. Here, he's describing their strengths and strategies. For more information on this framework, see chapter 11.

45. The remaining two pillars are discussed here: staff and support.

strengths are its claims-free service, direct service to all of Wellington's locations, and safety (with the best safety record in the business). Almost 60 percent of Wellington's shipments through IC are sent directly from origin to destination without being transferred in between.

IC's strategy is to provide convenient, low-risk service and to "take the worry out of shipping," as their slogan goes. They have a "soup-to-nuts" approach to working with customers, so they handle all the customer's logistical and administrative requirements from preshipping to inspections and acceptance in Wellington's warehouses and customer facilities. Consequently, they develop great loyalty among Wellington's shipping personnel. Also, they make points through their outstanding safety program, and their key customers are willing to pay a slight premium for it.

IC's account manager for Wellington is Dennis Araujo, a vice president of IC and past vice president of the Council of Logistics Management. A 40-year veteran, he is near legendary in transport circles and is very well connected. I've seen Dennis at every industry function I've attended in the past 15 years, and he's a frequent conference speaker on supply chain management and LTL transport topics. IC's hold on Wellington will remain solid until Dennis retires, primarily because of his relationship with the senior executives. He is well supported among the senior and middle ranks of management. The good news is that he's due to retire in 2 years.[46] If IC can make a smooth transition when he leaves, they'll hold position in Wellington for years to come. But Wellington's staff is getting younger, and Dennis doesn't connect as well with the younger managers coming up through the ranks at Wellington. He needs to bring on a generation X partner to transfer some account responsibility, and he's not likely to stomach that. My take is that IC's position will weaken among the bottom ranks of Wellington managers during the next 2 years, and IC may become vulnerable.

Consolidated Freightlines

Consolidated is a company on the rebound. They lost considerable market share in the late 1980s and early 1990s because they held on to their hub-and-spoke system longer than most of the other majors. Since abandoning that system in 1997, they've been reducing costs, getting their rates in line, and rebuilding market share. Still, they have the image of being somewhat behind the times. They are the only major LTL truck line that has not made an aggressive move to Internet commerce, and the rest of their operation has a similar, "old-line" image.

---

46. At this point, the plan identifies a potential vulnerability. In terms of the four pillars framework, this key person's pending retirement amounts to a crack in the pillar of staff. Jargon aside, this represents an opportunity for PERU.

Their strengths have traditionally been in refrigeration and container shipping. In fact, their aging management team made a number of innovations in refrigeration and container shipping back in the 1960s and 1970s. They remain a leader in intermodal container shipping and have a vast international network. Nearly 17 percent of containerized shipping coming into the U.S. is handled by Consolidated, its dedicated dock and warehouse facilities, and their rail partners in intermodal transport. These strengths make them a formidable competitor in intermodal shipping, and they are making a strong comeback in tractor trailer shipping (up 23 percent from last year according to sources in ATA).

Their strategy has always focused on technical innovation, and they've prided themselves in the past (and rightly so) on their numerous technical achievements and advances in transportation. There are some signs now that they are losing this edge. They were named "Most Innovative Carrier" by the U.S. Transport Council 5 years in a row from 1989 to 1993, but that honor has gone to other carriers since. They also try to gain advantage through top-to-top contacts. One effective strategy has been for them to name ex-CEOs from their key customers as members of Consolidated's Board of Directors. That strategy has paid off handsomely in the past, but it's also caused some push backs in the last few years, most notably by the Wells Transport lawsuit filed in 1997. In that suit, Wells claimed that Consolidated was guilty of unfair practices, and the suit was settled out of court.

A more recent strategy that Consolidated apparently has adopted is to target some of our routes in the Midwest and try to take our market share by lowballing their rates. We've been pointing out what they're doing to Wellington's buyers and told them that the low rates won't last, but the strategy has had some success. We need to counter it.

Consolidated recently has named Josie Pritchett as its account manager for Wellington. She is relatively new and doesn't have a lot of support inside Wellington at this time. Consolidated's sales group has gone through some shake-ups in the past 18 months following Joe Thompson's departure, and it doesn't appear that the dust has settled yet. My guess is that they're in for some tough times in the next 12 months as Pritchett gets her feet on the ground.

Consolidated has enjoyed a lot of support inside Wellington in the past, especially in the East and Midwest regions and Canada. Their support in the Midwest has eroded, but they remain the carrier of choice with Maynard Lutts and Carla Dawes.

Consolidated probably will remain strong in containers and refrigeration, but they are vulnerable in trailer loads during this period of internal upheaval. Also, they do not yet have their costs managed as effectively as they need to. Some customers still complain about their rates, so this would be a prime time to attack them on their established Wellington LTL routes.

Index

Printed in the United States
203579BV00004B/1-12/A

9 780814 410110